The income approach to property valuation

The income approach to property valuation

Andrew Baum and David Mackmin

Third Edition
David Mackmin

First published in 1979 by Routledge & Kegan Paul Ltd
Second edition 1981
Reprinted with corrections 1986
Reprinted in 1987

Third edition published by Routledge 1989
Reprinted in 1991
11 New Fetter Lane, London EC4P 4EE

Typeset by Leaper and Gard, Bristol
Printed and bound in Great Britain by
Mackays of Chatham PLC, Chatham, Kent.

British Library Cataloguing in Publication Data

Baum, Andrew

The income approach to property valuation.–
3rd ed.
1. Real property – Valuation – Great Britain
2. Real estate investment – Great Britain
I. Title   II. Mackmin, David
332.63′24′0941   HD1387   80–42182

ISBN 0-415-04388-3

0-415-04389-1 Pbk

Contents

Preface to first edition

For many years there was only one recognised UK book covering the subject of property valuation.

This in itself might have suggested that the subject area was finite; more recently, however, four further books have been published. This may well indicate that valuers are now prepared to recognise not only the individual's right to express an opinion of value, but also his right to express his opinion of *how* to value.

A lack of basic mathematical ability often prevents valuers from understanding modern or alternative approaches to valuation and their natural instinct has been to fall back on the methods used by their predecessors. We do not deride these approaches, but we hope that the trainee, newly qualified and the seasoned valuer will all be in a better position to understand, as well as be interested by, alternative approaches to property valuation after reading this book.

The book emphasises analytical aspects of property investment, concentrating on an income approach to valuation, and attempts to question blind acceptance of established techniques. We will be satisfied if the text stimulates thought amongst those involved in property investment, and in particular those studying at universities, polytechnics or part-time for professional examinations. This book is not a primer: but it covers a large element of the syllabuses for all three examinations of the Royal Institution of Chartered Surveyors.

We must add that anyone who gives professional advice or makes an investment decision based on any part of this book does so entirely at his or her own risk. It should not be presumed that the book represents the views of the Department of Land Management at the University of Reading, and (needless to say) the responsibility for any error or omission rests entirely with the other author!

Preface to second edition

In this edition of *The Income Approach to Property Valuation* we hope to have corrected the errors and omissions that evaded the most vigilant proof reading of the first edition. We are grateful to those readers who have drawn our attention to sections which lacked clarity or were otherwise in need of correction or improvement.

We have taken this opportunity to restructure the book, to provide a more logical sequence, to reflect current valuation practice and to include a more detailed consideration of development appraisal.

The chapter dealing with landlord and tenant legislation has been rewritten to incorporate the changes made by the Housing Act 1980.

As the text is intended to be illustrative we have decided not to amend examples merely to reflect changes in VAT rates and market movements since the publication of the first edition.

We thank Richard Ellis, Chartered Surveyors, for permission to use material previously appearing in some of their own publications.

Finally, we would like to apologise for referring on occasions to the valuer in the male gender only.

Andrew Baum B.Sc. M.Phil. A.R.I.C.S.
David Mackmin B.Sc. M.Sc. A.R.I.C.S. A.R.V.A.
Reading

Preface to the third edition

In the ten years since the first edition much has changed in the property market and a number of issues raised in the first edition have been the subject of research and discussion in practice and in education. This third edition has provided the opportunity to bring the section on investment valuation methodology up to date.

The text and a number of examples have been amended to reflect changes in taxation and legislation as at November 1988, and expanded in some areas where readers have expressed difficulty in following the logic of an argument. However, as the book is primarily concerned with principles and techniques, I have not amended examples by a factor of ten merely to reflect changes arising from inflation.

This edition makes reference to VAT, but its production preceeded the Finance Bill 1989. The effect of the VAT changes must now be built into the Income Approach by the practising valuer. Hopefully this edition is as readable as previous editions. Those seeking a more detailed discussion of the main issues are referred to the Routledge sister publications *Property Investment Appraisal* and *Statutory Valuations*.

David Mackmin B.Sc. M.Sc. F.R.I.C.S.
Reading

Acknowledgements

We wish to thank the Royal Institution of Chartered Surveyors for permission to reproduce in whole or part certain past examination questions, Surveyors Publications for permission to reprint their leaflet 'The Valuation of Commercial, and Industrial Property: Conditions of Engagement', the *Estates Gazette* and Peter J. Byrne for permission to reprint with minor amendments the article in Chapter 9, Her Majesty's Stationery Office for permission to reproduce extracts from a number of current Acts of Parliament, and Gooch and Wagstaff for supplying and permitting us to reproduce a sample investment purchase report.

We express our sincere thanks to Michael Gilbert of Kel Computing for his help with Chapter 8 and to all who have helped and encouraged us, in particular Peter Byrne and David Jenkins for their criticisms.

Introduction

Cairncross in his *Introduction to Economics* expresses his view that 'economics is really not so much about money as about some things which are implied in the use of money. Three of these – exchange, scarcity and choice – are of special importance.' Legal interests in land and buildings, which for our purposes will be known as property, are exchanged for money and are scarce resources. Those fortunates with surplus money have to make a choice between its alternative uses; if they choose to buy property they will have rejected the purchase of many other goods and services and will then have to make a choice between different properties.

Valuation is the vocational discipline within economics that attempts to aid that choice in terms of the value of property: that is, value within the framework of the specialised market that has evolved for the exchange of property rights, as well as value to a particular person or institution with known objectives, currently referred to as an appraisal.

Property is purchased for use and occupation or as an investment; but in both cases the purchaser measures the expected returns or benefits to be received from the property against the cost outlay. The valuer's task is to express these benefits in money terms and to interpret the relationship between costs and benefits as a rate of return, thus allowing the investor to make a choice between alternatives.

Since 1945 property and the construction industry have grown in importance and property is indiscriminately considered to be a 'safe' investment in inflationary times. The growth in pension schemes, life funds, property unit trusts and the like has completed the transition of the property market into a multi-million pound industry. As a result there has been a growth in demand for property to be valued and revalued for investors and for portfolio and asset valuation purposes.

Property as an investment is different to other forms of investment. The most obvious difference is its fixed location geographically and hence the importance of the quality of that location for the land's current or alternative uses as determined by its general and special accessibility and its interrelationship with other competing and complimentary buildings, locations and land uses. Once developed, the quality of the investment is influenced by the quality of the permitted planning use and the quality of the physical improvements (buildings) on the site. In addition and essential to the assessment of exchange value is the quality of the legal title – is it freehold or leasehold? The owner of a freehold title effectively owns all the land described in the title deeds in perpetuity, including everything below it to the centre of the earth and everything above. Freehold rights may be restricted by covenants in the title and/or by the rights of others such as rights of way. A leaseholder's rights are limited in time, the length of the lease, and by the terms and conditions (covenants) agreed between landlord and tenant and written into the lease or implied or imposed by law or statute.

To be competent the valuer must be aware of all the factors and forces that make a market and are interpreted by buyers, sellers and market makers in their assessment of market worth. In an active market where many similar properties with similar characteristics and qualities are being exchanged, a valuer will, with experience, be able to measure exchange value by comparing that which is to be valued with that which has just been sold. This direct or comparative method of valuation is used almost exclusively for the valuation of vacant possession freehold residential property. Differences in age, condition, accommodation and location can all, within reason, be reflected by the valuer in his assessment of value. Differences in size can sometimes be overcome by adopting a unit of comparison such as price per hectare or rent per square metre.

The more problematic properties are those for which there is no ready market; those which display special or unique characteristics; those which do not fully utilise the potential of their location and are therefore ripe for development, redevelopment or refurbishment; those that are tenanted and are sold as investments at prices reflecting their income generating potential; and leasehold properties.

For each of these broad categories valuers have developed methods of valuation that they feel most accurately reflect the market's behavioural attitude and which may therefore be considered to be rational methods.

In the case of special properties such as oil refineries,

glassworks, hospitals and schools the usual valuation method is the cost or contractor's method. It is the valuer's method of last resort and is based on the supposition that no purchaser would pay more for an existing property than the sum of the cost of buying a similar site and constructing a similar building with similar utility written down to reflect the physical, functional and locational obsolescence of the actual building.

Properties with latent development value are valued using the residual or development (developer's) method. The logic here is that the value of the property (site) in its current state must equal the value of the property in its developed or redeveloped state less all the costs of development including profit but excluding the land. In those cases where the residual sum exceeds the existing use value then in theory the property will be released for that higher and better use.

All property that is income producing or is capable of producing an income in the form of rent, and for which there is both an active tenant market and an active investment market, will be valued by the market's indirect method of comparison. This is known as the investment method of valuation or the income approach to property valuation and is the principal method considered in this book.

The income approach and the income-based residual warrant special attention if only because they are the valuer's main weapon in the valuation of the most complex and highly priced investment properties.

The unique characteristics of property make property investment valuation more complex an art and science than that exercised by brokers and market makers in the market for stocks and shares. As property, stocks and shares are the main investments available there is, however, bound to be some similarity between the pricing (valuation) methods used in the various markets and some relationship between the investment opportunities offered by each. A basic market measure is the investment yield or rate of return. The assessment of the rate of return allows or permits comparison to be made of investments within each market and between different investments in different markets. There is a complex interrelationship of yields and patterns of yields within the whole investment market, and in turn these yields are the key to pricing or valuation methods. Understanding those market relationships and methods can only follow from an understanding of investment arithmetic.

. Part One of this book therefore considers the basic investment arithmetic used by valuers. Part Two applies that knowledge to the valuation of income-producing property. Part Three considers some of the techniques used in the field of risk analysis. Throughout it is assumed that the reader has some knowledge of who buys property, why they buy it and what alternative investment opportunities there are, and also that he or she will have some knowledge of the nature of property as an investment. The reader should have some awareness of the social, economic and political factors that influence the market for and the value of property.

Our purpose in writing this book has been aptly summarised, coincidentally, by Robert Chartham in *Sex Manners for Advanced Lovers*, which we misquote with apologies.

> What we are trying to aim at is to put forward suggestions of techniques which may not have occurred to some who have already transformed themselves into highly proficient (seasoned) *valuers*, in the hope that they will be encouraged to try them out to discover for themselves whether or not they are of any help to them, their partners *or their clients*.

Part one

Chapter one

Valuation mathematics

If it is possible to summarise the functions of a valuer, it might be said that a valuer attempts to estimate the future benefits to be enjoyed from the ownership of a freehold or a leasehold interest in land or property, expressing those future benefits in terms of present worth. To do this a valuer must have a knowledge of the mathematics of finance and the theory of compounding and discounting.

The necessary calculations for the mathematics of finance require the use of one or more of the six functions of £1.

1 The amount of £1, or the future worth of £1 invested today allowing for compound interest at a given rate.
2 The amount of £1 per period, or the future worth of £1 invested at regular intervals of time with compound interest at a given rate.
3 The sinking fund factor, or that fraction of £1 which must be invested at regular intervals of time to produce £1 in a given period with compound interest at a given rate.
4 The present value of £1, or the present worth of £1 to be received in the future, discounted over a given period at a given rate of interest.
5 The present value of £1 per period, or the present worth of a series of payments of £1 due at regular intervals for a given period of time, discounted at a given rate of interest. This is known by property valuers as the years' purchase single rate.
6 The instalment to amortise £1, mortgage requirement or annuity, or the equal periodic payment required for both principal and interest on a loan of £1 for a given period of time and with interest at a given rate.

This first chapter deals with the basic mathematics of each function and its uses, and the interrelationship of the various functions.

3

At the present time there are several volumes of tables for the six (and other) functions available. Some of these tables are based on the assumption that income may be received or invested quarterly, but for most of this chapter the simplifying assumption will be made that payments or receipts are made or received at the beginning or end of the year in one instalment. It is also assumed that the tables work from the basis that the unit of money is always £1. All tables are based on the basic compound interest table, the amount of £1. Each function will be considered in the above order but will be referred to by the designation used by property valuers.

Single rate tables

1   The amount of £1

The amount of £1 is an unusual name for a familiar concept – compound interest. This accumulates both on the original capital sum invested and also on the interest added to it. Instead of a percentage, interest is expressed as a decimal (i) or (r), e.g. 5% = 5 ÷ 100 = 0.05.

If £1 is invested for 1 year at i interest, at the end of that year it will have accumulated to $(1 + i)$.

At the end of the second year $(1 + i)$ will have earned interest at i; so at the end of the second year it will have accumulated to $(1 + i) + i(1 + i)$, which can be expressed as $(1 + i)^2$.

At the end of n years the accumulated sum will be $(1 + i)^n$. This is the amount of £1, or A.

$$A = (1 + i)^n$$

where n is the number of years (or periods) of accumulation and i is the rate of interest, expressed as a decimal, per interest-earning period.

Example 1.1   Calculate to four places of decimals the amount of £1 after 5 years at 8%.

$$A = (1 + i)^n \qquad i = 0.08; \; n = 5$$

$$\therefore A = (1.08)^5$$

$$= (1.08) \times (1.08) \times (1.08) \times (1.08) \times (1.08)$$

$$= \underline{1.4693}$$

£1 will accumulate to £1.47 after 5 years at 8% compound interest.

2 The amount of £1 per annum

Regular investment such as that catered for by building societies is often undertaken by means of a standing order, authorising a fixed amount to be paid regularly into the account by the investor's bank. Each payment will accumulate at compound interest, so the accumulation of such payments could be calculated by a series of amount of £1 calculations. This would obviously be tedious.

The amount of £1 per annum table deals with this type of accumulation. It shows the amount to which £1, invested at the end of each year, will accumulate at i interest after n years.

The table is simply the summation of a series of amounts of £1. If each £1 is invested at the end of the year, the nth £1 will be invested at the end of the nth year and will thus earn no interest whatsoever. It must be worth £1. Each preceding £1 will earn interest for an increasing number of years thus: the $(n - 1)$ £1 will have accumulated for 1 year, and will be worth $(1 + i)$.

The $(n - 2)$ £1 will have accumulated for 2 years, and will be worth $(1 + i)^2$.

The first £1 invested at the end of the first year will be worth $(1 + i)^{n-1}$.

The series will read as follows:

$$1 + (1 + i) + (1 + i)^2 \ldots (1 + i)^{n-1}$$

This is a geometric progression. When summated it can be expressed as

$$\frac{(1 + i)^n - 1}{i}$$

and this is the formula for the amount of £1 per annum (A £1 p.a.).

Example 1.2 Calculate to four places of decimals the amount of £1 per annum for 5 years at 8%.

$$A \text{ £1 p.a.} = \frac{(1 + i)^n - 1}{i} \qquad i = 0.08; \; n = 5$$

$$\therefore A \text{ £1 p.a.} = \frac{(1.08)^5 - 1}{0.08} = \frac{1.4693 - 1}{0.08}$$

$$= \frac{0.4693}{0.08} \qquad = \underline{5.8666}$$

Example 1.3　If Mr A invests £60 in a building society at the end of every year, and at the end of 20 years has £4,323, at what rate of interest has this accumulated?

Annual sum invested	£60
A £1 p.a. for 20 years @ i%	x
Capital value (CV)	£4,323

$$x = \frac{£4,323}{£60} = 72.05$$

Looking through any amount of £1 p.a. tables, it will be seen that 72.05 is the relevant value for 20 years at *12%*. This is the rate of compound interest at which the investment has accumulated.

3　Annual sinking fund

Investors, particularly property investors, will often have a known expense to meet at some time in the future. Property requires regular maintenance; a premium may be payable by a tenant to a landlord at any time in the future in return for the grant of a lease; or a substantial part of a property may require complete renewal.

Such obligations must be reflected in the purchase price of the investment. As a result, the investor will have to estimate the magnitude and timing of the expense. The investor could invest a lump sum now which with interest would cover the expense when it arises, but it may be more convenient to set aside part of the income earned by the investment itself (i.e. rent) in a regular account or sinking fund which would accumulate to the required sum.

Example 1.4　An investor is considering the purchase of a small shop in which the window frames have begun to rot. It is estimated that in 4 years' time they will require complete replacement at a cost of £1,850. The shop produces a net income of £750 p.a. How much of this income should be set aside each year to meet the expense assuming an assured return of 7%?

Amount to be set aside	x
A £1 p.a. for 4 years @ 7%	4.44
Cost	£1,850

$$£1,850 = 4.44x$$
$$x = £416.67 \text{ p.a.}$$

This annual sum is termed a 'sinking fund', or ASF for short.

The use of annual sinking fund tables enables this sum to be calculated more easily.

Sum required	£1,850
ASF to replace £1 in 4 years @ 7%	0.22523
ASF	£416.67 p.a.

It can be seen that this calculation performs the function of the A £1 p.a. in reverse. In the first calculation the amount set aside was found by dividing the capital sum required by the A £1 p.a. In the second case the annual sum was found by the product of the capital sum required and the ASF. It follows that the ASF table is the reciprocal of A £1 p.a.

$$A \text{ £1 p.a.} = \frac{(1 + i)^n - 1}{i} = \frac{A - 1}{i}$$

$$\therefore \text{ASF} = \frac{i}{(1 + i)^n - 1} = \frac{i}{A - 1}$$

Example 1.5 Calculate the ASF to accumulate to £1 after 5 years @ 10%.

$$\text{ASF} = \frac{i}{(1 + i)^n - 1} = \frac{0.10}{(1.10)^5 - 1} = \frac{0.10}{1.61051 - 1}$$

$$= \frac{0.10}{0.61051} = \underline{0.1637975}$$

Example 1.6 Calculate the ASF necessary to produce £1 at the end of 15 years at 3% using the amount of £1 table.

All tables are based on compound interest, the amount of £1. In the ASF formula

$$\text{ASF} = \frac{i}{A - 1} = \frac{i}{(1 + i)^n - 1}$$

A is quickly identified as $(1 + i)^n$. For given values of i and n this constituent part of the ASF formula will give the amount of £1 for n years at i.

Amount £1 for 15 years @ 3% $= (1.03)^{15} = 1.558$

Thus $\text{ASF} = \dfrac{i}{1.558 - 1} = \dfrac{0.03}{0.558} = \underline{0.05376}$

4 The present value of £1

As any sum invested today will be worth more than the same sum receivable at some future date due to the accumulation of compound interest so £1 receivable in the future cannot be worth £1 at the present time. What it is worth will be the sum that could be invested now to accumulate to £1 at that future date. That sum will depend on the rate of interest that could be received and the length of time for which the use of the £1 is forgone. The present value of £1 table takes these factors into account and quantifies this present sum.

If £1 were invested now at i for n years, then at the end of the period it would be worth $(1 + i)^n$.

If £x were to be invested now at i for n years and assuming it will accumulate to £1

Then $x(1 + i)^n = £1$

and $x = \dfrac{1}{(1 + i)^n}$

This is the formula for the present value of £1 (PV), and is the reciprocal of the amount of £1.

$$PV = \frac{1}{(1 + i)^n} = \frac{1}{A}$$

Proof:
PV £1 in 7 years @ 10% = 0.51316
A £1 in 7 years @ 10% = 1.9487
0.51316 × 1.9487   = 1.00

Example 1.7 If Mr X requires a rate of return of 10%, how much much would you advise him to pay for the right to receive £200 in 5 years' time?

$$PV = \frac{1}{(1 + i)^n} = \frac{1}{(1.10)^5} = \frac{1}{1.6105} = 0.6209$$

0.6209 × £200 = £124.18

5 Present value of £1 per annum

The amount of £1 p.a. was seen to be the summation of a series of amounts of £1. Similarly, the present value of £1 per annum is the summation of a series of present values of £1. It is the present value of the right to receive £1 at the end of each year for n years at i.

The present value of £1 receivable in one year is $\dfrac{1}{(1 + i)}$, in two

years it is $\dfrac{1}{(1 + i)^2}$, and so the series reads

$$\frac{1}{(1 + i)} + \frac{1}{(1 + i)^2} + \frac{1}{(1 + i)^3} \cdots \frac{1}{(1 + i)^n}$$

This is again a geometric progression and can be expressed as

$$\frac{1 - \dfrac{1}{(1 + i)^n}}{i}$$

when summated. This is the formula for PV £1 p.a.

$$\text{PV £1 p.a.} = \frac{1 - \dfrac{1}{(1 + i)^n}}{i} \quad \text{or} \quad \frac{1 - \text{PV}}{i}$$

Example 1.8 Calculate the present value of £1 per annum at 5% for 20 years given that the present value of £1 in 20 years @ 5% is 0.3769.

PV £1 in 20 years @ 5% = 0.3769

$$\text{PV £1 p.a.} = \frac{1 - \text{PV}}{i}$$

$$= \frac{1 - 0.3769}{0.05} = \frac{0.6231}{0.05} = \underline{12.462}$$

Example 1.9 How much should A pay for the right to receive an income of £675 for 64 years if he requires a 12% return?

Income	£675
PV £1 p.a. for 64 years @ 12%	8.3274
CV	£5,621

The present value of £1 p.a. is usually referred to by valuers as 'years' purchase'. The Oxford English Dictionary gives a date of 1584 for the first use of the phrase 'at so many years' purchase' used in stating the price of land in relation to the annual rent in perpetuity. This term is less than helpful when relating it to other tables. However, the terms are interchangeable and both terms will be used.

Valuation mathematics

The PV £1 p.a. increases as the number of years increases. However, it approaches a maximum value as a certain time period is reached. This time period is actually infinity, but is often as a simplification assumed to be reached at 100 years. In valuation language it is referred to as 'perpetuity'. The maximum value of PV £1 p.a. is the present value of £1 p.a. in perpetuity, or the years' purchase in perpetuity (YP perp.). This will give the present value of the right to receive £1 at the end of each year in perpetuity at i.

Property investments will often produce perpetual incomes (see Chapter 3).

Example 1.10 In the formula $\dfrac{1 - \text{PV}}{i}$ what happens to PV as the time period increases? What effect does this have on the YP figure? Derive the formula for years' purchase in perpetuity and compare with $\dfrac{1 - \text{PV}}{i}$

Table 1.1

Years	PV @ 10%	PV £1 p.a. @ 10%
10	0.3855	6.1446
20	0.1486	8.5136
30	0.0573	9.4269
40	0.0221	9.7791
50	0.0085	9.9148
75	0.00078	9.9921
100	0.00007	9.9993

From Table 1.1 two facts are apparent. The first of these is that the PV decreases as n increases; and the second is that, in accordance with logic, YP increases with time. It follows that the PV inherent in the YP formula has a role to play, as it reduces the value of the YP as n decreases and thus allows YP to increase as n increases. As n approaches perpetuity, PV tends towards 0 (the present value of £1 receivable in an infinite number of years' time is infinitely small) and $\dfrac{1 - \text{PV}}{i}$ tends towards $\dfrac{1 - 0}{i}$. The formula for YP in perpetuity is therefore $\dfrac{1}{i}$

For example: at a rate of 10%, YP perp $= \dfrac{1}{0.10} = 10$.

10

Example 1.11   A freehold property produces a net income of £1,500 p.a. If an investor requires a return of 8%, what price should be paid? The income is perpetual: a YP in perpetuity should be used

Income	£1,500	
YP perp. @ 8%	12.5	$\left(\dfrac{1}{0.08} = 12.5\right)$
CV	£18,750	

A third present value of £1 per annum variant is 'the years' purchase of a reversion to a perpetuity'. It shows the present value of the right to receive £1 at the end of every year in perpetuity, after a given period of time, at i.

The table thus combines two functions: it calculates the present value of the right to receive a perpetual income starting immediately (YP in perpetuity) and then defers that value (present value of £1) at the same rate of interest.

$$\text{YP rev. perp.} = \text{YP in perp.} \times \text{PV £1}$$

$$= \frac{1}{i} \times \frac{1}{(1 + i)^n}$$

$$= \frac{1}{iA}$$

Example 1.12   Calculate in two ways the present value of a perpetual income of £600 p.a. beginning in 7 years' time using a discount rate of 12%.

Income	£600
YP perp. @ 12%	8.33
CV	£5,000
PV £1 in 7 years @ 12%	0.45235
CV	£2,262

$$\text{or YP rev. perp.} = \frac{1}{iA} = \frac{1}{i(1 + i)^7} = \frac{1}{0.12(1.12)^7} = \frac{1}{0.12(2.2107)}$$

$$= \frac{1}{0.265284} = 3.7695$$

Income	£600
YP rev. perp. in 7 years @ 12%	3.7695
CV	£2,262

Note: It can also be found by deducting the YP for 7 years at 12% from the YP in perpetuity at 12%.

The use of this present value or discounting technique to assess the price to be paid for an investment or the value of an income-producing property ensures the correct relationship between future benefits and present worth; namely that the investor will obtain both a return on capital and a return of capital at the target rate or market-derived rate of interest used in the calculation. This point is important and can be missed when PV factors are summated to produce the PV of £1 p.a. and when valuers rename a well-known investment function 'years' purchase'!

For example, if an investor is offered five separate investment opportunities on five separate occasions of £10,000 in a year's time, £10,000 in 2 years' time, £10,000 in 3 years' time, £10,000 in 4 years' time and £10,000 in 5 years' time, and seeks a 10% return on each occasion, the prices offered will be £9,090, £8,264, £7,513, £6,830, and £6,209 respectively. The calculation and proof can be shown thus:

| | Returns due in | | | | |
	1 year	2 years	3 years	4 years	5 years
	£10,000	£10,000	£10,000	£10,000	£10,000
PV £1 in *n* years at 10%	.9090	.8264	.7513	.6830	.6209
	£9090	£8264	£7513	£6830	£6209
A £1 in *n* years at 10%	1.100	1.210	1.3310	1.4641	1.6105
	£10,000	£10,000	£10,000	£10,000	£10,000

In each case the present worth or price equivalent today represents that sum of money which, if it had been saved and had earned the specified rate of interest for the specified number of years would have accumulated to £10,000. In the case of each exchange of money today for a known future sum it can be shown that although no interest is received for 1, 2, 3, 4 or 5 years, each future receipt of £10,000 repays the investor's respective initial cash commitment and the extra amount provides the precise equivalent of the interest forgone for the period. Hence the return on capital at 10% has been achieved and the initial capital has been returned.

The offer of a single investment opportunity of £10,000 at the end of each year for 5 years is the same exercise summated to give a present worth or price today of £37,908. For convenience it is found by multiplying £10,000 by the PV £1 p.a. for 5 years at 10% (£10,000 × 3.7908 = £37,908).

Clearly a return of the initial £37,908 must be achieved and a return of 10% must be enjoyed. The proof is shown in the table below.

Year	Capital outstanding	Return at 10%	Income	Balance or return of capital
1	37,908.00	3,790.80	10,000	6,209.20
2	31,698.80	3,169.88	10,000	6,830.12
3	24,868.68	2,486.87	10,000	7,513.13
4	17,355.55	1,735.55	10,000	8,264.45
5	9,091.10	909.11	10,000	9,090.89

(*Note*: Rounding error due to working to 2 decimal places.)

Discounted cash flow (DCF)

DCF is an aid to the valuation or analysis of any investment producing a cash flow. In its general form, it has two standard products – NPV and IRR.

(a) Net present value (NPV)　　Future net benefits receivable from the investment are discounted at a given 'target rate'. The sum of the discounted benefits is found and the initial cost of the investment deducted from this sum, to leave what is termed the net present value of the investment, which may be positive or negative. A positive NPV implies that a rate of return greater than the target rate is being yielded by the investment; a negative NPV implies that the yield is at a rate of return lower than the target rate. The target rate is the minimum rate which the investor requires in order to make the investment worth while, taking into account the risk involved and all other relevant factors.

It will be governed in particular by one factor: the investor's cost of capital.

Investments may require the initial outlay of a large capital sum, and investors will often be forced to borrow money in order to accumulate that sum. The interest to be paid on that loan will be the investor's cost of capital at that time. It is clear that the rate of return from an investment where the initial capital has been borrowed should be at least equal to the cost of capital, or a loss will result.

An alternative way of looking at this is that the investor will always have alternative opportunities for the investment of his capital. Money may be lent quite easily to earn a rate of interest

13

based on the cost of capital. The return from any investment should therefore compare favourably with the opportunity cost of the funds employed, and this will usually be related to the cost of capital.

For these reasons, the target rate should compare well with the cost of capital. From this basis, a positive or negative NPV will be the result of the analysis and upon this result the investment decision may be made.

Example 1.13 Find the NPV of the following project, using a target rate based on a cost of capital of 13%

Outlay £10,000	£	PV £1 @ 13%	Discounted sum
Returns in year 1	5,000	0.8849	4,425
2	4,000	0.7831	3,133
3	6,000	0.6930	4,158
			£11,716
		Less outlay	£10,000
		NPV	£1,716

The investment yields a return of 13% and, in addition, a positive NPV of £1,716. In the absence of other choices, this investment may be accepted.

However, it is more usual for the investment decision to be one of choice.

Example 1.14 An investor has £1,400 to invest and has a choice between investment A and B. The following returns are anticipated:

Income flow	A	B
	£	£
Year 1	600	200
2	400	400
3	200	400
4	400	600
5	400	600

The investor's target rate for both investments is 10%, the investments are mutually exclusive (only one of the two can be undertaken); which investment should be chosen?

Income flow		£	PV £1 @ 10%	Discounted sum
A	Year 1	600	0.9091	545
	2	400	0.8264	330
	3	200	0.7513	150
	4	400	0.6830	273
	5	400	0.6209	248
				£1,546
			Less outlay	£1,400
			NPV	£146

Income flow		£	PV £1 @ 10%	Discounted sum
B	Year 1	200	0.9091	182
	2	400	0.8264	330
	3	400	0.7513	300
	4	600	0.6830	409
	5	600	0.6209	373
				£1,594
			Less outlay	£1,400
			NPV	£194

From this information investment B should be chosen. Each investment gives a return of 10% plus a positive NPV: B produces the greater NPV. If either investment had been considered to be subject to more risk, this fact should have been reflected in the choice of target rate. And both investments involve the use of the same amount of capital.

However, this will not always be the case, and, when outlays on mutually exclusive investments differ, the investment decision will not be so simple. An NPV of £200 from an investment costing £250 is considerably more attractive than a similar NPV produced by a £25,000 outlay. How can this be reflected in an analysis? A possible approach is to express the NPV as a percentage of the outlay.

Example 1.15   Which of these mutually exclusive investments should be undertaken when the investor's target rate is 10%?

A	Outlay £5,000	B	Outlay £7,000
Year 1	£3,000		£4,000
2	£2,000		£3,000
3	£1,500		£2,000

15

			PV £1 @ 10%		
A	1	£3,000	0.9091		£2,727
	2	£2,000	0.8264		£1,653
	3	£1,500	0.7513		£1,127
					£5,507
				Outlay	£5,000
				NPV	£507

			PV £1 @ 10%		
B	1	£4,000	0.9091		£3,636
	2	£3,000	0.8264		£2,479
	3	£2,000	0.7513		£1,503
					£7,618
				Outlay	£7,000
				NPV	£618

At first sight, B might appear to be more profitable, but if NPV is expressed as a percentage of outlay the picture changes.

$$A = \frac{£507}{£5,000} \times 100 = 10.14\%$$

$$B = \frac{£618}{£7,000} \times 100 = 8.83\%$$

On this basis, A and not B should be chosen.

The NPV method is a satisfactory aid in the great majority of investment problems but suffers from one particular disadvantage. The return provided by an investment is expressed in two parts – a rate of return, and a cash sum in addition which represents an extra return. These two parts are expressed in different units which may make certain investments difficult to compare.

This fault is not present in the following method of expressing the results of a DCF analysis.

(b) The internal rate of return (IRR) This is the discount rate which equates the discounted flow of future benefits with the initial outlay. It produces an NPV of 0 and may be found by the use of various trial discount rates.

Example 1.16   find the IRR of the following investment.

Outlay £6,000: Returns Year 1   £1,024
                      2   £4,000
                      3   £3,000

Trying 10%		PV £1 @ 10%	
Year 1	£1,024	0.9091	£931
2	£4,000	0.8264	£3,306
3	£3,000	0.7513	£2,253
			£6,490
		Outlay	£6,000
		NPV	£490

At a trial rate of 10%, a positive NPV results. £490 is too high –
an NPV of 0 is the desired result. The trial rate must be too low, as
the future receipts should be discounted to a greater extent.

Trying 16%		PV £1 @ 16%	
Year 1	£1,024	0.8621	£883
2	£4,000	0.7432	£2,972
3	£3,000	0.6407	£1,923
			£5,778
		Outlay	£6,000
		NPV	−£222

This time the receipts have been discounted too much. A negative
NPV is the result, so the trial rate is too high. The IRR must be
between 10% and 16%.

Trying 14%		PV £1 @ 14%	
Year 1	£1,024	0.8772	£899
2	£4,000	0.7695	£3,076
3	£3,000	0.6750	£2,025
			£6,000
		Outlay	£6,000
		NPV	£0,000

As the NPV is 0, the IRR must be 14%.

Calculation of the IRR by the use of trial rates will be difficult when the IRR does not happen to coincide with a round figure, as in the following illustration.

Outlay £4,925
Trying 11%

			PV £1 @ 11%	
Cash flow	Year 1	£2,000	0.9009	£1,802
	2	£2,000	0.8116	£1,623
	3	£2,000	0.7312	£1,462
				£4,887
			Less outlay	£4,925
			NPV	−£38

The trial rate is too high: Trying 10%

			PV £1 @ 10%	
	Year 1	£2,000	0.9091	£1,818
	2	£2,000	0.8264	£1,652
	3	£2,000	0.7513	£1,503
				£4,973
			Less outlay	£4,925
			NPV	£48

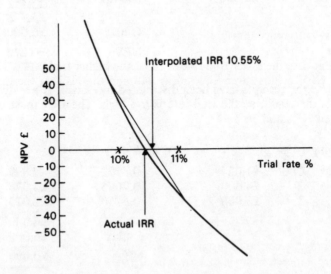

Figure 1.1

18

The IRR is therefore between 10% and 11%. Published tables may not give PV figures between 10% and 11%; the continued use of trial rates to make a more accurate estimation of the IRR will therefore be impracticable. The analysis has shown that the IRR lies between 10% and 11%, but the accuracy of such an analysis is limited.

A graph of NPVs plotted against trial rates will usually take the form shown in Figure 1.1. The graph shows how the IRR (producing an NPV of 0) lies between 10% and 11%. If the graph is drawn accurately, it will be possible to estimate the IRR in this way. This process is both difficult and time-consuming and will not guarantee complete accuracy. The graph takes the shape of a gentle curve and although a straight line may be assumed between two sufficiently close trial rates and the IRR estimated to a fair degree of accuracy, it is not precise. This process is known as linear interpolation.

Linear interpolation can also be carried out by the use of the following formula, which simply assumes a straight-line relationship between the trial rates and the resulting NPVs.

IRR = Lower trial rate

$$+ \frac{\text{NPV at lower trial rate}}{\text{NPV at lower trial rate} + \text{NPV at higher trial rate}}$$
$$\text{(ignoring signs)}$$

× Difference in trial rates

In this case the lower trial rate is 10%; the higher trial rate is 11%; the NPV at the lower trial rate is £48 and the NPV at the higher trial rate is −£38. The difference in trial rates is 1%.

$$\text{IRR} = 10\% + \frac{48}{48 + 38} \times 1\%$$

$$= 10\% + \frac{48}{86} \%$$

$$= 10\% + 0.558\%$$

$$= \underline{10.558\%}$$

This result is a more accurate representation of the geographical interpolation which yielded a result of 10.55%.

This method will provide a satisfactory answer in the majority of cases. However, it must be borne in mind that a graph of NPVs plotted against trial rates will result in a curve, and not a straight line between two points. Because of this, linear interpolation is inaccurate to a certain extent, and the result should not be expressed to too many decimal places. An IRR of 10.56% will be sufficiently reliable and precise for most purposes. Such calculations, however, are more readily undertaken using an investment calculator, the correct figure being 10.56087452%. When NPV and IRR results are compared, difficulties may arise:

Example 1.17   On the basis of NPV and IRR methods rank the following investments, using a rate of 10% in each case.

A		B	
Outlay £5,000		Outlay £10,000	
Year 1	£600	Year 1	£3,432
2	£2,000	2	£3,432
3	£4,000	3	£3,432
4	£585	4	£3,432

(a) NPV: trial rate 10%

PV £1 @ 10%

A. Year 1	£600	0.9091	£545
2	£2,000	0.8264	£1,653
3	£4,000	0.7513	£3,005
4	£585	0.6830	£399
			£5,602
		Less outlay	£5,000
		NPV	£602

PV £1 @ 10%

B. Year 1	£3,432	0.9091	£3,120
2	£3,432	0.8264	£2,836
3	£3,432	0.7513	£2,578
4	£3,432	0.6830	£2,344
			£10,878
		Less outlay	£10,000
		NPV	£878

On the basis of the NPV method, the investor should choose B.

(b) IRR: It is clear from the above calculations that each investment has an IRR exceeding 10%.

A Trying 15%				B Trying 14%			
Year 1	£600	0.8696	£522	Year 1	£3,432	0.8772	£3,011
2	£2,000	0.7561	£1,512	2	£3,432	0.7695	£2,639
3	£4,000	0.6575	£2,632	3	£3,432	0.6750	£2,317
4	£585	0.5718	£334	4	£3,432	0.5921	£2,033
			£5,000				£10,000

Deducting the outlays of £5,000 and £10,000 the results are:

NPV = 0 IRR = 15%   *NPV = 0   IRR = 14%*

Therefore choose A.

IRR and NPV methods give different rankings in this case. Which investment should be chosen? In investment B, an extra £5,000 has been employed. It produces certain extra benefits.
The difference between A and B could be tabulated.

	A	B	B – A
Outlay	£5,000	£10,000	£5,000
Receipts: Year 1	£600	£3,432	£2,832
2	£2,000	£3,432	£1,432
3	£4,000	£3,432	−£568
4	£584	£3,432	£2,848

The final column could be called the increment of B over A. This in itself becomes a cash flow on which an NPV or IRR analysis could be carried out. The cost of capital is 10%, and, as it has been assumed to represent the investor's target rate, it is also assumed that this is a rate of return that could be earned elsewhere. If the increment earns a return of less than 10%, the investor would be wise to invest £5,000 in project A and obtain 10% interest elsewhere with the remaining £5,000.

Another way of looking at this is to remember that the cost of capital also represents the cost of borrowing money. If the investor's £10,000 has been borrowed, a return of less than 10% on the increment of £5,000 of project B over project A means that the loan charges on this £5,000 are not being covered and the loan of the second £5,000 was not worth while.

21

However, if the increment can be shown to produce a return in excess of 10%, the loan charges will be covered. Investment B thus uses the whole £10,000 to good effect. If project A were chosen, the extra £5,000 could only earn 10%, as it is assumed that no return in excess of the cost of capital could be earned without incurring an extra element of risk.

Such an analysis is called *incremental analysis*.

Incremental flow:		PV £1 @ 10%	
Year 1	£2,832	0.9091	£2,575
2	£1,432	0.8264	£1,183
3	−£568	0.7513	−£427
4	£2,848	0.6830	£1,945
			£5,276
			−£5,000
		NPV* =	£276

The IRR of the increment exceeds 10%, so investment B should be chosen. The first £5,000 employed is as profitable as it would be if used in investment A; the second £5,000 is used more profitably than is possible elsewhere. B is therefore preferable to the investment of £5,000 in A plus the investment of £5,000 at the cost of capital rate of interest of 10%.

Discounted cash flow tables in certain sets of valuation tables are simply extensions of the present value of £1 and present value of £1 per annum tables: this illustrates the point that DCF is nothing more than a present value exercise.

6   Annuity £1 will purchase

This shows the amount that will be paid back at the end of each year for n years at i, in return for £1 invested. It calculates the annuity that can be bought for £1.

An annuity entitles the investor to a series of equal annual sums. It may be perpetual or for a limited term.

When money is invested in a building society, interest accumulates on the principal which remains in the account. But when an

---

*Any project incorporating frequent sign changes can produce more than one IRR. This arises from the polynomial nature of the equation.

annuity is purchased the purchase price is lost forever to the investor. The return from building society investment year by year is all interest on capital. But the return from an annuity represents partly interest on capital and partly the purchase price being returned bit by bit to the investor. These constituent parts will be referred to as return on capital (interest) and return of capital.

The original capital outlay must be returned by the end of the investment. If not, how could the rate of interest earned by an annuity investment be compared with the rate of interest earned in a building society? One retains the original capital outlay for the investor to recoup at any time, so the other (the annuity) must likewise return all the investor's capital.

The amount of an annuity will depend on three factors: the purchase price, i and n.

Example 1.18 What annuity will £50 purchase for 5 years if a 10% yield is required?

Sum	£50
Annuity £1 w.p. for 5 years @ 10%	0.2638
Annuity	£13.19

The £13.19 has two constituent parts. The return on capital is 10% of the outlay, i.e. £5 p.a. This leaves £8.19 extra. This must be the return of capital. But 5 × £8.19 does not return £50 because each payment is in the nature of a sinking fund which needs to be accumulated at compound interest (in this case 10%).

Proof:	
ASF	£8.19
A £1 p.a. for 5 years @ 10%	6.1051
CV	£50

This shows that the return on capital and return of capital are both achieved, as a sinking fund is inherent in the annuity.

Return on capital = i
Return of capital = SF

The formula for the annuity £1 w.p. is thus $i +$ SF, where i is the rate of interest required and SF is the annual sinking fund required to replace the capital outlay in n years at i.

Example 1.19 Calculate the annuity £1 will purchase for 10 years at 10%, if £6.1446 will purchase £1 at the end of each year for 10 years.

£1 will purchase $\frac{1}{6.1446}$ = £0.1627. Therefore the annuity £1 will purchase for 10 years at 10% is £0.1627.

The annuity factor can also be calculated from the formula i + SF. As the sinking fund factor is the annual factor of £1 needed to amortise £1 so the total partial payment required for recovery of capital and for interest on capital must be the amortisation factor plus the interest rate.

Therefore the annuity £1 will purchase for 10 years at 10% is:

$$i = 0.1$$
$$\text{plus the ASF to replace £1 in 10 years @ 10\%} = \underline{0.0627}$$
$$\underline{\underline{£0.1627}}$$

The majority of individuals interpret annuity to mean a life annuity. A life annuity is a policy issued by a life assurance office whereby the annuitant will receive for the rest of his life a given annual income in exchange for a given capital sum. The calculations undertaken by the life offices' actuaries have to take account of a number of special factors including the life expectancy factor. Such problems are outside the scope of this book, which is primarily concerned with annuities certain, that is the exchange of capital for a known income for a fixed and known period of time.

But whether one is considering a life annuity or the income flow from property certain terms are common to both.

In arrears: This means that the first annual sum will be paid (received) 12 months after the purchase or taking out of the policy. The payments could be weekly, monthly, quarterly or for any period provided they are in arrears.

In advance: This means that the payments are made at the beginning of the week, month, year, etc.

An immediate annuity: The word immediate is used to distinguish a normal annuity from a *deferred* annuity. An immediate annuity is one where the income commences immediately either 'in advance' or 'in arrears', whereas in the case of a deferred annuity capital is exchanged today for an annuity 'in advance' or 'in arrears', the first such payment being deferred for a given period of time longer than a year. In assurance terms one might purchase at the age of 50 a life annuity to begin at the age of 65. This would be a deferred annuity.

The majority of annuity tables are based on an 'in arrears' assumption.

The distinction between 'return on' and 'return of' capital is important in the case of life annuities because the capital element is held by the Inland Revenue to be the return of the annuitant's capital and therefore is exempt from income tax. In practice the Inland Revenue have had to indicate how the distinction is to be made. Quite clearly a precise distinction is not otherwise possible, because of the uncertain nature of the annuitant's life.

The distinction in the case of certain property valuations undertaken on an annuity basis is important, because the Inland Revenue are not allowed to distinguish between 'return on' and 'return of' capital other than for life annuities. Thus tax may be payable on the whole income from the property and the desired return may not be achieved unless this factor is accounted for in the valuation.

Example 1.20 What annuity will £4,918 purchase over 6 years at 6%?

	£4,918
Annuity £1 w.p. for 6 years @ 6%	0.2033
	£10,000 per annum

Example 1.21 What annuity will £1,000 purchase over 3 years at 10%?

	£1,000
Annuity £1 w.p. for 3 years @ 10%	0.402
	£402 per annum

Prove that the investor recovers his capital in full and earns interest from year to year at 10%.

Year	Capital outstanding	Interest at 10%	Income	Return of capital
1	1,000	100	402	302
2	698 (1,000 − 302)	69.80	402	332.20
3	365.80 (698 − 332.20)	36.58	402	365.42*

* Error of 0.38 due to rounding.

25

Example 1.22 What sum would have to be paid today to acquire an annuity of £1,000 for 6 years in arrears at 8% to begin in 2 years' time?

The 'in arrears' assumption means that the first £1,000 will be paid in 36 months' time.

```
  0     0     0   1,000 1,000 1,000 1,000 1,000 1,000   £
  L_____L_____L_____L_____L_____L_____L_____L_____L
 Now    1     2     3     4     5     6     7     8    years
```

Annuity income	£1,000
PV £1 p.a. for 6 years @ 8%	4.622
Cost of immediate annuity	£4,622
Defer 2 years × PV £1 in 2* years @ 8%	0.857
	£3,961

* The PV table assumes payment in arrears.

An annuity may be payable in advance. This should cause no difficulty as the PV of £1 per annum payable in advance at rate i for n periods is simply £1 plus the PV of £1 per period, payable in arrears at rate i for $(n - 1)$ periods. Alternatively one can multiply the PV £1 p.a. in arrears for n periods by the factor $(1 + i)$ (see incomes in advance).

Example 1.23 Calculate the capital cost of an annuity of £500 for 6 years due in advance at 10%.

'in advance'

```
 £500  £500  £500  £500  £500  £500
  L_____L_____L_____L_____L_____L_____L
    £500  £500  £500  £500  £500  £500
```

'in arrears'

Annuity income		£500
PV £1 p.a. for 5 years $(n - 1)$ @ 10%	3.79	
plus	1.00	4.79
		£2,395

or

		£500
PV £1 p.a for 6 years @ 10%	4.3553	
by factor $(1 + i)$	× 1.1	4.79
		£2,395

or £500 in advance for 6 years is £500 in arrears for 5 years plus an immediate £500

	£500
PV £1 p.a. for 5 years @ 10%	3.79
	£1,895
	+£ 500
	£2,395

Annuities may be variable. The present worth of variable income flows could be expressed as

$$V = \frac{I_1}{PV_1} + \frac{I_2}{PV_2} + \frac{I_3}{PV_3} \dots + \frac{I_n}{PV_n}$$

Whilst it is possible to have a variable annuity changing from year to year it is more common to find the annuity changing at fixed intervals of time.

Example 1.24   How much would it cost to purchase today an annuity of £1,000 for 5 years followed by an annuity of £1,200 for 5 years on a 10% basis?

Immediate annuity		£1,000	
PV £1 p.a. for 5 years @ 10%		3.79	£3,790
Plus deferred annuity		£1,200	
PV £1 p.a. for 5 years @ 10%	3.79		
PV £1 for 5 years @ 10%	× 0.62	2.3498	£2,820
			£6,610

It will be shown later that this approach is the same as that used by valuers when valuing a variable income flow from a property investment.

In the formula $i + SF$, i will remain the same whatever the length of the annuity. But the value of each year of the annuity will reduce as time increases due to the effect of SF. For a perpetual annuity, SF will be infinitely small, and tends towards 0. A perpetual annuity therefore $= i$.

27

Example 1.25 What perpetual annuity can be bought for £1,500 if a 12% return is required?

$$
\begin{array}{lr}
& \text{Invested sum} \quad £1,500 \\
(i = 0.12) \quad \text{Annuity £1 w.p. @ 12\% perp.} & \underline{0.12} \\
& \text{Annuity} \quad \underline{£180} \text{ p.a.}
\end{array}
$$

The formula for a perpetual annuity is i; the formula for a year's purchase in perpetuity is $\dfrac{1}{i}$ and is therefore the reciprocal. Is this true of all YPs?

$$\text{Annuity £1 w.p. for 5 years @ 10\%} = 0.2638$$

$$\text{YP for 5 years @ 10\%} = 3.7908$$

$$3.7908 = \frac{1}{0.2638}$$

The present value of £1 p.a. and the annuity £1 will purchase tables are therefore reciprocals.

It would follow that a second YP formula would hold, i.e. $\dfrac{1}{i + \text{SF}}$, as the limited term annuity formula is $i + \text{SF}$.

This is easily proved. Annuity £1 w.p. $= i + \text{SF}$:

hence   capital $\times (i + \text{SF}) = \text{Income}$

Now income $\times \text{YP} = \text{Capital}$

$$\therefore \qquad \text{YP} = \frac{1}{i + \text{SF}}$$

This formula will be further discussed under Dual Rate Tables.

Example 1.26 How much should A pay for the right to receive £1 p.a. for 25 years at 10%?

$$\text{YP} = \frac{1}{i + \text{SF}} = \frac{1}{i + \dfrac{i}{(1 + i)^n - 1}} = \frac{1}{0.10 + \dfrac{1.10}{(1.10)^{25} - 1}}$$

$$= \frac{1}{0.10 + 0.0101651} = \frac{1}{0.1101651} = \underline{£9.077}$$

28

Check $\quad YP = \dfrac{1 - PV}{i} = \dfrac{1 - 0.092296}{0.10} = \underline{£9.077}$

The function of SF in this YP formula is exactly the same as that of PV in the original – that is, to reduce the value of the YP figure as *n* decreases. The years' purchase figure must include a sinking fund element, as the valuation of an investment involves equating the outlay with the income and the required yield, so that both a return on capital and a return of capital are received.

Example 1.27   Value an income of £804.21 p.a. receivable for 3 years at a required yield of 10%. Show how both a return on and a return of capital are received.

Income	£804.21
YP for 3 years @ 10%	2.4869
CV	£2,000

Income = £804.21

Return *on* capital	Return *of* capital
= 0.10 × £2,000	= £804.21 − £200
= £200 p.a.	= £604.21

Sinking fund	£604.21
A £1 p.a. for 3 years @ 10%	3.31
CV	£2,000

This can also be demonstrated by a table:

Year	Capital outstanding	Income	Interest on capital	Return of capital
1	£2,000	£804.21	£200	£604.21
2	£1,395.79	£804.21	£139.58	£664.63
3	£731.16	£804.21	£73.12	£731.09*

* Error of £0.07 due to rounding to two decimal places.

A rate of return is received on outstanding capital (i.e. that capital which is at risk) only. The table assumes that some capital is returned at the end of every year so that the amount of capital outstanding reduces year by year. Interest on capital therefore decreases and more of the fixed income is available to return the capital outstanding. The last column shows how the sinking fund accumulates. £604.21 is the first instalment: £664.63 represents the second instalment of £604.21 plus one year's interest at 10%. £731.09 represents the third and final sinking fund instalment of £604.21 plus one year's interest at 10% on £1,268.84 (£664.63 + £604.21). The three summate to the original outlay of £2,000.

The above type of table is also used to show how a mortgage is repaid.

Mortgages

When a property purchaser borrows money by way of a legal mortgage it is usually agreed between the parties that the loan will be repaid in full by a given date in the future. Like anyone else lending money, the building society or mortgagee will require the capital sum to be repaid and will require interest on any outstanding amounts of the loan until such time as the loan and all interest are received. This is comparable to the purchase of an annuity certain from an assurance office. Indeed, conceptually, from the point of view of the mortgagee it is the purchase of an annuity. It follows that the mortgagee will require a return on capital and the return of capital.

The repayment mortgage allows the mortgagor (borrower) to pay back a regular sum each year, often by equal monthly instalments. Usually this sum is partly interest on capital, and partly return of capital. In the early years of the mortgage most of the payment represents interest on the loan outstanding and only a small amount of capital is repaid. But over the period of the loan, as more and more capital is repaid, the interest element becomes smaller and the capital repaid larger.

For the purpose of explanation, interest is assumed fixed throughout the term, but although fixed interest mortgages can occasionally be obtained the majority now make provision for the rate of interest to be varied up or down on due notice to the mortgagor. This requirement is now considered essential by most building societies in order that they may maintain a suitable margin between interest paid to depositors and interest charged to borrowers.

The distinction between 'return on' and 'return of' capital is of practical importance. Residential mortgagors may, up to certain limits, be allowed tax relief on interest paid but not on capital repaid. The distinction is even clearer in the case of the endowment mortgage, where interest is paid to the lender but capital is repaid by means of an assurance policy maturing at the end of the mortgage term. Tax relief may be allowed against the interest payments but not against the assurance premiums. The endowment mortgage tends to be cheaper (net of tax reliefs) at lower rates of interest and repayment mortgages cheaper at rates over 12% gross.

The valuer who can understand the concept of the normal repayment mortgage and can solve standard problems that face mortgagors and mortgagees should readily understand most investment valuation problems. The following examples are indicative of such mortgage problems.

Example 1.28   The sum of £10,000 has been borrowed on a repayment mortgage at 12% for 25 years. (i) Calculate the annual repayment of interest and capital. (ii) Calculate the amount of interest due in the first and tenth years. (iii) Calculate the amount of capital repaid in the first and tenth years.

The formula for the annuity £1 will purchase is $i + SF$. Its reciprocal, the PV £1 p.a. is $\dfrac{1}{i + SF}$ or $\dfrac{1 - PV}{i}$.

The mortgagee is effectively buying an annuity. There is in effect an exchange of £10,000 for an annual sum over 25 years at 12%. What is the annual sum?

	£10,000
Annuity £1 will purchase 25 years @ 12%	0.1275
Annual repayment	£1,275

or £10,000 ÷ PV £1 p.a. for 25 years @ 12%
$$\frac{£10,000}{7.8431} = £1,275$$

As interest in the first year is added immediately to capital borrowed, then:

£10,000 × 0.12 = £1,200 interest due in first year

As the total to be paid is £1,275 so the amount of capital repaid will be £1,275 − £1,200 = £75 in the first year.

The amount of interest in the tenth year will depend upon the amount of capital outstanding at the beginning of the tenth year, i.e. after the ninth annual payment.

Although a mortgage calculation is on a single rate basis, as the formula is $i + SF$ one can assume that £75 p.a. is a sinking fund

31

accumulating over 9 years at 12%.

	£75
Amount of £1 p.a. for 9 years @ 12%	14.7757
Capital repaid is	£1,108.1775

Capital outstanding is £10,000 less £1,108 = £8,892

or calculate the worth at 12% of the right to receive 16 more payments of £1,275.

	£1,275
PV £1 p.a. for 16 years @ 12%	6.974
	£8,892

Capital outstanding is £8,892

∴ interest will be £8,892 × 0.12 = £1,607

And capital repaid in year 10 is £1,275 − £1,067 = £208

In passing it may be observed that the capital in year 1 plus compound interest at 12% will amount to £208 after 9 years.

Year 1 capital	£75
Amount £1 for 9 years @ 12%	2.7731
	£208

As interest on a mortgage is based on capital outstanding from year to year, the change in capital repaid from year to year must be at 12%.

	£75
Amount of £1 for 24 years @ 12%	15.1786
Capital repaid in last year	£1,138

As the annual payment is £1,275, £1,275 − £1,138 represents the interest due in the last year of the mortgage, namely £137.

In most cases the rate of interest will change during the mortgage term. If it does, the mortgagor will usually have the choice of extending the term or repaying at a higher rate. More recently, because of a high rate of interest, borrowers have borrowed on the longest possible term. Increases in the interest rate will then leave the borrower with no choice other than to increase the annual payment, as otherwise the mortgage would never be repaid.

Example 1.29 Given the figures in example 1.28 advise the borrower on the alternatives available to him if the interest rates go down to 10% at the beginning of year 10.

Either: (a) He continues to pay £1,275 per annum and therefore repays the mortgage earlier

or: (b) He reduces his annual payment.

(a) *No change in annual payment*

Amount of capital outstanding at beginning of year 10 is (as before) £8,892.

This will be repaid at an annual rate of £1,275.

$$\frac{£8,892}{£1,275} = \text{PV £1 p.a. for } n \text{ years @ } 10\% = 6.9739$$

Interpolation in the PV £1 p.a. tables at 10% gives n as between 12 and 13 years, i.e. he repays the loan before the due date.

(b) *Change in annual payment*

Capital outstanding is	£8,892
Annuity £1 w.p. for 16 years @ 10%	0.1278
	£1,136

A change in interest at the beginning of year 10 means that, including the payment in year 10, there are 16 more payments due. The capital outstanding × annuity £1 will purchase for 16 years, or divided by PV £1 p.a. for 16 years, at 10% (the new rate of interest) will give the new annual payment. This might be known as the *annual equivalent* of £8,892 over 16 years at 10%.

Currently tax relief on mortgage interest is available up to a mortgage ceiling of £30,000 per mortgaged property. This relief for basic tax payers at 25% is usually handled by the mortgagee under the mortgage interest relief at source scheme (MIRAS). The mortgagee does this by calculating the repayments on a net of tax basis. The net of tax relief payment in example 1.28 might be:

Interest relief at 12% gross less tax at 25% = 9% net.

∴ Repayment on	£10,000
Annuity £1 w.p. for 25 years @ 9%	0.1018
	£1,018

Those claiming relief at the higher rate of 40% will have to make arrangements for this direct with the Inland Revenue through an adjustment to their tax codes. Double tax relief is available to those able to arrange a mortgage through a personal pension scheme. Tax rates and tax relief on mortgages are reviewed annually by the Chancellor.

Dual rate tables

In single rate annuity and years' purchase tables the sinking fund inherent in the formulae is providing for replacement of capital at the same rate per cent as the remunerative or investor's rate of return on capital. As such the sinking fund is notional and ensures that the correct value is assigned to the investment.

If the original capital outlay has to be replaced by the end of the life of the investment by reinvestment, for example, if the investor wishes to maintain a given income flow by purchasing a comparable investment, this can be achieved by creating a sinking fund. Such a situation is rarely engineered in practice. Despite this fact, the conventional technique employed in the valuation of limited term property investments is founded upon this assumption.

The technique is only used by valuers to value wasting assets such as leasehold interests (see Chapter 4). A leasehold interest is a terminating or wasting asset and comes to an end after a given number of years. While a freehold interest may be likened to saving in a building society (the principal is retained in the ownership of the investor) and all income represents a return on capital employed, a leasehold interest may be likened to a limited term annuity. The sum originally invested is spent in return for an income for a given number of years. At the end of that time nothing remains.

In order, therefore, to compare the return from an investment in a leasehold interest with an investment in a freehold interest it is argued that the original outlay must be returned at the end of the lease so that a similar, equal income flow may be acquired. This process may continue into perpetuity so that a perpetual income may be enjoyed and the return becomes comparable with that receivable from a freehold investment.

There would seem to be no problem at first glance because a single rate YP includes a sinking fund to replace initial outlay. But two problems are encountered if an actual sinking fund is to be arranged. While a single rate YP assumes that the sinking fund accumulates at the same rate as the yield from the investment, the rate of interest at which a sinking fund will accumulate does not necessarily relate to the yield given by the investment itself. Two rates may thus be needed. Second, the sinking fund must replace initial capital outlay and so the possible effect of tax on that part of the income that represents capital replacement cannot be ignored (see later) nor can the effect of tax on sinking fund accumulations.

Because the sinking fund must be available at the required point in time with no doubt as to its security, a safe rate of interest is assumed to be earned by the sinking fund. In 1977–78 this fluctuated between 6 and 10% (building society rates) but valuers were using $2\frac{1}{2}$–4%, the practice of the 1930s. This low figure is often justified by the argument that the accumulation must be net of tax (see later); but as building society accounts earn a higher return net of tax, are safe and are much more liquid than a sinking fund need be, so rates higher than 4% could be justified, but 4% is hardly ever exceeded in conventional valuations. During 1988 bank deposit accounts were again yielding as little as 2% net of tax on small deposits so the vagaries of the savings market will sometimes justify the adherence to a low net of tax accumulative rate. The overriding qustion lies not with the rate per cent but with the concept.

As already stated, there is no reason to suppose that the 'accumulative rate' will equate with the yield from the investment or the 'remunerative rate'. Where it does not, the YP figure will be 'dual rate'.

The *only* formula for a dual rate YP catering for the difference in accumulative and remunerative rates is

$$\frac{1}{i + \text{SF}}$$

The formula $\dfrac{1 - \text{PV}}{i}$ can only be used in the case of a single rate

YP; $\dfrac{1}{i + \text{SF}}$ can be used for single or dual rates.

In very rare cases annuities are calculated on a dual rate basis. This means that the investor requires a return on capital at one rate of interest but intends to recover his capital at a lower rate of interest.

Using the formula $i + \text{SF}$ the calculations are no more complex, initially than those for a normal annuity.

Example 1.30 What annuity will £1,000 purchase if interest is at 10% but the return of capital is to be at 2.5% for 10 years?

35

$$i = \quad 0.1000$$

ASF to replace £1 in 10 years @ 2.5% = $\quad \underline{0.0892}$

$$0.1892$$

Therefore £1,000 × 0.1892 = $\quad$ £189.20 per annum

It will be noted that the dual rate introduces a different meaning of rate of return. Previously it was shown that the investor's return was normally assumed to be on capital outstanding from year to year. The dual rate assumes a return on initial capital throughout. Thus:

Capital	Interest at 10%	ASF at 2.5%
£1,000	£100	£89.20
£1,000	£100	£89.20
for each year from 1 to 10.		

The ten amounts of £89.20 have to be assumed to be reinvested in a fund accumulating at 2.5%. Thus:

	£89.2 p.a.
Amount of £1 p.a. for 10 years @ 2.5%	11.2034
Capital replaced	£1,000

The investment is arithmetically perpetuated and it can be seen that on these terms a 10 year annuity of £189.20 p.a. is equal to a £100 perpetual annuity. The spendable income (total income less sinking fund) providing in each case a 10% return on the £1,000.

Example 1.31 How much would it cost to purchase today an annuity of £1,000 for 5 years followed by an annuity of £1,200 for 5 years on a 10% and 2½% basis?

Annuity		£1,000	
PV £1 p.a. for 5 years @ 10% and 2.5%		3.445	£3,445
Plus deferred annuity		£1,200	
PV £1 p.a. for 5 years @ 10% and 2.5%		£3,445	
PV £1 for 5 years @ 10%	× 0.62	2.136	2,563
			£6,008

Example 1.32   Value a limited income of £1,500 p.a. for 6 years where your client requires a yield of 11% and the best safe accumulative rate is 3%. Show how a return on and a return of capital are received.

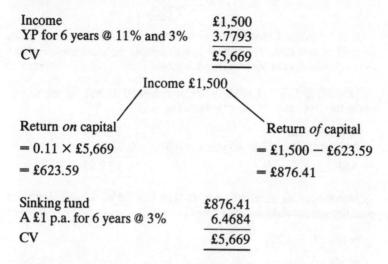

Income	£1,500
YP for 6 years @ 11% and 3%	3.7793
CV	£5,669

Income £1,500

Return *on* capital

= 0.11 × £5,669

= £623.59

Return *of* capital

= £1,500 − £623.59

= £876.41

Sinking fund	£876.41
A £1 p.a. for 6 years @ 3%	6.4684
CV	£5,669

Example 1.33   'Sinking funds, in dual rate YPs, are affected by tax in two ways.' How is this dealt with? Explain by reference to a specimen valuation.

1. The use of dual rate YPs assumes that sinking funds are taken out in practice. Such sinking funds are designed to replace the initial outlay on an investment. Because the sinking fund has to perform this function without question it is assumed to accumulate at a low, safe rate. In addition, it is assumed to accumulate at a net-of-tax rate.

If an investor pays basic rate tax at 25%, and the rate of interest earned by the sinking fund is subject to this rate of tax, then a gross accumulative rate will be reduced to a net accumulative rate. For example, given that ASF is £150 p.a. and the gross accumulative rate is 5% with tax at 25%, then:

After one year £150 × 5% = £7.50 interest is earned.
25% reduces this to (0.75 × £7.50) = £5.625.
£5.625 is only 3.75% of £150 – so the gross rate of 5% has been reduced to a net accumulative rate of 3.75%.

Such a calculation is easily accomplished by applying a tax adjustment factor of $(1 - t)$ to the original gross rate.

37

Thus 5% gross with 25% tax $= 5\% (1 - t)$

$$= 5\% (1 - 0.25)$$
$$= 5\% (0.75)$$
$$= \underline{3.75\%}$$

If the required sinking fund instalment is calculated on gross instead of net rates of interest it will simply be inadequate whenever interest on the sinking fund is taxed.

[*Example 1.34*   £1,000 must be replaced within 10 years. The accumulative rate is 6%: calculate the ASF.

Sum required	£1,000
ASF to replace £1 in 10 years @ 6%	0.075868
ASF	£75.87

However, this accumulation is taxed at 25%. It will therefore actually accumulate at $6\% (1 - t)$

$= 6\% (1 - 0.25)$
$= 6\% (0.75)$
$= 4.5\%$

ASF	£75.87
A £1 p.a. for 10 years @ 4.5%	12.29
CV	£932.44

The sinking fund is insufficient to replace the initial outlay of £1,000, due to the effect of tax on the sinking fund accumulation. The SF must from the start be calculated in the light of the tax rate, i.e.

Sum required	£1,000
ASF to replace £1 in 10 years @ 4.5%	0.08137
ASF	£81.37
A £1 p.a. for 10 years @ 4.5%	12.29
CV	£1,000

The sinking fund has this time been correctly calculated to accumulate after the effect of 25% tax on the interest accumulating on the sinking fund. Accumulative rates must be net of tax to compensate for this first effect that tax has on the accumulation of the sinking fund.]

2. Tax also affects income from property. Rates of return from most investments are quoted gross of tax, because individual tax rates vary and net-of-tax comparisons may, as a result, be meaningless. The remunerative rate $i\%$ in a dual rate YP is therefore a gross rate of interest.

But a sinking fund is tied to the promise that it must actually replace the initial capital outlay, so that a comparable investment may be purchased. The effect of tax on the income cannot therefore be ignored.

[*Example 1.35*   Value a profit rent of £2,000 p.a. (see Chapter 4) receivable for 10 years using a remunerative rate of 10% gross and an accumulative rate of 3% net. The investor pays tax at 25p in the £ on all property income. Show how the calculation is affected.

Ignoring tax on income:	£2,000
YP for 10 years @ 10% and 3%	5.341
CV	£10,682

But income is taxed at 25p in the £:

$$\text{Net income} = £2,000 \times (1 - t)$$
$$= £2,000 (1 - 0.25)$$
$$= £2,000 (0.75)$$
$$= £1,500.$$

From this net income a net remunerative rate of 7.5% [10% (1 − t)] and a sinking fund to replace initial outlay must be found.

CV	£10,682	
Net income	£1,500	

Return *on* capital   Return *of* capital

(or *spendable income*)   (or *sinking fund*)

Net = 0.075 × £10,682		= £1,500 − £801.15	
= £801.15		= £698.85	
	Sinking fund	£698.85	
	A £1 p.a. for 10 years @ 3%	11.4639	
		£8,011.55	

This fails to replace the initial outlay of £10,682. Why? Because, as the income is reduced by 25%, both spendable income and sinking fund must be reduced by 25%. The spendable income then becomes a net spendable income representing a net return on capital and still conforms to the investor's requirements. But the *net* sinking fund must replace £10,682 – the fact that the gross sinking fund would notionally replace the initial outlay is no comfort for the investor left several thousand pounds short. It must therefore be ensured that the *net* sinking fund still replaces the initial outlay. Thus:

Gross sinking fund $\times (1 - t) =$ net sinking fund

Gross sinking fund $=$ net sinking fund $\times \dfrac{1}{1 - t}$

If, having calculated the desired amount that should remain as a net sinking fund, this amount is multiplied by the 'grossing-up' factor of $\dfrac{1}{1 - t}$, the required amount of net sinking fund will remain available after tax. Thus:

Net SF $\times \dfrac{1}{1 - t} \times (1 - t) =$ net SF.

Thus more must be set aside as gross sinking fund, i.e. the net SF $\times \dfrac{1}{1 - t}$. This will necessarily mean the amount of income remaining as spendable income will be reduced, and the investor's requirements of a 10% return will not be fulfilled. A new valuation is therefore required, reducing the price paid so that a grossed-up sinking fund may be provided and a 10% return (gross) can still be attained.

A new YP figure must be calculated using a 10% remunerative rate, a 3% net accumulative rate, and a grossing-up factor applied to the SF of $\dfrac{1}{1 - t}$. The dual rate YP formula adjusted for tax will be

$$\frac{1}{i + \left(\text{SF} \times \dfrac{1}{1 - t}\right)}$$

In this case this becomes $\dfrac{1}{0.10 + \left(0.08723 \times \dfrac{1}{1 - 0.25}\right)}$

$$= \frac{1}{0.10 + \left(0.08723 \times \frac{1}{0.75}\right)} = \frac{1}{0.10 + 0.11630} = \frac{1}{0.2163}$$

$$= 4.6232$$

Revaluation:	Income		£2,000
	YP for 10 years @ 10% and 3% adj. tax @ 25%		4.6232
		CV	£9,246

Proof:	CV	£9,246
	Gross income	£2,000
	Net income	£1,500

Net spendable income	Sinking fund
0.075 × £9,246	£1,500 − £693.45
= £693.45	= £806.55

Sinking fund	£806.55
A £1 p.a. for 10 years @ 3%	11.4639
CV	£9,246

The result of using a tax-adjusted YP has been to reduce the capital value from £10,680 to £9,246. This has enabled the investor to gross-up the sinking fund to compensate for the effect of income tax and leave enough spendable income to provide a 10% gross and 7½% net return on capital.]

The effect of tax on a sinking fund is thus twofold.

1 Tax is levied on the *interest* accumulating on the sinking fund. To allow for this a net accumulative rate must be used.
2 Tax is levied on the *income* from which a sinking fund is drawn. So that the correct net sinking fund remains after tax a grossing-up factor is used. A tax-adjusted dual rate YP caters for this, and ensures that the correct valuation is made.

Interrelationship of tables

The student's knowledge of this may be tested by problems requiring the use of information provided by one particular table to calculate a related figure from another table. A knowledge of the formulae is essential. It can be seen that the amount of £1 is represented in each formula:

$$1 \quad PV = \frac{1}{A} \qquad\qquad 4 \quad YP = \frac{1 - \dfrac{1}{A}}{i} \text{ or } \frac{1}{i + \dfrac{i}{A-1}}$$

$$2 \quad A \text{ £1 p.a.} = \frac{A-1}{i} \qquad\qquad 5 \quad A \text{ £1 w.p.} = i + \frac{i}{A-1}$$

$$3 \quad ASF = \frac{i}{A-1} \qquad\qquad 6 \quad A = (1+i)^n$$

It can also be seen that the six tables fall into three sets of reciprocals. It is the understanding of these two facts that provides the key to the solution of the following type of problem.

Example 1.36 Showing your workings, calculate to four places of decimals:

(i) PV £1 p.a. @ 5% for 20 years using the figure given in the valuation tables for PV £1, 20 years @ 5%.

$$PV = \frac{1}{A}: \qquad\qquad PV \text{ £1 p.a.} = \frac{1 - PV}{i}$$

PV £1 in 20 years @ 5% $= 0.37689$

$$PV \text{ £1 p.a. for 20 years @ 5\%} = \frac{1 - 0.37689}{0.05}$$

$$= \frac{0.62311}{0.05}$$

$$= 12.4622$$

(ii) ASF necessary to produce £1 after 15 years @ 3% using the amount of £1 table.

$$ASF = \frac{i}{A-1} \qquad\qquad A \text{ £1 15 years @ 3\%} = 1.558$$

$$ASF \text{ to replace £1 in 15 years @ 3\%} = \frac{0.03}{1.558 - 1} = \frac{0.03}{0.558}$$

$$= 0.0538$$

(iii) YP 70 years @ 5% and 2½% given that the ASF to produce £1 in 70 years @ 2½% = 0.0053971.

$$YP = \frac{1}{i + SF}$$

where i is the remunerative rate and SF is the annual sinking fund to produce £1 for n years at i

$$= \frac{1}{0.05 + 0.0053971}$$

$$= \frac{1}{0.0553971} = \underline{18.0515}$$

Some problems may not allow such simple substitution.

Example 1.37 Given that A £1 p.a. for 7 years @ 4% = 7.8983, find YP for 7 years @ 4%.

$$A \text{ £1 p.a.} = \frac{A-1}{i} \qquad ASF^* = \frac{i}{A-1}$$

$$\therefore A \text{ £1 p.a.} = \frac{1}{SF}$$

$$YP = \frac{1}{i + SF}$$: the value of SF in this formula is the reciprocal of the amount of £1 p.a. for 7 years @ 4%, i.e. 7.8983.

$$\therefore YP = \frac{1}{0.04 + \dfrac{1}{7.8983}}$$

$$= \frac{1}{0.04 + 0.1266}$$

$$= \frac{1}{0.1666}$$

$$= \underline{6.00}$$

*ASF is the same as SF.

The problem may be complicated further by changing the relevant number of years.

Example 1.38 Given that ASF 16 years @ 4% = 0.04582, find the annuity £1 will purchase for 14 years @ 4%.

This obviously presents a difficulty. It is no longer sufficient just to isolate A, as it will represent the wrong number of years in the annuity figure.

Valuation mathematics

In the compound interest formula $(1 + i)^n$, n is the exponent and the expression means that $(1 + i)$ is multiplied by itself n times. Exponents have certain properties and a knowledge of these can be useful when manipulating the various valuation formulae.

1 Any number raised to the zero power equals 1.

2 A fractional exponent is the root of a number

$$(1 + i)^{\frac{1}{2}} \text{ or } (1 + i)^{0.5} = \sqrt{(1 + i)}$$

$$(1 + i)^{0.2} = \sqrt[5]{(1 + i)}$$

3 When a number being raised to a power is multiplied further by itself the exponents are added:

$$(1 + i)^4 \times (1 + i)^6 = (1 + i)^{10}$$

Similarly $(1 + i)^{10} \div (1 + i)^5 = (1 + i)^5$.

Thus $\dfrac{\text{A £1 for 16 years @ 4\%}}{\text{A £1 for 2 years @ 4\%}} = \text{A £1 for 14 years @ 4\%}$

$$\text{ASF} = \frac{i}{A - 1} = 0.04582$$

$$A - 1 = \frac{0.04}{0.04582} = 0.873 \qquad A = 1.873$$

$$\frac{1.873}{(1 + i)^2} = \text{A £1 for 14 years @ 4\%}$$

$$\frac{1.873}{(1.04)^2} = \frac{1.873}{1.0816} = 1.7317$$

Thus A £1 w.p. for 14 years @ 4% $= i + \dfrac{i}{A - 1}$

$$= 0.04 + \frac{0.04}{1.7317 - 1}$$

$$= 0.04 + \frac{0.04}{0.7317} = 0.04 + 0.05467$$

$$= 0.09467$$

Nominal and effective rates of interest

The rates of return provided by different investments are usually compared by means of the annual rate of interest quoted. For example, building societies usually quote net rates of interest earned in savings accounts, such as 10% per annum, representing the return provided by the investment.

Sometimes, however, such information should be qualified by

the frequency of payment of interest. Where interest is not paid annually, the quoted rate of interest will often be misleading.

For example, building society A pays 10% per annum, interest paid annually. 10% per annum in this case is the quoted or stated rate, which is called the *nominal* rate of interest. Because interest is paid annually, 10% is also the actual rate of interest earned in one year, or the *effective* rate of interest.

Consider, on the other hand, building society B which pays 10% per annum with interest paid half-yearly. 10% per annum paid half-yearly indicates that two instalments of 5% per 6 months are actually paid. Hence the nominal rate of 10% per annum will differ from the effective rate of interest, as the interest paid after 6 months will itself earn interest over the second half of the year.

The total accumulation of £1 invested in an account for one year will therefore be $£(1.05)^2 = £1.1025$. Interest is 10.25 pence, accumulated on £1 invested. The effective rate of interest is therefore 10.25%, and building society B is more generous than building society A.

Investments are therefore best compared by means of the annual effective rate of interest. Building societies, banks and all other finance companies are required to disclose this annual percentage rate (APR). The APR may be based on sums which include arrangement costs.

Incomes in advance and non-annual incomes

Example 1.39 How should a valuer deal with the valuation of incomes received in advance? Most years' purchase valuation tables assume that the unit of income is received at the end of the year. The same may apply to PV and A £1 p.a. tables.

However, this is not always a realistic assumption. Rent from property is usually paid in advance. Tables giving 'in arrear' figures may be used alongside common sense to provide related 'in advance' figures.

1 PV £1: normally assumes that the sum is to be received at the end of year n. If the sum is received at the start of year n instead, this will coincide with the end of year $(n - 1)$. Thus

   the PV of £1 receivable in advance $= \dfrac{1}{(1 + i)^{n-1}}$.

2 Amount of £1 p.a. normally assumes that each £1 is invested at the end of each year. If this becomes the start of each year instead an extra £1 will accumulate for n years – but the £1 paid at the end of the nth year will now be paid at the start of

year *n*. The series becomes

$$(1 + i)^n + (1 + i)^{n-1} \ldots (1 + i)^2 + (1 + i)$$

and can be summated to $\left(\dfrac{(1 + i)^{n+1} - 1}{i}\right) - 1$

3 Year's purchase or PV £1 p.a. usually assumes income to be received at the end of each year. But if it comes in advance, the series will read

$$1 + \frac{1}{(1 + i)} + \frac{1}{(1 + i)^2} \cdots \frac{1}{(1 + i)^{n-1}}$$

This is summated to $\dfrac{1 - \dfrac{1}{(1 + i)^{n-1}}}{i} + 1$

Example 1.40 Calculate YP for 6 years @ 10% in advance.

$$\frac{1 - \dfrac{1}{(1 + 0.10)^{6-1}}}{1} + 1$$

$$= \frac{1 - \dfrac{1}{1.6105}}{0.10} + 1 = 3.79 + 1 = \underline{4.79}$$

Alternatively, this could be given by YP for 5 years @ 10% + 1: (3.79) + 1 = 4.79, or by YP for 6 years @ 10% × (1 + *i*).

Example 1.41 Calculate the amount of £1 in 7 years 6 months at an interest rate of 3% per half year.

i has always represented an annual interest rate. But, as long as *i* and *n* relate to the same time period, that time period can be anything.

In the example, the interest rate (*i*) is per half year, so *n* should represent periods of half a year.

$i = 0.03$

$n = 15$ periods

$$A = (1 + i)^n$$
$$= (1 + 0.03)^{15}$$
$$= 1.557967$$

The same logic may be applied to all six functions as specified at the beginning of this chapter.

Incomes receivable quarterly in advance

It was stated at the beginning of this chapter that some valuation tables are based on the assumption that income may be received or invested quarterly.

At the current time it is much more common to find income from property (rent) paid in advance, as mentioned earlier (see also p. 77). In fact such income is usually paid quarterly in advance, and this is the basis of valuation tables by Bowcock and Rose. By far the most common application of such a basis is to years' purchase tables.

The formula for the years' purchase to be applied to an income receivable quarterly in advance, single rate, is:

$$YP = \frac{1 - \dfrac{1}{(1+i)^n}}{4\left[1 - \dfrac{1}{\sqrt[4]{(1+i)}}\right]}$$

where i is the annual effective rate of interest.

For example, the single rate years' purchase, quarterly in advance, at an annual effective rate of 10% for 20 years, is 9.038, compared with the equivalent annual in arrears years' purchase of 8.5136, reflecting the advantages of receiving income both earlier and more regularly.

The formula for the years' purchase to be applied to an income receivable quarterly in advance, dual rate with a tax adjustment, is:

$$YP = \frac{1}{4\left[1 - \dfrac{1}{\sqrt[4]{(1+i)}}\right] + \dfrac{4\left[1 - \dfrac{1}{\sqrt[4]{(1+s)}}\right]}{[(1+s)^n - 1][1 - t]}}$$

where i is the annual effective remunerative rate, s is the annual effective accumulative rate, and t is the tax rate.

For example, the dual rate years' purchase, quarterly in advance, at an annual effective remunerative rate of 10%, an annual effective accumulative rate of 3%, adjusted for tax at 40%, for 20 years is 6.3555, compared with the annual in arrears equivalent figure of 6.1718.

It is strictly correct that such factors should be applied to incomes which are received quarterly in advance, in order that it is demonstrable that the yield indicated by the valuation is actually provided by the investment. The use of other tables might provide valuations which are acceptable in the market, but it should be noted that such valuations are based upon slightly misleading rates of return.

Continuous compounding

When interest is added more frequently than annually, the compound interest $(1 + i)^n$ is adjusted to $\left(1 + \dfrac{i}{m}\right)^{mn}$, where m is the number of times per year that interest is added, i is the nominal rate of interest per year and n is the number of years.

If, for example, the nominal rate of interest is 100% per annum, then within the formula i becomes 1, and £1 invested for one year will accumulate to $£\left(1 + \dfrac{1}{m}\right)^m$. The greater the number of times in the year that interest is added, the greater will be the total sum at the end of the year: but there must be a limit, because while the number of periods becomes infinitely large the rate of interest per period becomes infinitely small. Potentially, m might tend towards infinity. This would imply the immediate reinvestment of earned interest, or *continuous compounding*.

Mathematically the maximum sum to which £1 could compound in 1 year at 100% per annum is given by the following series:

$$1 + \frac{1}{1} + \frac{1}{1 \times 2} + \frac{1}{1 \times 2 \times 3} + \frac{1}{1 \times 2 \times 3 \times 4} \cdots \frac{1}{m!}$$

which is a convergent series summating to 6 places, to 2.718282. This value is known as the exponential constant, or e

Now, to return to the general case:

$$A = \left(1 + \frac{i}{m}\right)^{mn}$$

Let $\dfrac{i}{m} = \dfrac{1}{t}$: then t is the reciprocal of the rate of interest per (m) period. As the number of payments per year becomes larger and tends towards infinity, t does likewise and interest can be said to be compounding continuously.

Then: $A = \left(1 + \dfrac{1}{t}\right)^{mn}$

$$m = ti, \text{ so } A = \left(1 + \frac{1}{t}\right)^{nti} \text{ or } \left[\left(1 + \frac{1}{t}\right)^{t}\right]^{in}$$

As t tends towards infinity, $\left(1 + \frac{1}{t}\right)^{t}$ becomes e (see above). Thus £1 invested at i with interest compounding continuously over n years will accumulate to e^{in}.

Example 1.42 To what sum will £1 compound over 2 years at 10% per year nominal rate of interest assuming continuous compounding?

$e^{in} = 2.718282^{(0.1)(2)}$	No.	Log.
$= 2.718282^{(0.2)}$	2.718282	0.4343
$= \sqrt[5]{2.718282}$	$\div 5$	0.08686
$= \underline{£1.221}$	1.221	Anti-log

£1 accumulating at 10% per year with interest added annually would compound to $(1.10)^2$ or £1.21.

The present value of £1 $= \dfrac{1}{(1 + i)^n}$ or $(1 + i)^{-n}$. It follows then that where interest is compounding continuously PV $= e^{-in}$.

The foregoing demonstrates that the rate of interest used in calculations of compounding and discounting must be *the effective rate for the period.*

Part two

Chapter two

The income approach

Introduction

Valuation by direct capital comparison with sales in the market is the preferred method of valuation for most saleable goods and services. Valuation by this method is reliable provided that the sample of comparable sales is of sufficient size to draw realistic conclusions as to market conditions.

This requires full knowledge of each transaction. Such a situation rarely exists in the market for investment property, and in the absence of directly comparable sales figures the valuer turns to the investment method. The investment method is used for valuing income-producing property whether freehold or leasehold, because as a method it most closely reflects the behaviour of the various parties operating in the property market.

Initially, the valuer will pay regard to the income or net benefits to be derived from the ownership of an interest in property, because investors are primarily concerned with the income and the risks attaching to that income when making investment decisions.

Valuation was earlier summarised as the estimation of the future benefits to be enjoyed from the ownership of a freehold or a leasehold interest in land or property, expressing those future benefits in terms of present worth. The valuer must therefore be able to assess these future net benefits (income) and be able to select the appropriate rate of interest in order to discount these benefits to derive their present value. The income approach to property valuation requires the valuer to concentrate on the assessment of the income pattern and the rate(s) of interest to be used to discount that income-flow.

Definitions

In a discipline that is derived from urban economics and investment analysis one would expect to find some common agreement as to the meaning of terms used by practitioners. This does not exist, so that additional problems may arise when advice is given to investors who are more acquainted with terms used by other financial advisers. The advice of the most expert valuer is of minimal value if it is misinterpreted, so a definition of terms used from here on may be useful.

The definitions that follow may not achieve universal acceptance but are adhered to within this text.

Market value is the price that one would expect under specified market conditions. It is sometimes defined as the most probable selling price. However defined, the definition must assume competitive market conditions, i.e. more than one buyer and seller operating within a market with full or reasonably full knowledge of the market; rational behaviour among market participants; normal market sale conditions, i.e. not a forced sale; an open market, i.e. no collusion; normal financing; and all other terms and conditions of the sale should be assumed to be normal. Hence it is the most probable selling price as between willing buyer and seller under normal market conditions. Indeed its definition assumes a sale to the most probable puchaser or type of purchaser, a point that tends to be forgotten.

Under unusual market conditions, such as those which existed in the early 1970s, it may be difficult to identify prospective purchasers within the market. Thus, although there is a price at which every property will find a buyer, it can be extremely difficult to judge the market value in a distorted and inactive market. Nevertheless, the need for market valuations remains, a good example being the demand for asset valuations for accounting purposes. The Royal Institution of Chartered Surveyors through its Asset Valuations Standards Committee has issued guidance notes containing the following definition of *open market value*.

The open market value is intended to mean the best price at which an interest in a property might reasonably be expected to be sold by Private Treaty at the date of valuation assuming:
(a) a willing seller;
(b) a reasonable period within which to negotiate the sale, taking into account the nature of the property and the state of the market;
(c) values will remain static throughout the period;
(d) the property will be freely exposed to the market;
(e) no account is to be taken of an additional bid by a special purchaser.

This definition is incorporated in the RICS leaflet 'The Valuation of Commercial and Industrial Property' (see Appendix A). While this has become an accepted definition, 'the most probable selling price' conveys more succinctly the object of a market valuation.

Value in use is the present worth of all future benefits to the owner of the interest in that property. If all the information relates to a specific client or potential investor then value in use equals investment value to that investor. Only if the specific purchaser is normal or typical within the market will value in use equal market value as defined above.

Value in exchange is market value. If a good or service is incapable of being exchanged for other goods or services it has no market value.

Price is an historic fact except when qualified in such a phrase as 'offered at an asking price of . . .'. Under perfect market conditions value in use would equate with value in exchange and price would be synonymous with value. The property market is not perfect and price and value cannot always be said to be equal.

Valuation is the art or science of estimating the value of interests in property. According to the dictionary, the word valuation is interchangeable with the word Appraisal. The latter word is in vogue as meaning 'the provision of full advice on the suitability or otherwise of a specific property as a potential investment purchase to a specific investor' as such there is the implication that an appraisal is more comprehensive than a valuation.

Valuation report is the formal presentation of the valuer's opinion in written form. As a minimum it must contain a sufficient description to identify the property without doubt; a value definition; a statement as to the interest being valued and any legal encumbrances; the effective date of the valuation; any special feature of the property or the market that the valuer has taken special note of; and the value estimate itself.

These definitions may be confusing to the reader and not obviously that important, but in practice they may be very important. Even more important is the valuer's instruction and the importance of communication between valuer and client. 'How much is it worth?', 'What price should I offer?', 'Is it worth £*x* million?', 'What figure should we include in our accounts for the value of our property assets?' and 'Is that the same as their market worth?', are questions which may give rise to different responses from the valuer and might result in the valuer expressing different opinions for the same property interest for different purposes.

However, in all cases where a property is income producing or capable of being let at a rent then an investment or income approach to its valuation for the specified purpose will be the valuer's best method of valuation.

The investment method

The investment method is a method of estimating the present worth of the rights to future benefits to be derived from the ownership of a specific interest in a specific property under given market conditions. In property valuation these future rights can usually be expressed as future income (rent) and/or future reversionary capital value. The latter is in itself an expression of resale rights to future benefits. The process of converting future income flows to present value capital sums is known as capitalisation, which in essence is the summation of the future benefits each discounted to the present at an appropriate market-derived discount rate of interest. The terms discount rate and capitalisation rate are increasingly preferred to 'rate of interest', 'interest rate' or 'rate of return'. The use of the term 'rate of interest' should be restricted to borrowing, being the rate of interest charged on borrowed funds.

In Chapter 1 a distinction was made between return on capital and return of capital. The interest rate or rate of return refers to return on capital only and is sometimes referred to as the remunerative rate to distinguish it from the return of capital or sinking fund rate. Technically a discount rate ignores capital recovery but in general valuation usage discount rate and capitalisation rate are synonymous and are assumed to mean any annual percentage rate used to convert a future benefit (income flow or lump sum) into a present worth estimate.

It is necessary to discount future sums at a rate to overcome liquidity preference, time preference and the risks associated with uncertainty about the future: that is, the uncertainty of receiving the future income, uncertainty as to the value of the future income in terms of purchasing power, and uncertainty as to the stability of the property market in the future. A capitalisation rate reflects all these factors and more and is referred to as an all risks yield (ARY).

In its simplest form income capitalisation is merely the division of income (I) by the annual rate of capitalisation (R). A rate of capitalisation is expressed as a percentage – say 10% – but all financial analyses and calculations require this ratio to be expressed as a decimal. 10% becomes 0.10, 8% = 0.08, and thus

Value (V) = I/i

Example 2.1 Calculate the present worth of a freehold interest in a property expected to produce a rental of £1,000 p.a.

in perpetuity at an annual rate of capitalisation of 10%

$V = I/i = 1{,}000/0.10 = £10{,}000$

In preference to dividing by i valuers will multiply by a capitalisation factor being the reciprocal of the capitalisation rate. Thus:

$V = I \times 1/i = 1{,}000 \times 1/0.10 = 1{,}000 \times 10 = £10{,}000$

The capitalisation factor in valuation is termed years' purchase (see Chapter 1).

The capitalisation of an infinite income, dividing by a market rate of capitalisation, is a simple exercise known as capitalisation in perpetuity. Where, however, the income is finite, then allowance must be made for recovery of capital. Two concepts exist in UK valuation practice: the internal rate of return and the sinking fund return. Each allows for the systematic return of capital over the life of the investment but each approach is based on different assumptions.

The internal rate of return assumes that capital recovery is at the same rate as the return on capital i. It reflects the normal investment criterion of a return on capital outstanding from year to year and at risk, with the capital being returned from year to year out of income. Where capital recovery is at the same rate as the risk rate the table used is the present value of £1 per annum (YP single rate) which in turn is the reciprocal of the annuity £1 will purchase. Thus any finite income stream can be treated as an annuity calculation. This concept is the more acceptable because the present worth of any future sum is that sum which if invested today would accumulate at compound interest to that future sum, and hence the present worth of a number of such sums is the sum of their present values.

If the sums are equal and receivable in arrears then

$$V = I \times \frac{1 - PV}{i}$$

If the sums vary from year to year then

$$V = \sum \frac{I_1}{(1 + i)} + \frac{I_2}{(1 + i)^2} + \frac{I_3}{(1 + i)^3} \cdots \frac{I_n}{(1 + i)^n}$$

Mathematically there need be no distinction between the two concepts as capital recovery can always be provided within a capitalisation factor by incorporating a sinking fund to recover capital:

$$PV\ £1\ p.a. = \frac{1}{i + SF}$$

But if it can be shown that investors insist on a return on initial outlay throughout the life of the investment, then the sinking fund concept is the more acceptable. Further, if it can be shown that investors expect a return of capital at a different rate to the return on capital then this can be allowed for in the formula (see p. 34).

The arithmetic manipulation of figures in capitalisation exercises is not, of course, valuation. Valuation is a process which requires careful consideration of a number of variables before figures can be substituted in mathematically proven formulae. Any assessment of present worth or market value can only be as good as the data input allows and that factor is dependent upon the education, skill and market experience of the valuer. Ability to analyse and understand the market is of paramount importance.

Valuation has been likened to a science, not because of any precision that may or may not exist, or because in part it involves certain basic mathematics, but because the question 'How much?' poses a problem that requires a solution. The scientific approach to problem solving is to follow a systematic process. There may well be short cuts within the process. Indeed the discounting exercise itself, because it is repetitive, can frequently be carried out by pre-programmed calculators and computers. Short cuts exist if data are already available, but adoption of a systematic approach provides the confidence that full account has been taken of all the factors likely to affect the value of a property.

Valuation process

First, the valuer should define the problem. 'What are the client's real requirements?' 'Why does he want a valuation?' 'What is the purpose of the valuation?' These questions should establish whether the client requires a market valuation, or a valuation for company asset purposes, insurance, or rating.

The date of the valuation must be ascertained. If a value is required for book purposes at a certain date, an 'in advance rental' may require an 'in arrears' valuation and vice versa.

In order to produce a market valuation the valuer requires a precise knowledge of the market and the property. The second step in the valuation process is the collection of all the data considered necessary to complete a proper valuation. Given specific economic and market conditions the valuer will be considering four principal qualities: the quality of the legal title, the quality of the location, the quality of the building, the quality of the lease(s) and tenant(s) in occupation or those that can be assumed in the case of a new or owner-occupied property.

The following schedule and Figure 2.1 provides some idea of the mass of data that needs to be collected and assessed in order to arrive at an objective opinion of the property's marketable qualities which in turn colour the valuer's judgement as to the income generating capabilities of the property and its suitability as an investment.

The property:	Site measurements
	Building measurements:
	External, internal, number of floors
	Elevation, orientation
	Services: heating, lighting, air
	conditioning, lifts, etc.
	Age and design
	Suitability of premises for present use
	Adaptability
	Accessibility to markets, amenities,
	labour
Legal:	Freehold or leasehold. Details of title
Interest to be valued	restrictions such as restrictive
	covenants
	Details of any leases or sub-leases,
	tenants, rent levels, lease terms
Planning	Permitted uses
Economic:	
General	State of economy
Regional and local	Population structure
	Average wages
	Principal employment
	State of local industry
	Economic base of area
	Level of unemployment
	Town and regional growth prospects
	Transportation, existing and planned
	Current planning proposals
	Building societies, savings banks and
	general level of investment in the
	town and region
	Position of town in regional hierarchy
Market:	Total stock of similar property
	Comparison of subject property to the
	stock
	New stock in course of construction
	and planned

Vacancy rates
General level of rents and rates
Tenant demand for similar property
Alternative investments: Other properties
      Stocks and shares
Legislation: Planning control
      Landlord and tenant control over
        rents
      Safety, health and working conditions
        controls

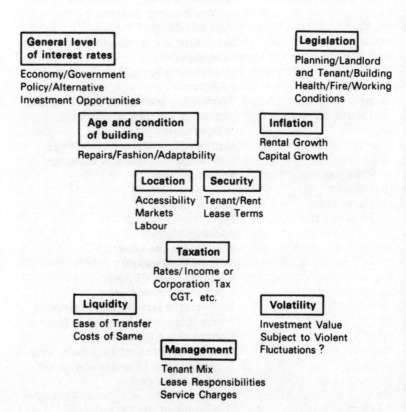

**General level
of interest rates**

Economy/Government
Policy/Alternative
Investment Opportunities

Legislation

Planning/Landlord
and Tenant/Building
Health/Fire/Working
Conditions

**Age and condition
of building**

Repairs/Fashion/Adaptability

Inflation

Rental Growth
Capital Growth

Location   **Security**

Accessibility Tenant/Rent
Markets   Lease Terms
Labour

Taxation

Rates/Income or
Corporation Tax
CGT, etc.

Liquidity

Ease of Transfer
Costs of Same

Volatility

Investment Value
Subject to Violent
Fluctuations ?

Management

Tenant Mix
Lease Responsibilities
Service Charges

Figure 2.1 Factors determining investors' yield requirements and valuers'
capitalisation rates

Such data are collected for analysis if considered significant in terms of value. The valuer needs to know what other properties are in the market, whether they are better in terms of location, etc., who are in the market as potential purchasers and as potential tenants, and whether the market for the subject property is active.

To collect the level of information required entails either very sound local knowledge, or the need to make enquiries of the local planning authorities, rating authorities, highway authorities, bus companies, British Rail and local census statistics.

Thus one finds that the major firms of surveyors and valuers will now hold on file considerable detailed information on the City and West End of London, including in some instances very detailed street-by-street information, and similar information on the main provincial cities. This information source is kept up to date by research members extracting relevant information from national and local papers, local council minutes, etc.

Having collected the information shown above, it is then necessary to consider the market. 'A major danger in assessing the direct property market lies in failing to identify the main segments into which the market is divided according to the value, reversionary terms, etc. ... of a property' (Greenwell & Co. Property Report, October 1976). The valuer must be able to identify the most probable type of purchaser if the most probable selling price is to be assessed. The alternative comparable properties on the market that may be in competition for investors' or owner-occupiers' funds need to be considered. What is the current level of demand within that sub market? What new construction work is in hand? These and other questions will indicate what market data are required as preparatory material for the valuation.

The most difficult aspect in an income capitalisation exercise is the determination of the correct capitalisation rate. Every property investment is different, and if the available data on sales are insufficiently comparable then it may become difficult to justify the use of a selected rate. Too frequently valuers assume that if property sales, with 7 year rent review patterns, analyse on a 7% basis, then this can be assumed to be an accepted rate for that *type of property*. It is in fact the accepted rate only for that type of property *let on 7 year review* with the *first review* at a *comparable* date in the future and with a comparable level of rental increase.

The valuation process can be redefined* as shown in the following diagram.

---

*See *The Appraisal Process* by D.H. Mackmin.

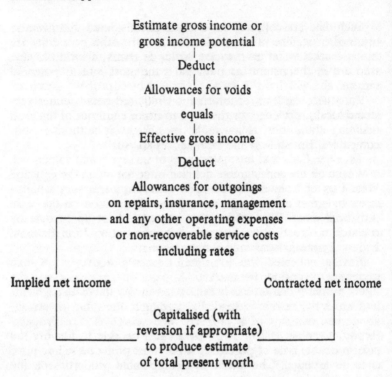

Estimate gross income or
gross income potential
|
Deduct
|
Allowances for voids
|
equals
|
Effective gross income
|
Deduct
|
Allowances for outgoings
on repairs, insurance, management
and any other operating expenses
or non-recoverable service costs
including rates

Implied net income ⎤ ⎡ Contracted net income

Capitalised (with
reversion if appropriate)
to produce estimate
of total present worth

Within this process the three main variables likely to have the greatest effect on the final estimate of value can be identified: income (rent), operating expenses, and capitalisation rate. It is our presumption that a valuer practising in a well-run valuation department will be able to provide reliable figures for these items readily, and should be able to substantiate these figures from available analysed data.

Income or rent

Capitalisation is the expression of future benefits in terms of their present worth. Valuation therefore requires the valuer to consider the future: but current UK valuation practice reflects a distrust of making predictions. The convention has developed of using initial yields on rack rented property as the capitalisation rates to be applied to current estimates of future rental income, thereby building into the capitalisation rate the market's forecast of future expectations. The forecast is still made but the valuer has avoided any explicit statement. Some American appraisers now consider this approach to be outmoded and argue that it should only be used if a level constant income flow is the most probable income pattern.

The RICS research report (Trott, 1980) on valuation methods recommends the use of growth explicit models for investment analysis and suggests that a greater use should be made of growth explicit DCF models in the market valuation of property investments.

Whenever the investment method is to be used, whether in relation to tenant-occupied property or owner-occupied property, an initial essential step is the estimation of the current rental value of that property. If the property is already let this allows the valuer to consider objectively the nature of the present rent roll. Initially the most important task must be the estimation of rental income.

If the property is owner-occupied then it is necessary to assess the imputed rental income.

No property investment decision can be taken without a detailed assessment of present and expected income. This assessment requires analysis of current rents being paid, rents being quoted and the vacancy rate of comparable properties.

Detailed analysis of the letting market must precede analysis of a specific letting. Thus if it can be demonstrated within the market for office space that such space users will pay a higher rent for ground floor space than for space on a higher floor then this may be reflected in the way in which a letting of a whole office building is analysed in terms of rent per square metre. If the rent of luxury flats and apartments can be shown to have a closer correlation with the number of bedrooms than with floor area then analysis might be possible on a per bedroom basis. If floor area is to be used then continuing analysis will indicate whether or not bids are influenced by the size of, for example, the hall and bathroom, or whether their existence is sufficient and the bid unaffected by the amount of space occupied.

Reliable estimates of current rents can only flow from analysis of rents actually being paid, and under no circumstances should a valuation be based on an estimate of rent derived from analysis of an investment sale where there is no current rack rent passing. This is because rent analysed in this manner depends upon the assumption of a capitalisation rate. For example, if the only information available on the transaction is that a building of 500 m^2 has just been sold for £50,000 with vacant possession, the only possible analysis is of sale price per square metre.

In most cases analyses of rent being paid should be on the basis of net lettable space, but agricultural land is often quoted on a total area basis inclusive of farm dwellings and buildings.

Net lettable space becomes more meaningful if it is taken to mean the net area of the building suitable for use for the purpose let. This definition excludes circulation space within the building such as stairwells, landings, lifts and ancillary facilities such as wash rooms. The rent analysed on this basis reflects the quantity and quality of the facilities provided, which should of course be noted on any data record sheet for future use. The precise set of rules for measuring buildings of different use types will vary from valuer to valuer and from area to area, but the old adage 'as you analyse so should you value' should be adhered to in terms of building measurement.*

There is a growing tendency for shop premises to be let at a fixed rental plus a percentage of profit or turnover. Where a valuation is required of property let on such terms full details of total rents actually collected, checked against audited accounts for a minimum of 5 years, should be used as the basis for determining income cash flow for capitalisation purposes.

Due to the heterogeneous nature of property it is customary to express rent in terms of a suitable unit of comparison thus:

Agricultural land	rent per hectare
Office and factory premises	rent per square metre
Shops	rent per square metre overall or per square metre front zone

Three alternative approaches have been developed for analysing shop rents: overall analysis, arithmetic zoning and natural zoning.

(a) Overall analysis

The rent for the retail space is divided by the lettable rental space to obtain an overall rent per m². This is a simple approach but is complicated by the practice of letting retail space together with space on upper floors used for storage, sales, rest rooms, offices or residential accommodation at a single rental figure. In these circumstances it is desirable to isolate the rent for the retail space. Some valuers suggest there is a relationship between ground floor space and space on the upper floors – this will only be the case where the user is the same or ancillary (e.g. storage). Here custom

---

*See RICS code of measurement for guidelines.

or thorough analysis will indicate the relationship, if any, between ground floor and upper floor rental values. Where the use is different the rent of the upper floor should be assessed by comparison with similar space elsewhere and deducted from the total rent before analysis. Thus if the upper floors comprise flats then the rent for these should be assessed by comparison within the residential market and then deducted from the total rent. Overall analysis tends to be used for shops in small parades and for large space users. In the latter case it is reasonable to argue that tenants of such premises will pay a pro rata rent for every additional square metre up to a given maximum. The problem here is that what one retailer might consider to be a desirable maximum could be excessive for all other retailers. Such a point should be reflected as a risk accounted for by the valuer in his selection of capitalisation rate.

(b) Arithmetic zoning

This approach is preferred in many cases to an overall rent analysis because, in retailing, it is the space used to attract the customer into the premises that is the most valuable (namely the frontage to the street or mall). Again the rent for the retail space should be isolated before analysis.

Example 2.2   Analyse the rent of £5,000 being paid for shop premises with a frontage of 6 m and a depth of 21 m.

Overall = £5,000 ÷ (6 × 21) = £39.68 per m^2

Zoning: Assume zones of 7 m depth and £x per m^2 rent for zone A

Then Zone A = 6 × 7 = 42 m^2 at £x = 42.0x

Zone B = 6 × 7 = 42 m^2 at £$\frac{1}{2}x$ = 21.0x

Zone C = 6 × 7 = 42 m^2 at £$\frac{1}{4}x$ = 10.5x

$$\overline{73.5x}$$

£5,000 ÷ 73.5 = x

£68.0 = x

The rental value for zone A is therefore £68 per m^2.

The observant reader will realise that the space could be divided into any number of zones – only convention suggests that these should not exceed three and that the first two should be approximately 7 m deep (see RICS code of measurement).

Certainly in practice retailers do not see the premises divided into rigid zones. Every rental estimate must be looked at in the light of the current market and common sense – who would be the most probable tenant for premises 7 m wide by 100 m deep? Is there any user who operates in such space, or is the last 50 m waste or valueless space for most retailers in that locality?

(c) Natural zoning*

This method can only effectively be used to analyse rents within a shopping street or centre where information is available on a number of units, as it requires comparison between units. Once more the rents for retail space are isolated from the rent for the premises as a whole. For example, consider the rent of two adjoining premises, one of 6 m × 21 m, let at £5,000 per annum, the other 8 m × 25 m, let at £6,500 per annum.

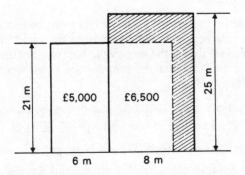

The method here argues that if retailers are paying £5,000 for 6 m × 21 m and £6,500 for 8 m × 25 m then £1,500 represents the rent for the area hatched in the sketch. Even here the logic may collapse if somewhere within the parade there is a shop 6 m × 20 m let at £6,750 p.a.

In terms of the analysis of retail space, warehouse accommodation and factory space, most valuers have, almost certainly, too limited a knowledge of the specific requirements of different retailers and of different manufacturers. Where one is dealing with standard shop units, for example within a shopping mall, the unit of comparison can often be left as the 'shop unit'. Rent will be a factor of location/position and not size.

---

*See R. Emeny and H.M. Wilks, *Principles and Practice of Rating Valuation*, Estates Gazette, 1982.

The developing technique, although not yet found to be any more satisfactory than those listed, is multi-variate analysis when the dependent variable rent is considered against a number of independent variables which could include size, location, distance from car parks, bus station, etc.

It would be ideal if all rental estimates could be based on true comparables, i.e. those of the same size, design, facilities, location, etc. This is rarely the case in practice. With experience, adjustments can be made for some of these variations, but wherever possible estimates of rent should be based on close comparables.

As far as office records are concerned, strict procedures should be adhered to so that the format of data is consistent. In this respect it is recommended that all rents are analysed net of landlords' outgoings (see below) and that apart from obvious factors such as the address of the property the record should contain details of facilities included (e.g. central heating, air conditioning) and the lease terms.

The valuer must be in possession of all the facts of a given letting before any rental figure can be analysed. In the case of residential and commercial property statute intervenes to protect the tenant in several ways (see Chapter 7). Thus a tenant of business premises who carries out improvements would not expect to pay an increase in rent for these improvements on the renewal of the lease. The valuer must therefore know the basis upon which a given rent was agreed before he can make proper use of the information. An earlier lease might have been surrendered or the tenant might have undertaken to modernise the premises. Either of these could have resulted in a rental lower than a market rental being agreed between the parties. And of increasing concern is the lease definition of rent where there is provision for a rent review – there is almost certainly a difference between 'full market rental' and a 'reasonable rent', the latter inferring something less than the maximum rent achievable if offered in the open market.

It is arguable, in inflationary times, that the rent agreed for a 20 year lease without review will differ from that agreed for the same lease with 10 year, 7 year or 5 year reviews (see Chapter 6). For preference, comparability should entail estimating rents from analyses of lettings with similar review patterns. If this is not possible it must be remembered that capitalisation is the discounting of income flows at a market derived rate and that it is the combination of income and discount rate which produces the estimate of present worth.

Rental value will also be affected by a number of other lease clauses. Particular attention should be paid to those dealing with alienation – assignment and sub-letting; user; repair and service charges. Although the Landlord and Tenant Act 1988 now ensures that landlords do not unduly delay the granting of consents in conditional cases, the position in relation to an absolute prohibition on alienation remains unchanged. In the latter case there will be an adverse affect on rents. User restrictions in shopping centres and multiple tenanted commercial property can have a beneficial effect on rents. Where they are too restrictive they will have a detrimental effect on rents. Responsibility for repairs and the nature of any service charge provisions must be considered twice: firstly to see if they are affecting market rents, and secondly to see if they leave the landlord with a liability which must be estimated and deducted as a landlord's expense before capitalisation. (Where VAT is charged on rents the valuer must ensure that it is the rent net of VAT that is used for valuation purposes.)

Landlords' expenses

Where investment property is already subject to a contracted lease rent, and/or where it is customary to quote rents for a specific type of property on gross terms, it is essential to deduct landlords' outgoings (operating expenses) before capitalising the income. Any investment valuation must be based on net income. This conventionally means an income net of all the expenses that the owner of an interest in property is required to meet out of the rents received from ownership of that interest in that property. These expenses are not usually considered to include income or corporation tax.

Expenses may be imposed upon the landlord by legislation, or they may be contractual, as in an existing lease. But an inspection of the property may suggest that, though neither party is statutorily or contractually liable, there are other expenses that will have to be met by the owner of that interest in the property. The valuer must identify all such liabilities and make full allowance for them in his valuation. In order to do this, he must refer to all existing leases in respect of the property.

The principal items of expenditure can be broadly classified under the headings of insurance, management, taxes, running expenses and repairs. Of these only the cost of complying with repairing obligations should cause any real difficulty in accurate assessment.

Insurance

The valuer armed with plans and his own detailed measurements of the building will be able to estimate or obtain an accurate quotation for all *insurances*, particularly fire insurance. Fire insurance is an extremely involved subject, complicated by the variation in insurance policies offered. A valuer should therefore acquaint himself with the terms and conditions of policies offered by two or three leading insurance companies and should always assess the insurance premium in accordance with those policies. If reinstatement value is required this can be referred to a building surveyor or preferably a quantity surveyor, or may be based on adjusted average figures extracted from *Spon's Architects' and Builders' Price Book*. Due to the 'averaging provisions' of most policies it is better to be over insured than under insured, and hence to overestimate rather than underestimate this item.

Quotations for other insurances necessary on boilers, lifts, etc., can always be obtained from a broker or insurance company.

A deduction for insurance will rarely be necessary as the lease will usually contain provisions for the recovery of all insurance charges from the tenant in addition to the rent. In most cases the wording of a 'full repairing and insuring lease' leaves the responsibility for insurance with the owner, but the cost of insurance with the tenant.

Management

This refers to the property owner's supervising costs equivalent to the fee that would be due to a management agent for rent collection; attendance to day-to-day matters such as the granting of licences to assign/sub-let or to alter the premises; inspections of the premises, and instructions to builders to carry out repairs. It is usually considered to be too small to allow for in the case of premises let to first class tenants on full repairing and insuring terms. The valuer must use his discretion but it is suggested that if the valuer or his firm would charge a fee for acting as managing agents, then a similar cost will be incurred by any owner of the property and a deduction for management should therefore be made. The valuer must have full details of the current rent roll in order to value a property, and as management fees are based on total sums collected the allowance for management can be accurately assessed. Value added tax should be added to the fee where appropriate. If VAT is payable on rents it will impose an additional management cost which will be reflected in the fees negotiated by managing agents.

Where the management fee is recoverable as part of a full service charge no deduction need be made in a valuation of the landlord's interest.

Taxes

The Uniform Business Rate is paid by the occupier of business premises. Inspection of the lease will indicate the party to that lease who has contracted to meet the 'rates' demand. If premises are let at an inclusive rental (i.e. inclusive of rates) then rates should be deducted. If let exclusive of rates then no deduction is necessary. If the letting is inclusive and there is no 'excess rates clause' then the deduction must represent the average annual figure expected up until the end of the lease or next review, not a figure representing current rates. If an excess rates clause is included then the sum to be deducted is the amount of rates due in the first year of the lease or the lowest sum demanded during the current lease. This is because such a clause allows for the recovery from the tenant of any increase in rates over and above the amount due in the first year of the lease.

Other 'rates' may inclue water rates, drainage rates, and rates for environmental and other purposes.

It has always been the custom in the UK to value before deduction of tax on the grounds that income and corporation tax are related to the individual or company, and not to the property. However, if market value implies the most probable selling price, there is automatically an implication of the most probable purchaser. The valuer without this knowledge cannot be held to be assessing market value; thus it is held by some that the tax liability of the most probable purchaser should be reflected in the valuation (see Chapter 5).

For simplicity, no deduction will be made for tax in most of this text.

Running expenses

Where the owner of an interest is responsible for the day-to-day running of a property such as a block of flats, an office building let in suites, or a modern shopping centre, a deduction from rent may be necessary to cover the cost of items such as heating, lighting, cleaning and porterage. Current practice is to include provision for a separate service charge to be levied to cover the full cost of most running expenses. The valuer must therefore inspect the leases to check the extent to which such expenses are recoverable. Older leases tend to include partial service charges, in which case the total income from the property should be assessed and the total cost of services deducted.

All the items falling under the general head of 'running expenses' are capable of accurate assessment by reference to current accounts for the subject property; by comparison with other properties; by enquiry of electricity, gas and oil suppliers; by enquiry of staff agencies; and so on. The valuer operating within a firm with a large management department is at a distinct advantage, as that department should be able to provide fairly detailed analyses of comparable managed property.

Where a full service charge is payable this is usually adjustable in arrears. In other words, the annual service charge is based on last year's expenses. During periods of rapidly rising costs the owner will have to meet the difference between service cost and service charge and if this is a significant recurrent amount it represents a reduction in the owner's cash flow and should be taken into account in a valuation.

Increasingly these points are being met by more complex service charge clauses and schedules which provide for interim increases, for example to cover the uncertain energy element in running expenses.*

Repairs

A detailed consideration of existing leases will indicate those items of repair that have to be met by the landlord out of rental income. The sum to be deducted from an annual income before capitalisation must be an annual averaged figure. Thus liability to redecorate a building every 5 years should be estimated and averaged over the 5 years. A check should be made against double accounting – if the cost of repair to boilers, lifts, etc., is covered by a service charge then no allowance should appear under repairs for such items. If indeed the cost of redecoration is recoverable by a direct proportionate charge to tenants then no deduction need be made.

Where an allowance has to be made every effort is required to estimate the amount as accurately as possible. An excess allowance will lead to an under-valuation, inadequate allowance to an over-valuation.

Advice, if needed, should be obtained from builders and building

---

*The statutory requirements relating to service charges and management charges in residential property are complex. Readers involved or interested in the residential sector must refer to all current Housing and Landlord and Tenant legislation.

surveyors as well as by comparison with other known repair costs for comparable managed property.

Essential works

Any obvious immediate renewals or repairs as at the date of the valuation should be allowed for by a deduction from the estimate of capital value to reflect the cost (see Chapter 6 for future costs).

Averages and percentages

Valuers should use averages with care. An example of this is the use of average heating costs per square metre. The valuer is required to value a specific property, not an average property. The requirement is to estimate the average annual cost of heating that specific property.

Some valuers, texts, and correspondence courses suggest that it is a reasonable approach to base insurance premiums and repair costs on a percentage of full rental value. This approach is not recommended unless the valuer can prove that the figure adopted is correct. To do this requires a knowledge of absolute costs and expenses. A percentage allowance may be wildly inaccurate; a high street shop could be worth £10,000 a year and a block of 20 flats could be worth £10,000 a year, but the latter will almost certainly cost more to keep in repair. Two properties may let at identical rents, but one may be constructed of maintenance free materials, the other cheaply constructed with short-life material. A thousand square metres of retail space in Exeter and a thousand square metres of space in Oxford Street, London, may cost the same to maintain but have very different full rental values. A large old building may let at the same rent as a small modern building and clearly the repairs will differ.

Similar points may be made in respect of the use of percentages to estimate insurance premiums.

Voids

Where there is an over-supply of space within a given area the probability of voids occurring when leases fall in is increased. If a single investment building is let in suites to '*n*' tenants, voids may occur sufficiently regularly for a valuer to conclude that the average occupancy is only, say, 95%. In such cases having estimated the full rental value the figure should be reduced to the level of the most probable annual amount. Voids are less likely to affect operating expenses so a pro rata allowance on operating costs should not be made. Indeed in some exceptional cases it may have to be increased to allow for empty rates, non-recoverable service costs and additional security.

In the case of a building let to a single tenant, a void is only likely to occur at the end of the current lease. If this is a reasonable expectation then the income pattern must be assumed to be broken at the review date for the length of time considered necessary to allow for finding a new tenant. Additional allowances may have to be made for negative cash flows if local taxes and other running expenses have to be met by the owner during this period.

Purchase expenses

Rent charges

In the few cases where rent charges occur these should be allowed for in a valuation by making a capital deduction. The sum to be deducted is the redemption cost, calculated in accordance with the Rent Charges Act, 1977.

Stamp duty, solicitors' fees, surveyors' fees, etc.

It has long been valuation practice when giving investment advice to include in the total purchase price an allowance to cover stamp duty, solicitors' fees and surveyor's fees, and any other expenses to the purchaser occasioned by the transaction including VAT. This in total currently amounts to 2¾–3% of the purchase price.

It should be remembered that analysis of a transaction might also take these expenses into account to reveal the purchaser's yield on his total outlay rather than the yield he realises on the purchase price alone.

Chapter three

The income approach to freeholds

The main legal interests bought and sold in property are freehold and leasehold interests. As investments, the former have an assumed perpetual life span although on many occasions the valuation should include a reversion to site value at the end of the building's economic or physical life; the latter have a limited life span fixed by the lease term. Having identified the interest to be valued the valuer must then determine not only the current income but also future income and the income flow pattern. Two distinct approaches have developed for assessing the open market value of an income producing property. The first, as already indicated (Chapter 2), is to assume a level continuous income flow and to use an overall or all risks capitalisation rate or growth rate derived from the analysis of comparable sales on similar terms and conditions (i.e. 5 year or 7 year rent review patterns) to calculate present worth. The second has been named the discounted cash flow (DCF) approach.

The first or normal approach is favoured by many on the grounds that it is more correctly a market valuation. As such it relies on an active property market and an ability to analyse and obtain details of comparable capitalisation rates. Those in favour of the DCF approach argue that, when there is insufficient activity within the defined sub-market, valuation can still be undertaken on the DCF approach and, further, that most valuers using the normal approach fail to recognise the sub-markets involved. For example, it is assumed that if initial yields on rack rented properties are, say, 7% then the capitalisation rates to be used for valuing property with an early reversion to a rack rent can be closely related to 7%. The argument against this is that if there is no evidence of capitalisation rates from sales of investments with early reversions it may be because there is no market for such investments. The strongest criticisms of the normal approach are that it fails to specify explicitly the income flows and patterns assumed by the valuer, and that it applies growth implicit all risk yields to fixed contracted tranches of income. The DCF approach requires the valuer to specify precisely what rental income and expenses are expected when, and for how long. The valuer is therefore forced to concentrate on the national and local economic issues likely to affect the worth of the specific property as an investment. There may after all be properties in a depressed economy for which rental increases in the foreseeable future are very unlikely.

Both approaches will be used in problems relating to the valuation of freehold interests in property. The examples will indicate the approach adopted.

The DCF approach accepts the idea of the opportunity cost of investment funds. Opportunity cost implies that a rate of return must be paid to an investor sufficient to meet the competition of alternative investment outlets for the investor's funds. This is the basis of the riskless rate of discount, a riskless rate being assumed to compensate for time preference only. Any investment with a poorer liquidity factor or higher risk to income or capital value will have to earn a rate over time in excess of the riskless rate. Analysts tend to adopt as their measure the current rate on 'gilt edged' stock. These are generally held to be fairly liquid investments and are safe in money terms if held to redemption. Additionally, if they are sold at a loss, or at a gain, it can be reasonably assumed that there will have been a similar movement in the values of most other forms of investment. Property, being considerably less liquid, is expected to achieve a return over time of 1–2% above the going rate on gilt edged stock.

The DCF method requires the valuer to 'forecast' rents and to discount those rents at a rate sufficiently higher than the riskless rate to account for the additional risks involved in the specific property investment. 'Forecast' here does not mean prediction nor does it necessarily imply a projection based on extrapolating or extending the past into the future. It is an estimate of the most probable rent due in *n* years' time based on sound analysis of the past and present market conditions. The current preference seems to be to assess an implied growth rate for rent from the relationship between all risk capitalisation rates and gilts plus a risk premium of 1–2%.

Capitalisation

The technique of converting income into a capital sum is extremely simple. In the case of freehold interests in property the income will fall into one of the following patterns.

The income approach to freeholds

A level annuity

If the income is *fixed* for a period much in excess of 60 years or in perpetuity, or if a property is let at its rack rental and there is market evidence of capitalisation rates, then it can be treated as a level annuity in perpetuity.

Net income $\div\ i =$ Capital value

Net income $\times \dfrac{1}{i} =$ CV

A 'stepped' annuity

If the income is fixed by a lease contract for 'x' years and is then due to rise, either by reversion to a rack rental to be valued, for simplicity, in perpetuity, or to rise to a higher level for 'y' years, then reverting to rack rental in perpetuity, the valuation may be treated as an immediate annuity plus a deferred annuity in one of two ways. The first is referred to as a term and reversion, the second as the layer method.

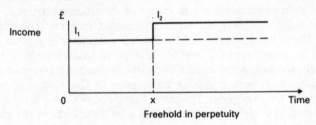

Freehold in perpetuity

Term and reversion

Net income	I_1	
YP for x years at $i\%$		£
Plus reversion to net income	I_2	
YP in perpetuity at $i\%$		
PV £1 in x years at $i\%$		£
		£

Layer method

Net income	I_1	
YP in perpetuity at $i\%$		£
Plus increased income		
Net income	$I_2 - I_1$	
YP in perpetuity at $i\%$		
PV £1 in x years at $i\%$		£
		£

Having estimated I_1 and I_2 as accurately as possible, the critical factor is the capitalisation rate $i\%$ which need not remain the same throughout. If it does remain the same, then each approach will produce the same value estimate.

A falling annuity

This can be treated in a similar manner to a rising annuity using either of the previous methods.

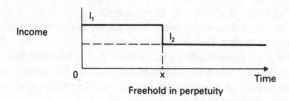

Freehold in perpetuity

Many valuers would adopt the layer method so that a higher capitalisation rate could be used for the income that will cease $(I_1 - I_2)$ as it is considered to be at great risk.

A variable annuity

It is fairly rare to find a completely variable income from property, i.e. one where the income changes from year to year. But the suggested technique is to treat the calculation as an NPV calculation (see p. 13), treating each payment as a separate reversion and discounting each to its present value at an appropriate rate of discount i.

Advance or arrears

It has always been the custom to assume annual 'in arrears' income flows and annual rates for capitalisation purposes. There is, however, a growing tendency, as property is let on 'in advance' terms, to value on such a basis (see p. 45). In this respect it is essential to determine the valuation date at the commencement, as in many cases this will fall between rental payments. Technically this is still an 'in advance' valuation as the assumption of open market value will generally imply an apportionment of rents received 'in advance' as at the date of completion of a sale, and for valuation purposes the valuation date may be treated as a sale completion date.

77

Second, it is necessary to be certain that in this respect the lease terms are being enforced. It is common to find rent due on 1 January 'in advance' being paid at a date later than 1 January.

Third, one should not lose sight of the fact that 'in advance' means one payment due immediately, i.e. its present value is the sum due, and thereafter the same sum is due for *n* periods in arrears.

The crucial point is the relationship between the income and the discount rate. The latter must be the correct 'effective' rate for the particular income pattern. For preference this should be derived from market analysis of comparable 'quarterly', 'yearly', 'in advance' or 'in arrears' transactions as investors may not in fact be prepared to accept the same effective rate.

If the appropriate comparable evidence is not available, then an 'in arrears' rate can be transposed to (say) an effective 'quarterly in advance' rate or a 'quarterly in advance' income changed to an 'annual in arrears' income.

It should be noted that the use of 'quarterly in advance' valuation tables for the valuation of incomes received on this basis may be questioned, as it is very rare that the valuation date will coincide exactly with the date when an instalment of rent is due. The income pattern may in fact resemble a 'quarterly in arrears' income.

If a property valuation is analysed on a precise basis, allowing both for the correct apportionment of rent as at the date of valuation and for the correct timing of future rents, then the rate of return will be higher than the rate per cent adopted in the valuation on an 'annual in arrears' basis. This realisation has encouraged some valuers to switch to 'quarterly in advance' valuations using published tables or programmed calculators and computers. Where this is done, valuers must be sure that they adopt the proper market relationship between income patterns and yields of comparables in their valuation work.

When the whole market relates to 'quarterly in advance' lettings and all valuers are analysing yields on a precise basis, then the market yields adopted by valuers for capitalisation work will be correct for 'in advance' valuations. Until then the valuer needs to be fully aware of the basis of the quoted market yield before transposing it to an 'in advance' valuation.

The reader should note that as the assessment of rental value, outgoings and capitalisation rates are all opinions, switching to 'in advance' valuation tables will not in itself achieve a better opinion of value. Attempts at such arithmetic accuracy may be spurious.

Save where stated, the 'annual in arrears' assumption has been used in all examples. This assumption is still commonplace in valuation practice, but accurate investment advice requires that estimation of the exact timing of income receipts is necessary in order to assess yields accurately. The introduction of computers enables the valuer to incorporate an accurate calendar within any valuation or analysis programme.

On examination it will be noted that certain property investments resemble certain other forms of investment and they can be distinguished by the future pattern of returns. Thus, property let on long lease without review could be compared to an irredeemable stock. Owner-occupied freehold commercial properties are comparable to equity shares, whereas freehold properties let on a short lease or with regular rent reviews (whilst in a sense resembling equity investments) must also reflect the stepped income pattern. Short fixed-income leasehold interests are comparable to any fixed-term investment such as an annuity.

Recognition of these relationships is essential if the valuer is to make correct adjustments to the capitalisation rates to be used in a valuation where the income pattern produced by the property is out of line with current market evidence.

Capitalisation and DCF methods

The traditional or conventional methods of freehold valuation are the term and reversion approach and the layer or hardcore method. These methods rely on an active market to guide the valuer on his or her choice of capitalisation rates. The traditional and the modern uses of these methods are illustrated in the following examples.

Example 3.1 Value a freehold shop in a prime trading position let at its full rental value of £20,000 per annum on full repairing and insuring terms. The lease is for 20 years with reviews every 5 years. Similar properties are selling on the basis of an all risks yield (ARY) or capitalisation rate of 5%.

Rent	£20,000
YP perpetuity @ 5%	20
	£400,000

Notes:

1. Although the lease is only for 20 years it is assumed that it would continue to let readily and that full rents will be receivable.

2. Although the rent is reviewable every 5 years there is no need to provide for this explicitly in a capitalisation approach as each reversion would also be to today's market or full rental value of £20,000.

3. All property incurs a management cost but customarily when property is let on FRI terms no deduction is made for management.

4. For some purposes the costs of acquisition (survey fees, legal fees and stamp duty) will be deducted to arrive at a net value. Where the net value plus fees adds up to £400,000, £20,000 represents a return on total outlay of 5% (see Chapter 9). The return on net value would be greater than 5%.

Example 3.2 If the rent in example 3.1 is payable in advance and the market is still looking for a 5% investment the valuation becomes:

Rent	£20,000
YP perpetuity @ 5% in advance	21
	£420,000

Notes:

1. £420,000 is being paid for the right to receive an immediate £20,000 and therefter £20,000 at the end of each year. This could only be the case if the valuation was undertaken on the rent due date. In such a case it is not the terms of the lease but the date of the valuation and the rent payment date that guides the valuer. In property sales the contract will usually provide for rental apportionment as between vendor and buyer (see Bornand, 1988).

2. Similar points and changes can be made to reflect quarterly rental arrangements.

Example 3.3 If the same property were let at £10,000 per annum on FRI terms with 2 years to run to a review or lease renewal the valuation could appear as:

Term and reversion

Term	£10,000	
YP 2 years @ 5%	1.86	£18,600
Reversion	£20,000	
YP perp. @ 5%		
× PV £1 in 2 years @ 5%	18.14	£362,800
		£381,400

	Layer		
Layer		£10,000	
YP perp. @ 5%		20	£200,000
Top slice		£10,000	
YP perp. @ 5% × PV £1 in 2 years @ 5%		18.14	£181,400
			£381,400

Notes:

1. See p. 76 for consideration of income tranches.

2. Because all the capitalisation and deferment or discounting rates have been left at 5% both conventional methods produce the same value figure.

3. In this case YP × PV of 18.14 comes from the YP of 20 multiplied by the PV factor of 0.9070. It could have been found by using the YP of a reversion to a perpetuity table or deducting the YP for 5 years from the YP in perpetuity (see Chapter 1).

Some valuers still insist on using different rates to reflect some personal view on security of income. This can be dangerous and can produce very peculiar results. This can apply to either traditional approach, as illustrated below.

Term	£10,000	
YP 2 years @ 4%	1.89	£18,900
Reversion	£20,000	
YP perp. def'd 2 years @ 5%	18.14	£362,800
		£381,700
Layer	£10,000	
YP perp. @ 4%	25	£250,000
Top slice	£10,000	
YP perp. def'd 2 years @ 5%	18.14	£181,400
		£431,400

The variation in the term and reversion is negligible and in a valuation would not be material when expressed as an opinion of, say, £380,000. In the layer method, failure to appreciate the effect of the change results in an underlet property being valued higher than the equivalent fully let property (see example 3.1). This cannot be correct. Practising valuers generally avoid such an error by capitalising the layer income at the ARY and increasing the rate on the top slice.

The reason for valuers wishing to change rates within a valuation rests with the historic evolution of the methods and the changing economy as reflected in the investment market (see Baum and Crosby, 1988). Valuers in the nineteenth century were primarily dealing with rack rented properties, largely agricultural, at a time when inflation was relatively unknown. A realistic and direct comparison could be made between alternative investments such as the undated securities (gilts) issued by government, the interest on deposits and farmland. The latter, being more risky, was valued at a percentage point or so above the secure government stock. Other property, such as residential and the emerging retail properties, were more risky but were let on long leases so they could be capitalised in perpetuity, again at an appropriate higher rate.

In the 1930s the depression made any contracted rent a better or more secure investment than an unlet property and there was real fear that at the end of a lease the tenant would seek to redress the position by requesting a lower rent or by vacating. Logic suggested the use of a lower capitalisation rate for secure contracted rents than unsecured reversions.

This approach continued unchallenged until the 1960s. In the meantime the market had changed in many ways and with the rise of inflation the investment market had identified a crucial difference between fixed-income investments such as gilts and those where the owner could participate in rental and capital growth such as equities and rack rented properties. This change was noted in the market and the reverse yield gap emerged. Nevertheless, valuers continued to use a capitalisation approach, varying yields to reflect the so-called security of income of contracted rents, the argument being that a tenant would be more likely to continue to pay a rent which was less than the estimated rental value because it represented a leasehold capital value (see Chapter 4). The market did not appear to recognise that the technique of the 1930s was one of using rates to reflect money risk, whereas those post the appearance of the reverse yield were capitalisation rates which reflected money risks and expectations of growth.

There are currently many arguments for not varying capitalisation rates in simple conventional valuations, but two will suffice. By the 1960s the property market for income-producing properties was being dominated by the major institutions. Valuers offering property investment opportunities were increasingly required to specify (a) the initial or year one rate of return and (b) the investment's internal rate of return. The former acted as a cut-off rate as actuarial advice at that time required all investments, depending upon the fund, to produce a minimum return – frequently

3–4%. The second caused confusion for valuers used to using perhaps four or five rates in a multiple reversionary property. The confusion arose because few valuers understood the concept of IRR, few knew how to calculate it and in the 1960s there was nothing more sophisticated than a slide rule to aid with the calculations.

The profession took a little longer to recognise that if the capitalisation rate is held constant it becomes the expected IRR. It can also be shown that for many term and reversion exercises using variable rates the IRR – now popularly called the equivalent yield – is almost the same as the ARY. As a result many valuers, whether using the term and reversion or layer method, now use an equivalent or same yield approach. It is, however, important to distinguish between the phrase *equivalent yield* and *equated yield.* In *Donaldson's Investment Tables* it is stated that:

> The equated yield of an investment may be defined as the discount rate which needs to be applied to the *projected* income so that the summation of all the incomes discounted at this expected yield rate, equates with the capital outlay . . . whereas an equated yield takes into account an assumed growth rate in the future annual income, an equivalent yield merely expresses the weighted average yield to be expected from the investment in terms of *current* rental value and without allowing for future growths in rental income.

Secondly it can be shown that variable rates pose their own problems. Bowcock uses a simple example of two properties each let at £100 per annum but one with a review in 5 years and the other with a review in 10 years, both with a reversion to £105 per annum. Traditionally the solution might appear as:

Term	£100	
YP 5 years @ 9%	3.8897	£388.97
Reversion	£105	
YP perp. def'd		
5 years @ 10%	6.2092	£651.96
		£1040.93
Term	£100	
YP 10 years @ 9%	6.4177	£641.77
Reversion	£105	
YP perp. def'd		
10 years @ 10%	8.8554	£404.82
		£1046.59

Clearly, there is something wrong with a method which places a higher value on the latter investment which includes a 10 year deferred income than the former with a 5 year deferred income. In practice, this potential error is not noted by valuers who subjectively adjust their rates to reflect (a) their view of the extent of the security of income, namely the difference between contracted rent and full rental value, and (b) the risk associated with the period of waiting till the rent review.

Some critics have also drawn attention to the problems of selecting the correct deferment rate in a variable yield valuation. Customarily the reversion has been deferred at the reversionary capitalisation rate. If this is done then it can be shown that the sinking fund provision within the YP single rate formula (at 9% in the above example) is not matched by the discounting factor (10% in the example) as a result the input rates of return of 9% and 10% will not be achieved. This can be corrected by deferring the reversion at the term rate.

The discerning valuer must conclude that it is safer and more logical to adhere to the same yield or equivalent yield approach. It is also the easiest yield to extract from sales evidence as the calculation is identical to that of the IRR. On a same yield basis there is no distinction to be made between the two capitalisation methods. However, the term and reversion seems the most acceptable theoretical method and preferable for valuations involving lease renewals when a void allowance or refurbishment cost may need to be built in. It is also easier to handle if outgoings have to be deducted. The layer method is possibly simpler and useful when handling certain investments where clients wish to know what price has been or is to be paid for the top slice.

Valuers are still faced with the problem of finding comparables. The more unusual the patterns of income the more difficult it is for the valuer to judge the correct capitalisation rate. For example, what would be the right equivalent yield to use for a property let at £10,000 p.a. with a reversion to £20,000 p.a. in 15 years? In most cases an equivalent yield approach is likely to be criticised when the yield used is lower than the opportunity cost of capital or gilt yield for investments with a fixed income running for 15 or more years.

The position today is that many investments with growth potential sell on a low yield basis compared to the fixed income returns on government stock. But the risk position has not changed, as all property is still riskier than holding cash or gilt stock. Thus with gilts at say 12% a property investor should arguably be looking for 13–14%. Purchasing at 5% is forgoing at least £8 per £100 invested per annum. Few people offered employment at £13,000 per annum would reject it in favour of one at £5,000 per annum unless they were certain that over a specified contract term the loss of £8,000 per annum would be compensated by regular and substantial increases in salary. The same is true of property. So capitalising at 5% must imply rental growth in perpetuity and the first criticism of the equivalent yield approach is that it fails to indicate rental growth explicitly by reverting to current rental values. Also, both the term income and the reversion are capitalised at the same ARY implying the same rental growth when clearly a lease rent is fixed by contract for the term. The only substantive arguments in defence of the equivalent yield approach are simplicity and that purely by chance it may over value the term just sufficiently to compensate for the undervaluation of the reversion (see Baum and Crosby, 1988).

Example 3.4 Using the facts from example 3.3, calculate the implied rate of rental growth assuming an opportunity cost rate or required equated return of 12%, and revalue on a modified DCF basis assuming the FRV of £20,000 is based on a normal 5 year review pattern. The relationship between ARYs and the equated yield or opportunity cost rate can be summarised as:

$$K = e - (\text{ASF} \times P)$$

where K = the capitalisation rate expressed as a decimal, e = the equated yield expressed as a decimal, ASF = the annual sinking fund to replace £1 at the equated yield over the review period (t), and P = the rental growth over the review period.

So given that $K = 0.05$ (5%), $e = 0.12$ (12%) and $t = 5$ years

then $0.05 = 0.12 - (0.1574097 \times P)$
$0.157409P = 0.12 - 0.05$
$0.1574097P = 0.07$
$P = 0.07/0.157409P$
$P = 0.444699$ (44.47% over 5 years)

The nature of compound interest was outlined in Chapter 1. Here there is a growth in rent, 'P', over 5 years of 44.47% and therefore:

$$P = (1 + g)^t - 1$$

where g = growth per annum expressed as a decimal and t = the rent review period (5), and therefore $1 + P$ must equal $(1 + g)^t$ to give

$$1.444699 \quad = (1 + g)^5$$

$$1.444699^{0.2} = (1 + g) \ [(\text{or } \sqrt[5]{1.444699} = (1 + g)]$$

$$1.076355 \quad = (1 + g)$$

Therefore $g \quad = 1.076355 - 1$

$$g\% = 7.6355\%$$

The figure 7.6355% represents the implied annual average rental growth in perpetuity.

Some commentators prefer the formulation:

$$(1 + g)^t = \frac{\text{YP perp. at } K - \text{YP } t \text{ years at } e}{\text{YP perp. at } K \times \text{PV } t \text{ years at } e}$$

or

$$g = [\sqrt[t]{(1 + (1 - \frac{K}{e})\ ((1 + e)^t - 1))}] - 1$$

This implies that the rent in 2 years time should be:

£20,000 × amount of £1 at 7.6355% for 2 years

£20,000 × 1.5854 = £23,170.80, say £23,170.

The property can now be revalued on a conventional basis and on a contemporary basis, in this case using a modified or short cut DCF (Baum and Crosby, 1988, provide a full critical comparison).

Term and reversion		
Next 2 years	£10,000	
YP 2 years @ 5%	1.86	£18,600
Reversion to	20,000	
YP perp. @ 5%	20	
	£400,000	
PV £1 @ 5%		
for 2 years	0.907	£362,800
		£381,400

Short cut DCF

Next 2 years	£10,000	
YP 2 years @ 12%	1.6901	£16,901
Reversion to	£23,170	
YP perp. @ 5%	20	
	£463,400	
PV £1 @ 12%		
for 2 years	0.7972	£369,422
		£386,323

The difference in opinion in practice on such a short reversionary property would be less significant as the valuations would probably be rounded to £382,000 and £385,000 respectively. However, it can be seen how the term and reversion produces a nearly acceptable solution by over valuing the term by £1,699 (£18,600 − £16,901) which to some extent compensates for the under valuation of the reversion of £6,622 (£369,422 − £362,800). The short cut DCF now reads like an investment valuation as all contracted income is discounted at a money market rate and the reversion is to an expected, albeit implied, rent, not to today's rental value.

The importance of this issue is greater when considering a longer reversionary property.

Example 3.5 Assuming the same facts as examples 3.3 and 3.4 but assuming a reversion in 15 years.
Then

£20,000 × Amount of £1 at 7.6355% for 15 years

£20,000 × 3.02 = £60,306.34

Term and reversion

	£10,000	
YP 15 years @ 7%	9.1079	£91,079
	£20,000	
YP perp. @ 7%	14.2857	
	285,714	
PV £1 in		
15 years @ 7%	0.3624	£103,542
		£194,621

Modified DCF

	£10,000	
YP 15 years @ 12%	6.8109	£68,109
	£60,306	
YP perp. @ 5%	20	
	1,206,120	
PV £1 in 15 years @ 12%	0.1827	£220,353
		£288,462

Here a subjective assessment had to be made as to the appropriate equivalent yield to use for a 15 year deferment. The modified DCF assesses the fixed lease income at the equated yield or opportunity cost, the reversion is to the implied rent in 15 years time and the value is deferred at the equated yield. If the DCF is arithmetically more correct (and it is) then an equivalent yield of less than $5\frac{1}{4}\%$ would have to be used to arrive at a figure of £288,462. It is extremely difficult in the absence of true comparables to arrive at a correct equivalent yield subjectively, but that appears to be the favoured approach and may involve the use of money rates for discounting the fixed term.

Currently, though, it is not possible to say that a modified DCF approach must be the preferred approach. It may be the more rational approach in that it is possible to argue that investors should be indifferent between the short and long reversionary properties if they are expected to produce the same equated yield. But this is difficult to support if the market is substantially discounting long reversions through the subjective approach of their investment surveyors; implying inconsistency over the choice of equated yields.

The modified DCF can be proved by using a full projected cash flow over, say, 100 years, discounted at 12% as in Table 3.1. Baum and Crosby discuss DCF techniques in more detail.

In practice such contemporary methods seem to be rejected in favour of the market methods. That implies that although valuers do not make the market they do in some instances have a strong influence. Current market practice favours the simple equivalent or same yield approach. This creates the probability that investors will conclude that some valuers are over, or undervaluing, properties and will sell or purchase in the market at market prices to take advantage of such market imperfections.

Table 3.1 DCF to 100 years allowing for a rental growth at 7.6355% and discounted at an equated yield of 12%. Year 96 could be taken to perpetuity by capitalising £21,717,164 at 5% in perpetuity and discounting for 95 years. This would bring the value figure into line with the modified DCF.

Period (years)	Income × A £1 at 7.6355%	PV £1 p.a. at 12%	PV £1 at 12%	Present value
0–15	10,000	6.8109	–	68,109
16–20	60,306	3.60477	0.18269	39,714
21–25	87,124	3.60477	0.10367	32,558
26–30	125,868	3.60477	0.05882	26,688
31–35	181,842	3.60477	0.03337	21,874
36–40	262,706	3.60477	0.01894	17,936
41–45	379,532	3.60477	0.01074	14,693
46–50	548,310	3.60477	0.00609	12,037
51–55	792,144	3.60477	0.00346	9,880
56–60	1,144,410	3.60477	0.00196	8,085
61–65	1,653,329	3.60477	0.00111	6,615
66–70	2,388,566	3.60477	0.00063	5,424
71–75	3,450,761	3.60477	0.00036	4,478
76–80	4,985,314	3.60477	0.00020	3,594
81–85	7,202,282	3.60477	0.00011	2,855
86–90	10,405,137	3.60477	0.00006	2,250
91–95	15,032,301	3.60477	0.000037	2,005
96–100	21,717,164	3.60477	0.000021	1,565
			Value	£280,360

Throughout this section it must be remembered that the growth rates used are implied and that the figures derived in no way predict the future. They merely provide the valuer with an additional tool with which to examine and, as will be seen later, to analyse the market. Such implied rents must be critically examined against the reality of the market place and realistic economic projections.

The following examples are based on questions set by the Royal Institution of Chartered Surveyors. They should not be assumed to be model answers, as they are used for illustration only, and adhere to traditional methodology (an approach still expected by many examining bodies). Examinees using equivalent yield or contemporary approaches must be very specific in the statements and assumptions made to accompany their solutions.

Example 3.6 Value the following for sale in the open market: a freehold semi-detached house built in 1933. It is let at £30 per week. The occupier pays the fire insurance and does internal repairs.

Assumptions:
1   £30 per week is the maximum recoverable rent on these terms.
2   There is sufficient market evidence to substantiate a capital-isation rate on initial rentals of 10%.
3   Points 1 and 2 exclude the need to revert to a future income.
4   Fees for managing this type of property are 10% of rents collected.

Market valuation:

Gross income p.a. (£30 × 52 weeks)[1]		£1,560
Less landlord's outgoings		
External repairs and decorations,[2] say	£150	
Management @ 10% on rent	£156	
Plus VAT on management & repairs at 15%	£45.90	£351.90
Net income rounded to		£1,200
Years' purchase in perpetuity @ 10%		10
Estimated capital value[4]		£12,000

Notes:
 1. £30 per week is a little more than £1,560 per annum if a per day basis is adopted.
 2. This figure is based on office records and experience: a rate of say 10% on £1,560 is not an accurate method of assessing repair costs.
 3. VAT on professional fees: it would be possible to round these figures, but as the rent is to the nearest £1 rounding has been left until the net income line. The current VAT rate should be used.
 4. If the capital value does not come to a round figure, it is conceivable that it too may be rounded in the light of market experiences. There may be an active market for this type of investment property, in which case valuation by direct capital comparison is feasible.
 5. The addition of VAT to rents may have to be accounted for in future years.

Example 3.7 Value freehold shop premises let on lease with 4 years to run at £7,000 per annum. The tenant pays the rates and the insurance and undertakes internal repairs. It is worth £12,500 per annum net today and rental values for this type of property are continuing to rise in this area.

Assumptions:
1 Current capitalisation rates on rack rented comparable premises are 8%.
2 Rents are due annually in arrears.

Market valuation:

Gross income per annum for 4 years		£7,000	
Less landlord's outgoings			
External repairs and decorations[1]	£500		
Management at 5% of £7,000[2]	£350		
Plus VAT at 15%	£127.5	977.5	
Net income,[4] say		£6,000	
Years' purchase for 4 years @ 7%[5]		3.39	£20,340
Plus reversion in 4 years to[6]			
Net income		£12,500	
YP in perpetuity deferred 4 years @ 8%[7]		9.19	£114,875
Estimate of capital value			£135,215

Value (say) £135,000[8]

Notes:

1 Based on office records, etc.
2 Based on fees charged by management department for comparable properties.
3 VAT will be a cost unless a VAT election is made.
4 It is very unlikely that this sum is precise. Accuracy to the nearest £ at this stage would be unrealistic, so this is rounded, suggesting accuracy to the nearest £100.
5 The relationship between the rates here and at 7 (7% and 8%) depends upon a number of assumptions as to the true behaviour of the market. The argument here is that the £6,000 is more secure in money terms, hence a lower rate is used.
6 In a normal market valuation the reversion is to full rental value (FRV) as estimated in today's terms. There is no deduction here as it is a net rent, although some valuers could allow for management at say 1–2% of rent collected.
7 YP in perp. deferred = YP perp. at 8% × PV £1 in 4 years at 8% or YP perp. at 8% less YP for 4 years at 8%.
8 This final estimate is rounded, as no valuer can truly value to the nearest £, figures of this magnitude would bear rounding to the nearest £1,000.
9 The idea of reducing the term capitalisation rate by 1% to reflect money security is almost certainly inappropriate during inflationary periods. Money security should give way to a reflection of purchasing power risk. Some purchasers will not differentiate between a property let below rack rental and one let at rack rental, because there is no real difference provided the sum paid for the investment reflects the difference in current income and any difference in expectation of future

rental change. But, on the latter point, is it reasonable to use the same discount rate for both the capitalisation of, and the 4 year deferment of the reversionary income? A modified DCF approach may be preferred or used as a check.

A number of valuers would comment that this rate and the deferment rate should be higher by 1–2% to reflect the greater uncertainty of receiving the future increased income. Of the two, the concept of increasing the deferment rate may seem the most logical as 8% could be applied to £12,500 if it was receivable today. But those who defend the former method argue that it results in an over-valuation of the term which helps to compensate for the under-valuation of the reversion. The point here in practice, and as indicated in the question, is that if the rent of £12,500 is continuing to rise, the true rent in 4 years' time will exceed £12,500 and the reversion has therefore been under-valued. Those who favour a DCF approach would argue that neither approach is defensible because, assuming the opportunity cost of money is 12%, capitalisation rates of 7% and 8% and deferment rates of 8% imply a particular expectation of growth in the incomes over the periods involved. The particular rates used in the examples may fortuitously have produced a result which is close enough to the correct value of the property.

10 A comparable conventional layer method valuation employing different rates may be laid out as follows:

Layer income	£6,000	
YP perp. @ 7%	14.29	£85,740
Marginal income[a]	£6,500	
YP perp. def'd 4 years @ 8%	9.19	£59,735
Estimate of capital value		£145,205

Value (say) £145,000

Notes:

(a) Reversionary income of £12,500 minus initial (layer) income of £6,000.

(b) *Parry's Valuation Tables* (Estates Gazette) 8th edition, page xxiii, lays down a rule for adjusting the capitalisation rates in a layer method valuation to produce the same figure of value as in example 3.2. The method requires the capitalisation rate for the marginal income $(I_2 - I_1)$ to be found from the ratio of $(I_2 - I_1)$ to the difference between the existing rent capitalised as if in perpetuity and the full rental value, also capitalised as if in perpetuity. But, as the method requires the valuer to make an initial assumption concerning the appropriate term and reversion rates it is much simpler to carry out a term and reversion valuation.

11 An equivalent yield valuation may be derived from either approach to find the single equivalent rate of interest which, if applied to both term and reversion (or layer and marginal) income, will produce the same valuation.

Valuation (term and reversion)   £135,215

Term:

Net Income	£6,000	
YP 4 years @ x%	a	£A

Reversion:

Net Income	£12,500	
YP perp. def'd 4 years @ x%	b	£B

$£(A + B) = £135,215$

By trial and error, x% may be found. In this case it is approximately 7.97%. This is the equivalent yield.

Valuation (equivalent yield)

Term:

Net income	£6,000	
YP 4 years @ 7.97%	3.31	£19,860

Reversion:

Net income	£12,500	
YP perp. def'd 4 years @ 7.97%	9.23	£115,375
		£135,235

12 Valuing throughout at 8% produces (£6,000 × 3.3121 + £12,500 × 9.18787 = £19,872 + £114,848 = £134,720 or say £135,000).

13 An equated yield valuation is a valuation which employs DCF techniques. This may be combined with a conventional valuation approach as a short cut or carried out fully as previously illustrated.

14 The conventional capitalisation approach is perfectly acceptable under normal conditions where property is let on normal terms with regular rent reviews, and where there is evidence of capitalisation rates. In such cases it is most logical to use an equivalent yield approach, whether it be in the format of the term and reversion, or the layer, method.

15 Where the income pattern is not normal, there is a strong case for using the DCF approach. DCF directs the valuer to concentrate upon an explicit consideration of the net current and future incomes, and upon the correct rate of interest to use to discount that specified cash flow.

Falling incomes

The problem considered in example 3.8 is that of falling incomes. This may be caused by changes in demand for space as occurred in the 1970s.

Example 3.8 Value a freehold office building let at £10,000 p.a. with 5 years to the review. The current rental value is £7,500 p.a. The following rental pattern emerges:

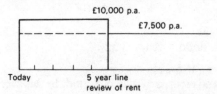

The valuer's immediate response is 'will rents rise to the contracted level by the review date?' If he feels confident in saying yes, then the valuation problem is removed and £10,000 p.a. can be treated as a perpetual income provided a current capitalisation rate can be derived from market comparables. However, reduction of the deferment period might cause problems.

The second question is whether the tenant can insist on a lower rent at the review date. If there is an upwards-only rent review clause then this might preclude a fall in rent. This will depend upon the amount of space occupied, whether or not there is a break clause in the lease, and the tenant's negotiating strength.

The valuer's conventional solution is to use the layer method assessing the income to be lost on a dual rate basis thus (see page 31 and Chapter 4):

Continuing income	£7,500	
YP perp. @ 8%	12.5	£93,750
Plus income to be lost	£2,500	
YP for 5 years @ 8% and 3% adj. tax @ 40%	2.54	£6,350
		£100,100

The philosophy here is that only £2,500 for 5 years will cease and that the capital value assigned to this income must be recovered at the low, safe sinking fund rate of 3% after allowing for the incidence of taxation on that part of the income which represents capital recovery. But the use of 8% implies a growth in the £7,500 from today, which is clearly false because it has already been stated that there will be no increase for at least 5 years.

A shortened DCF approach might well overcome this:

		£10,000	
PV £1 p.a. for 5 years @ 15%		3.35	
			£33,500
		£7,500	
PV £1 p.a. in perpetuity @ 8%	12.5		
PV £1 in 5 years @ 15%	0.50	6.25	£46,875
			£80,375

Valuers may still seek to criticise this approach on the grounds that part of the income ceases and no provision has been made for recovery of that part of the total value used to acquire that income. A moment's reflection on the meaning of PV £1 p.a. will indicate that capital is recovered. But there is the point that this ignores the effect of tax on income: to overcome this it would be preferable to rework on a net-of-tax DCF basis.

Sub-markets

The concept of open market value assumes the most probable selling price. This presumes a knowledge of the most probable purchaser which presumes detailed knowledge and understanding of the sub-markets. It also assumes sufficient market activity to extract, by analysis, details of returns expected by investors.

As an indication the following sub-markets can be noted:

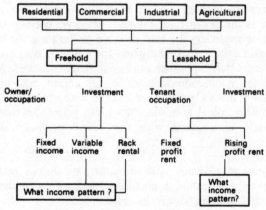

The valuation of leasehold interests is considered in the following chapter.

Chapter four

The income approach to leaseholds

The problem of valuing leasehold interests in property has ben vexing valuers for many years. In most other countries the debate is now closed, but in the UK there is still considerable disagreement between those who regard the 'dual rate' or reinvestment approach to be correct and those who would seek to treat a leasehold as they would treat any investment requiring analysis or valuation.

In this section the different views are set out with comments, and whilst the view of the authors may be apparent it would be wrong without empirical evidence to state categorically that one or other approach is the right one. Our advice is to identify the sub-market, identify the most probable type of purchaser and as far as possible adopt methods that parallel the investment aims of that most probable purchaser group.

A number of facts are not in dispute, namely:

1   A leasehold interest is of finite duration.
2   In investors' terms a lease can only have a market value if it produces an income and if it is assignable. The leasehold income is the profit rent, the rent actually received or potentially receivable less the rent payable to the superior landlord.
3   The profit rent must be adjusted for any expenses payable by the interest holder, but irrecoverable from the sub-lessee.
4   Where tax on income is payable, the capital cost of a finite investment has to be recovered out of taxed income.
5   The mathematical formulation of the years' purchase single rate may be equated with the years' purchase dual rate ($\frac{1}{i + \text{SF}}$), so that capitalisation of an income using either provides the investor with a return on initial outlay plus replacement of capital in a sinking fund, on the assumption of compound interest within the rates used.

The crux of the problem is how the purchaser of a leasehold interest should or does allow for capital recovery.

Dual rate adjusted for tax

The reasons generally given for valuing leaseholds on the dual rate basis for recoupment (recovery) of capital by reinvestment in a sinking fund at a low safe rate are:

1 That an investor requires a return on initial outlay throughout the lease term at the remunerative rate.
2 That he must fully recover all his capital by the end of the lease term and that to be certain of doing this he must reinvest in a sinking fund accumulating at a low, safe, net-of-tax rate.
3 That by so doing the investor has equated the finite investment with an infinite (freehold) investment in the same property base, i.e. the spendable income is perpetuated (see Chapter 1).

Example 4.1   Estimate the value of a 4 year unexpired lease. The profit rent is £100 per annum net.

Net of outgoings profit rent	£100
YP for 4 years @ 10% and 3% adj. tax @ 40%	2.00
	£200

Proof:
Annual sinking fund to replace £1 at 3% in
4 years $= 0.239$
∴ ASF to replace £200 $= 200 \times 0.239$
                                             $= £47.80$

Grossed-up to allow for tax on original
income of £100 $= 47.80 \times \dfrac{1}{1 - t}$

                                  $= 47.80 \times \dfrac{1}{1 - 0.40}$

                                  $= 47.80 \times \dfrac{1}{0.60}$

                                  $= £79.66$

Grossed-up sinking fund = say £80
∴ Spendable income $= £100 - £80$
                      $= £20$
                      $=$ a 10% return on ECV of £200

The £200 recovered over 4 years can be reinvested at 10% to produce a 10% return in perpetuity.

But:

1 Capitalisation on a single rate basis can be considered to give a return on initial outlay plus a sinking fund. Additionally it can be shown to give a return on capital at risk (see p. 29).
2 It can be shown that when a single rate years' purchase is used the investor will, at the implied rate, recover all his capital by the end of the term.
3 The investment may have been perpetuated and can be shown to be perpetuated on a single rate and dual rate basis. But a leasehold interest cannot be equated with a freehold interest if one merely recovers historic cost during periods of inflation.

Within conventional dual rate valuations two schools of thought are apparent. Initially both accept that the risk, or remunerative, rate for a leasehold should be 1–2% above the appropriate freehold rate. This is to allow for the additional problems of reinvesting in a sinking fund, reinvesting the accumulated sinking fund at the end of the lease term, and for the additional risks inherent in a leasehold investment relating to restrictions imposed by the lease terms and possible dilapidations. This philosophy would have ben sound in the late nineteenth and early twentieth centuries when leases were for long terms of 99 years or more. To assume some constant magical relationship today is inconsistent with the philosophy of market valuations, unless market transactions justify that rate.

Both schools assume that reinvestment must be at a low, net-of-tax rate and that the sinking fund premium or instalment must be met out of taxed income. But the schools seem to differ on the nature of the sinking fund.

The original theory is that capital replacement in order to be guaranteed must be in effect 'assured.' Hence reinvestment is assumed to be made in a sinking fund policy with an assurance company. Such a policy is a legal contract. The total sum assured will be paid out on the due date if all premiums have been met. The apparent rate of accumulation is between 2^{1}/2% and 4%. Such a policy is unaffected by any changes in tax rates, as such changes will only affect the investor's investment income.*

The second school argues in favour of reinvestment at safe rates. These will not necessarily be guaranteed but could conceivable include regular savings in a post office account, bank

---

*If a policy is taken out and a re-sale occurs part way through the term, the insured must either continue to pay the annual premium or accept a paid-up policy. In the latter case there would be a shortfall in capital recovery.

deposit account, or building society savings or investment accounts. A potential 'danger' is that without realisation the valuer can be implying an effective gross return on the sinking fund greater than the remunerative rate used in a valuation. Conventionally a 6% freehold yield might become a 7% leasehold yield, but 7% and 4% with a tax rate of 50p in the £ would imply that the investor could invest in a sinking fund and initially be better off than by purchasing the leasehold interest. It can be seen that the profit rent must grow at a rate sufficient to compensate for the opportunity cost of investing at 7% gross and not at 4% net. This would be perfectly tenable under certain market conditions.

Both approaches rely on the argument that the purchaser of a leasehold investment is unlikely to have the opportunity to reinvest at the remunerative rate. Apart from the fact that there is no need to reinvest if the investor accepts a return on capital at risk, there is the obvious point that relatively safe rates compared to the initial remunerative rate are readily available for regular saving. Further, most purchasers of leasehold investments invest in more than one unit, and may receive sufficient income each year to purchase further leasehold investments. The leasehold investor is then better advised to reinvest in further leaseholds (or freeholds) rather than in a sinking fund.

Historically there may have been some justifications for the dual rate approach. In the eighteenth, nineteenth and early twentieth century leaseholds were long leaseholds frequently ground leases or improved ground leases with no rent reviews; as such they were very comparable to investments in freeholds. Initially they were valued single rate at $^{1}/_{2}$–2% above the freehold rate to reflect the additional risk arising from lease covenants etc. The problem emerged in the 1920s and 1930s when lease length began to fall and when the gap between safe and risky investments became greater. This was in part a reflection of depression in the economy.

It was also a time when purchasers of leases were individuals buying for occupation or to hold as investments; there were few large investors in the market. By the mid 1930s valuers were split between single rate and dual rate although writers still made the point that sale prices could be analysed on either basis. The need to demonstrate parity with freeholds began to dominate, as did the concern for capital recovery when safe investments were yielding so little. For those who were seeking protection and perpetuation through reinvestment there was the added difficulty of finding reinvestment opportunities for small annual sums other than in a bank or post office. The result was a growing rationale for the conventional dual rate approach.

The position post 1950 was very different as inflation became part of life. Nevertheless, the dual rate method survived virtually unchallenged other than for the universal acceptance of the need for the tax adjustment. It survived with the low sinking fund even though most savers could achieve much higher returns than the 4% maximum used by valuers. It survived even though few sinking fund policies were taken out, even though occupiers were depreciating leaseholds as wasting assets in their accounts and even though investors accepted that they effectively provided for capital replacement by reinvestment in a general sense rather than on a per property basis.

A final point is that where the investment is made with borrowed funds or partially borrowed funds (e.g. 60% mortgage) reinvestment at the rates adopted in valuations by certain valuers will certainly be at levels lower than the interest charged on the borrowed capital. Clearly the investor would be better advised to pay off part of the loan rather than reinvest in a sinking fund.

One of the most disturbing elements of dual rate valuation is its concentration on today's profit rent and its failure to consider the future, in particular its failure to reflect the unique gearing characteristics of longer leaseholds. Taking, for example, property A held for 20 years at £10,000 p.a. without review and sub-let with 5 year reviews for £20,000 p.a.; and property B similarly held at £80,000 p.a. and sub-let at £90,000 p.a., the conventional dual rate approach would place the same value on both as they both produce a profit rent of £10,000 p.a. This completely hides the fact that with rental growth at any rate per cent the profit rents after each rent review grow at different rates. This problem of gearing can only be solved by valuing the head rent and occupation rent separately and by adopting a DCF or real value approach. Conventional dual rate methodology would, if applied constantly to every situation, provide the investor with some phenomenal investments and result in some vendors grossly underselling their investments.

The dual rate method was considered in depth in the RICS research report (Trott, 1980). A general conclusion being that it will continue to be used because 'that is how the market does it'; however for investment advice a DCF approach should be adopted and indeed, should always be used to check the dual rate approach to avoid the possibility of incorrect sales advice.

Variable profit rents

Variable profit rents present special problems in valuations where the sinking fund rate of return adopted is lower than the investment risk rate (remunerative rate).

The valuation of a leasehold investment may involve a variable profit rent in the following cases:

1. Where a leaseholder lets property to a sub-lessee for part only of the unexpired term. In this case there will be a fixed profit rent for *n* years and a reversion to a potential growth profit rent in *n* years.
2. Where a leaseholder lets property to a sub-lessee for the full unexpired term with a proviso for rent reviews in *n* years to a known sum or to full rental value.
3. Where a leaseholder has a right to a new lease under the Landlord and Tenant Act 1954 Part II, and where the rent for the new lease must be at full rental value adjusted for goodwill and/or approved improvements carried out by the lessee.*

In some cases the profit rent will be rising, while in others it will be falling. In both cases anomalies occur if, in the assessment of present worth, the flow of income is treated as an immediate annuity plus one or more deferred annuities, assessed on a dual rate basis. The valuation should be treated as an immediate variable annuity.

Wherever a leasehold valuation is required the valuer should exercise care in determining the true net profit rent, special attention being given to the allowance for expenditure on repairs and insurance when a sub-letting has taken place on terms differing from the head lease.

Whilst the valuer's subjective adjustments to the remunerative rates used in the three cases may well differ, the particular problem of variable profit rents will remain and is fully illustrated in the following problem.

Example 4.2   Using as an example a profit rent of £1,800 for 2 years rising to £2,000 for 5 years, demonstrate the problems encountered when valuing rising profit rents on a conventional dual rate basis. Demonstrate the alternatives to this approach.

Leasehold rate at FRV: 10% and 3% adj. tax @ 40%

Conventional valuation:†
Term:

Profit rent	£1,800	
YP for 2 years @ 9% and		
3% adj. tax @ 40%	1.0977	£1,976

---

*See Landlord and Tenant Act 1954 Part II and Law of Property Act 1969
†The use of variable remunerative rates causes further problems as does the deferment of the reversions at the reversionary remunerative rate. These issues can be overcome by adopting a same yield approach.

Reversion:

Profit rent	£2,000	
YP for 5 years @ 10% and 3% adj. tax @ 40%	2.416	
	£4,832	
PV £1 in 2 years @ 10%	0.8265	£3,994
		£5,970

What are the problems? None is apparent from this valuation. but compare the valuation of the following profit rent of £1,800 receivable for 7 years:

Profit rent	£1,800	
YP for 7 years @ 10% and 3% adj. tax @ 40%	3.1495	£5,669.60

Notice that the second investment is valued at £300 lower than the first. But what is the real difference? The first investment produces an extra £200 for 5 years deferred for 2 years.

Profit rent	£200
YP for 5 years @ 10% and 3% adj. tax @ 40%	2.416
	£483.2
PV £1 in 2 years @ 10%	0.8265
	£400.0

The difference in the two valuations is £300, yet the difference in rent is worth £400. There is obviously some kind of error.

The error can be demonstrated in the same manner much more dramatically. Take two profit rents with a 20 year life. One is of £1,000 for the whole period; the other rises to £1,100 after 10 years (and is therefore more valuable).

(1)		(2)		
Profit rent	£1,000	Profit rent	£1,000	
YP for 20 years @ 10% and 3% adj. tax @ 40%	6.1718	YP for 10 years @ 9% and 3% adj. tax @ 40%	4.2484	£4,248
	£6,172	Reversion to	£1,100	
		YP for 10 years @ 10% and 3% adj. tax @ 40% ×		
		PV £1 in 10 years @ 10%	1.573	£1,730
		(4.0752 × 0.386 = 1.573)		£5,977

The inferior investment is valued more highly by the conventional dual rate method, and the error becomes embarrassing.

It can be demonstrated without any need for comparison that an error does exist by checking that the sinking fund actually replaces the initial outlay. This will be done with reference to the original valuation.

Term:		
CV	£5,970	
Income	£1,800	
Spendable income		Sinking fund
0.09 × £5,970		£1,800 − £537.3
= £537.3		= £1,262.7 gross
		= 0.6 (£1,262.7) net
		= £757.6
A £1 p.a. for 2 years @ 3%		2.03
		£1,538

This £1,538 will then be allowed to accumulate interest for 5 more years, the period of the reversion.

$$\begin{array}{c} £1,538 \\ \text{A £1 in 5 years @ 3\%} \quad 1.1593 \end{array} = £1,783 \text{ replaced}$$

Reversion:		
CV	£5,970	
Income	£2,000	
Spendable income		Sinking fund
0.10 × £5,970		£2,000 − £597
= £597		= £1,403 gross
		= 0.6 (£1,403) net
		= £842
A £1 p.a. for 5 years @ 3%		5.3091
		£4,470 replaced

Total replacement of capital $A + B = £1,783 + £4,470 = £6,253$

Compare £6,253 with an initial outlay of £5,970 and it can be seen that there is an over-replacement of capital. Why? It can be shown that the replacement of capital for both term and reversion, when examined separately, is perfectly correct.

Term: (see p. 101)
CV	£1,976
Income	£1,800

Spendable income	Sinking fund	
0.09 × £1,976	£1,800 − £178	= £1,622 gross
= £178		× 0.6
		£973.2 net
	A £1 p.a. for 2 years	
	@ 3%	2.03
	Term capital replaced	£1,976

Reversion:

CV	£4,832		
Income	£2,000		
Spendable income		Sinking fund	
0.10 × £4,832		£2,000 − £483.2	£1,516.8 gross
= £483.2			× 0.6
			£910.08 net
		A £1 p.a. for 5 years	
		@ 3%	5.3091
		Reversion capital replaced	£4,832

It follows that the error must arise from the addition of term and reversion. This produces an extra accumulation of sinking fund resulting in an over-replacement of capital. The deferment of the reversion by a single rate PV is another expression of the same error. It is often said that the error results from the provision for two sinking funds or the interruption of the desired single sinking fund.

As a result the methods that have been devised to deal with this error attack the problem by attempting to ensure that the initial capital is accurately replaced by the sinking fund.

1 The sinking fund method

The problem which has been identified above is that the conventional dual rate method of valuing leasehold interests does not provide for accurate replacement of capital. The sinking fund method ensures that this must happen, its premise being that capital value is equal to the amount replaced by the sinking fund. The method calculates the amount of the net sinking fund and its accumulation which must necessarily be equal to the capital value of the investment.

Let CV = x

Term: Rent   =£1,800
Gross sinking fund = Income − spendable income

$$= £1,800 - 0.09x$$

(Return on capital = remunerative rate of
9%: return on capital = $0.09x$)

Net sinking fund $= (£1,800 - 0.09x)(0.6)$
$$= £1,080 - 0.054x$$

Reversion: Rent $= £2,000$
Gross sinking fund $= £2,000 - 0.10x$
$\therefore$ Net sinking fund $= £1,200 - 0.06x$

Calculate accumulation of net sinking funds:

Term:		£1,080 − 0.054x	
A £1 p.a. for 2 years			
@ 3%		2.03	
A £1 in 5 years @ 3% × 1.1593	2.3534		£2,541.65 − 0.127x
Reversion:		£1,200 − 0.06x	
A £1 p.a. for 5 years			
@ 3%		5.3091	£6,370.92 − 0.3185x
			£8,912.57 − 0.4455x

The capital value should equal the amount replaced and therefore
x should equal the sum of the sinking fund accumulations. So:

$$x = £8,912.57 - 0.4455x$$

$$1.4455x = £8,912.57$$

$$\therefore x = £6,165.74$$

This method can be checked by checking the accumulation of sinking funds on term and reversion.

Term:

CV	£6,166		
Income	£1,800		
Spendable income		Sinking fund	
0.09 × £6,166		£1,800 − £554.94 = £1,245.06 gross	
= £554.94		× 0.6	
		£747.04 net	
A £1 p.a. for 2 years @ 3%	2.03		
A £1 in 5 years @ 3%	1.1593		2.354
			£1,758.07

Reversion

CV	£6,166	
Income	£2,000	

Spendable income	Sinking fund		
0.10 × £6,166	£2,000 − £616.6 =	£1,383.40 gross	
= £616.60		× 0.60	
		£830.06 net	
A £1 p.a. for 5 years @ 3%		5.3091	£4,406.87
Capital replaced			£6,164.94*

*The marginal error here is due to the initial rounding to £6,166 and subsequent rounding in the calculations.

2 The annual equivalent method*

The purpose of this second method is to find that fixed income which would be equivalent to the rising profit rent which is to be valued. Equivalent incomes for both term and reversion are found and valued separately to allow for the use of different remunerative rates on term and reversion. It was originally suggested that the rate of interest used to capitalise and de-capitalise both incomes when finding the annual equivalent should be the accumulative rate, and this will be the approach that will be adopted, although it is open to question at the present time due to the problem of choosing a reasonable accumulative rate.

A Capitalise at low safe rate:

Term:			
Income		£1,800	
YP for 2 years @ 3%		1.9135	£3,444

Reversion:			
Income		£2,000	
YP for 5 years @ 3%	4.5797		
PV £1 in 2 years @ 3%	× 0.9426	4.3168	£8,633

B Find annual equivalent incomes:

Term:
   £3,444 ÷ YP for 7 years @ 3%
= £3,444 ÷ 6.2303
= £552.78

Reversion:
   £8,633 ÷ Yp for 7 years @ 3%
= £8,633 ÷ 6.2303
= £1,385.65

C Capitalise annual equivalents at market capitalisation rate:

*The current teaching of this and the sinking fund method is attributed to Dr M. J. Greaves previously of Reading University and the National University of Singapore.

Term:

Income	£552.78	
YP for 7 years @ 9% and 3% adj. tax @ 40%	3.2519	£1,797.59

Reversion:

Income	£1,385.65	
YP for 7 years @ 10% and 3% adj. tax @ 40%	3.1495	£4,364.10
		£6,161.69

D Proof:

Term:

CV	£1,797.59
Income	£1,800

Spendable income

Sinking fund

$0.09 \times £1,797.59$
$= £161.78$

£1,800 − £598.19* = £1,201.81 gross
× 0.6

£721.09 net

Reversion:

CV	£4,364.10
Income	£2,000

Spendable income

Sinking fund

$0.10 \times £4,364.10$
$= £436.41$

£2,000 − £598.19* = £1,401.81 gross
× 0.6

£841.09 net

*Total spendable income at 9% and 10% on term and reversion is £598.19
(£161.78 + £436.41).

Check sinking fund accumulations:

Term:

		£721.09	
A £1 p.a. for 2 years @ 3%	2.03		
A £1 in 5 years @ 3%	× 1.1593	2.354	£1,697

Reversion:

		£841.09
A £1 p.a. for 5 years @ 3%	5.3091	£4,465
		£6,162*

*Error due to rounding.

The proof employed in the sinking fund approach is not applicable in this case, where term and reversion must be kept separate when checking the sinking fund accumulation. In the first approach spendable income differs over term and reversion; but in the annual equivalent method, spendable income remains the same. If the remunerative rates were the same over term and reversion then either proof may be used; but when they differ, the annual equivalent valuation can only be checked by the particular approach outlined above.

3 The double sinking fund method*

This, the original of the three methods discussed here, involves more detailed arithmetic. The required sinking fund to replace a capital value of x is deducted from income to leave the amount of spendable income that will be enjoyed. The spendable income is then capitalised.

This ignores the sinking fund accumulation, which is then added back to produce a similar equation to that which is solved in the sinking fund approach. A constant sinking fund is ensured by this approach, overcoming the conventional method's fault.

1 Let CV $= x$

Then sinking fund to replace x = ASF to replace £1 in 7 years at 3% $\times x$

$$= 0.1305064x$$

Gross up for tax @ 40% $= 0.1305064x\left(\dfrac{1}{1 - t}\right)$

$$= 0.1305064x \times \frac{1}{0.6}$$

$$= 0.2175106x$$

∴ Spendable income is £1,800 $-$ 0.2175106x for term.
∴ Spendable income is £2,000 $-$ 0.2175106x for reversion.

2 Capitalise the spendable income
Term:

Income	£1,800 $-$ 0.2175106x		
YP for 2 years @ 9%		1.7591	£3,166.38 $-$ 0.3826228x

Reversion:

Income	£2,000 $-$ 0.2175106x		
YP for 5 years @ 10%	3.7908		
PV £1 in 2 years @ 10%	0.8264463	3.133	£6,265.79 $-$ 0.6814372x
			£9,432.17 $-$ 1.06406x

This (£9,432.17 minus 1.06406x) is the present value of the spendable income provided by the investment. It has been capitalised by a single rate YP which contains an inherent sinking fund at the remunerative rate. The capital value of the spendable income could thus be reinvested at the end of 7 years, while

*This method is attributed to A. W. Davidson one time Head of Valuation at Reading University.

another sinking fund has been provided to replace the capital value of the whole income flow – x. There are therefore two sinking funds, hence the name of the method.

An alternative view is to remember that income is split into two parts when it is received for a limited period – spendable income and sinking fund. It follows that capital value can be split into capitalised spendable income and capitalised sinking fund. Having found the first of these constituents the second should be added to give the total value of the investment.

What, then, is the present capital value of the sinking fund? It replaces x in 7 years. Its present value is x deferred for 7 years at the investor's remunerative rate(s): 9% for 2 years and 10% for the remaining 5.

3 Replaced CV = $\qquad\qquad\qquad\qquad\qquad\qquad\qquad x$

PV £1 in 5 years @ 10%	0.6209213	
PV £1 in 2 years @ 9%	0.84168	0.522617
		0.522617x

Thus if x is the capital value CV, then x must be equal to the total of 1, 2 and 3.

$$x = £9,432.17 - 1.06406x + 0.522617x$$
$$x = £9,432.17 - 0.541443x$$
$$1.541443x = £9,432.17$$
$$x = £6,119.05$$

Proof:

Term:

CV	£6,119.05
Income	£1,800

Spendable income	Sinking fund
0.09 × £6,119.05	£1,800 − £550.71 = £1,249.29 gross
= £550.71	× 0.6
	£749.57 net

Reversion:

CV	£6,119.05
Income	£2,000

Spendable income	Sinking fund
0.10 × £6,119.05	£2,000 − £611.91 = £1,388.09 gross
= £611.91	× 0.6
	£832.85 net

Check sinking fund accumulations:

Term:		£749.57	
A £1 p.a. for 2 years @ 3%	2.03		
A £1 in 5 years @ 3%	× 1.1593	2.354	£1,764.02

Reversion:		£832.85	
A £1 p.a. for 5 years @ 3%		5.3091	£4,421.68
			£6,185.70

(compare with CV of £6,119.05)

The proof suggests that capital value is not accurately replaced. But the rationale of the method must ensure accurate replacement of capital, and this leads to the conclusion that this method suffers from another fault. This is that although rates of return of 9% on the term and 10% on the reversion are required they are not accurately provided by this valuation. There is an over-replacement of capital and consequently the interest is under-valued, as in the conventional method, but to a reduced degree.

	CV	Replaced CV
Conventional dual rate:	£5,970	£6,253
Sinking fund:	£6,166	£6,165
Annual equivalent:	£6,162	£6,162
Double sinking fund:	£6,119	£6,186

It is therefore possible to conclude that the sinking fund and annual equivalent methods best overcome the problem posed by the conventional method of valuing variable profit rents, as they appear to provide for accurate replacement of capital and correctly allow for the required rate of return to be provided.

However, even the apparent accuracy of these solutions cannot be relied upon in all circumstances. For example, the sinking fund method becomes unworkable if the term income is particularly low; the spendable income over the period becomes negative, and considerable problems arise.

Harker, Nanthakumaran and Rogers of Aberdeen University in their discussion paper on 'Double sinking fund correction methods' (1988) support the sinking fund method and suggest a resolution to the negative spendable income problem.

Because the use of dual rate valuations can be seen to lead to difficulties, single rate leasehold valuations may be put forward as an alternative. Philip Bowcock has shown that even single rate valuations may be prone to error where more than one rate of interest is used. Nonetheless, the potential for arithmetic error in a single rate valuation is considerably less, and this type of valuation of leaseholds will now be considered.

Single rate valuation of leaseholds

If a single rate approach is to be used in a market place where purchasers are liable for tax on incomes then capital recoupment must be provided for out of taxed income. To do this the inherent sinking fund element must either be adjusted for tax, or tax deducted from the profit rent.* The latter approach is adopted here.

Example 4.3 Estimate the present worth of a profit rent of £100 for 4 years. Tax is at 40% and the investor requires a net of tax return of 7.75%.

Profit rent	£100	
Less tax at 40p	40	
Net of tax profit rent	£60	
YP for 4 years @ 7.75%	3.33	£200

The investor will obtain a return on his capital of 7.75% net and will recover his capital in full at 7.75%. Whether or not he reinvests part of the income is immaterial, as the investor has the opportunity of accepting a partial return of capital at the end of each year.

	Capital outstanding	Net income	Return on capital at 7.75%	Return of capital
Year				
1	£200	£60	£15.50	£44.5
2	£155.5	£60	£12.05	£47.95
3	£107.55	£60	£8.335	£51.66
4	£55.89	£60	£4.33	£55.67*
				£199.78

*Error due to rounding of figures.

*See Chapter 5 for consideration of net valuations.

Two valuers valuing an income of £100 would therefore both agree on a figure of £200. But valuer A would argue that the investment represented a 10% gross return allowing for replacement of capital at 4% net whilst valuer B given the information on income, tax and purchase price of £200 would argue that the only acceptable method of investment analysis where purchase price is known is to find the internal rate of return which over 4 years is in this case approximately 35% on gross income (see p. 114). No doubt investors do like to make investment decisions on like criteria and one might therefore suggest that the reason why some investors will buy leasehold interests is simply that they do show a high IRR.

'As you analyse, so should you value.' This tenet is often used by valuers as an argument in support of the retention of the dual rate approach to leasehold valuations. It is equally useful in advocating the use of single rate leasehold valuations.

Example 4.4 A 5 year leasehold investment producing a profit rent of £1,000 p.a. has been sold for £2,584. Analyse this market evidence and value a 50 year profit rent of £1,000 p.a.

A Dual rate: analysis

Income	£1,000	
YP for 5 years @x% and 3% adj. tax @ 40%	2.584	£2,584

Solve by tables or formula to find x: $x = 8\%$.

Valuation		
Income	£1,000	
YP for 50 years @ 8% and 3% adj. tax @ 40%	10.551	£10,551

B Single rate: analysis

Income	£1,000	
YP for 5 years @x%	2.584	£2,584

Solve by tables or formula to find x: $x = 26\%$

Valuation		
Income	£1,000	
YP for 50 years @ 26%	3.845	£3,845

The result of switching from a dual rate to a single rate basis is a valuation which is impossible to reconcile with market evidence. On current experience, it is much more likely that a price nearer to £10,551 would be paid for the 50 year investment.

Because of this inconsistency, because conventional dual rate valuations are adjusted for tax, and because the tax position of the purchaser is a vital factor in the market for leaseholds, the analysis and valuation should be carried out net of tax (see Chapter 5).

C Single rate (net of tax): analysis

Income	£1,000	
Less tax @ 40%	£400	
Net income	£600	
YP 5 years @ x%	(4.31)	£2,584

Solve the formula or tables to find the *net* rate of interest, x: x = 5.1%.

Valuation		
Income	£1,000	
Less tax @ 40%	£400	
Net income	£600	
YP 50 years @ 5.1%	18.0	£10,800

It can therefore be concluded that an alternative to dual rate valuations, which provides valuations consistent with current market experience, does exist: the single rate, net-of-tax, approach. It must be emphasised that the switch from dual rate to single rate will necessitate a change in the remunerative rates used, and that the difference between the freehold rates used with the (equivalent gross) leasehold rates for similar properties will be greater than the conventional 1–2% adjustment (see p. 98). A differential of 2–4% will be more appropriate to reflect the additional loss of security incurred by removing the assumption of a sinking fund accumulating at a low, safe rate.

The use of net single rate valuations of leasehold interests avoids the great majority of technical problems identified in the earlier discussion of dual rate valuations. The problem of choosing the appropriate rate of tax remains, particularly as some investors such as pension funds and charities are non-taxpayers.

Tax adjustment rate

What rate of tax should be used to adjust a gross profit rent to a net rent, or to gross-up a sinking fund to allow for tax?

The answer normally given is to use standard rates of income or corporation tax. Because the valuer's task is generally to determine market value, this implies a sale to the most probable purchaser,

113

which implies some knowledge of the market and therefore sufficient knowledge to adjust, both for analysis and valuation, at a rate appropriate to the most probable purchaser.

However, as tax is levied at different rates for different investors, an average tax rate (e.g. 40%) is used to reflect market interaction. But analysis of leasehold investments from a client's point of view must be carried out at that client's net-of-tax required rate of return.

Example 4.5 'Short leasehold investments are sound investments for charities because of their tax advantage.' Discuss.

Apart from the point that charities are more interested in income over the long term than short term, a number of points can be made. If the statement is true then charities must comprise a sub-market for this kind of investment. In that case the valuer needs to reflect the fact that the income is probably tax free; that they would be ill-advised to reinvest in a sinking fund policy with an assurance company because they will probably have difficulty in recovering the tax element on the 4% net accumulations of the policy; and that they would be best advised to reinvest in the safest gross funds* to avoid delay in recovery of taxed interest or dividends.

Example 4.6 Analyse the sale of a £100 profit rent for 4 years at a price of £200 from the point of view of a gross (i.e. non-tax-paying) fund.

$$\frac{£200}{£100} = \text{Multiplier of 2}$$

(a) Assume reinvestment in an equivalent safe gross fund at say 8%. Therefore the sinking fund to recover £200 will be:

£200 × ASF to replace £1 in 4 years at 8%

= £200 × 0.22

= £44

The gross spendable income = £100 − £44

$$= £56$$

$$\therefore \text{gross return} \qquad = \frac{56}{200} \times 100$$

$$= 28\%$$

---

*This term here is used to indicate any investment where interest or dividends are paid without deduction of tax.

114

(b) Without a reinvestment assumption analyse to find the internal rate of return.

Solve $\dfrac{1 - \left[\dfrac{1}{(1 + i)^4}\right]}{i} = 2.$

The present value of £1 p.a. in 4 years at 35% = 2, and therefore the IRR is 35%.

Charities, because of their tax position, may be interested in short leasehold investments, because, if they can buy at prices determined by absolutely conventional approaches the effective return will be sufficiently high to compensate for the disadvantages of the investment.

Categories of leasehold investment

There are a number of identifiable categories of leasehold interests, each of which requires a different approach due to the specific sub-market and profit rent pattern.

1 Long leaseholds, over (say) 30 years, at a fixed head rent

Where the head lessee is in occupation or has sub-let on a short lease the investment may be treated as one with potential income growth, i.e. a rising profit rent. Whether a dual rate or single rate approach is followed, the risk rate (remunerative rate) will probably be comparable to that for freehold rack rented properties with similar rent review patterns, but 1–2% higher. If the head lease is for a term certain in excess of 40 years, then it could be treated as directly comparable to the freehold, because the length of time involved reduces the sinking fund (recoupment of capital) to a very small percentage of the profit rent, which becomes nearly all spendable income, as in the case of a freehold investment. But the problem of gearing must be noted and a split valuation used as a check, if not as *the* method.

2 Fixed profit rent

Where the head lessee, or predecessor in title, has sub-let the property for the full unexpired term of the head lease without rent review, the profit rent is fixed. The valuation must reflect this factor and the profit rent must be capitalised at an appropriate cost of capital rate. This effectively allows for the depreciating worth of

115

each year's income in terms of purchasing power. A single rate approach is frequently the most effective method.

3 Occupation leases

If the most probable purchaser is a potential occupier then, although an investment valuation may be adopted, care must be taken to see that it reflects the objectives of that type of purchaser. For example, if the lease of retail premises in a prime trading position is to be sold with the benefit of vacant possession then the purchaser will very likely be another retailer. Retailers will not be looking for a property investment return of $x\%$ on the imputed profit rental; they will be seeking a first class outlet for their goods. Their bids are likely to be well above that of most property investors and an adjustment of several points in the capitalisation rate may be necessary. Indeed, analyses of such sales may produce very unusual rates of return whichever way the analysis is undertaken.

Summary

The historical evolution of the dual rate method is now shrouded in the mists of time. Textbooks and journals of the time move from single rate to dual rate with very little explanation and with virtually no consideration of the fact that it hinges on the acceptance of a return on initial outlay throughout the life of the investment. A concept apparently unique to the UK leasehold property investment market.

The emergence of the tax adjustment factor is better documented and is relevant to all short-term investments, however valued, where tax is charged on that element of income which is essentially capital recoupment.

The reluctance of the market to return to single rate seems as strong today as it was initially to shift from it to dual rate. A strength of dual rate lay in the ability to compare returns from freeholds with leaseholds. The reluctance today may be the fear of the unknown arising from the unique nature of every leasehold investment and the pressure on the valuer to find a unique solution. The solution lies in the proper use of discounting techniques where the unique growth expectations can be explicitly accounted for.

Chapter five

Taxation and valuation

It is customary in valuation to ignore the effects of income tax, on the grounds that investors compare investments on the basis of their gross rates of return. This may well be an acceptable criterion where tax affects all investments and all investors in a like manner. Although this is not the case in the property market only a few valuers would argue that tax should always be deducted from income before being capitalised at a net-of-tax capitalisation rate (a 'true net approach').

One of the most important points to note is that where the income from property is all *return on capital*, that is true spendable income, gross and net valuations will produce the same value estimate. Where part of the income is a part return of capital this, other than in the case of certain life annuities, is not exempt from taxation and in such cases the gross and net approaches may produce a different value estimate.

In addition, certain investments will produce fairly substantial growth in capital value over a relatively short term, due to a growth in income. In these cases, if the investment is resold, Capital Gains Tax (CGT) may be payable on the gain realised.

Example 5.1 Explain what is meant by 'net rates of interest' and discuss their uses in valuation, using numerical examples.

A net rate of interest is interest earned on deposited monies after the deduction of an allowance for the payment of tax on the gross interest earned. Here the phrase refers to any net-of-tax rates.

Thus £1,000 deposited with a bank, for example, earning interest at the rate of 10% per annum would, with tax at 40p in the £ (40%), produce a net rate of 6% ($10 \times (1 - t)$ where t is 0.4). As far as the valuer's use of the valuation tables is concerned, the switch from gross to net valuations should cause no problems. Thus, the present value of £1 in 5 years at 10% gross allowing for

117

tax at 40p in the £ can be found in tax-adjusted tables to be 0.74726, or in unadjusted tables at 6% ($10 \times £1 - t$) where t is 0.4) to be 0.747258. It should be obvious that where £100 is invested at 10%, and tax is payable, compounding can only take place at the net-of-tax rate.

It is also obvious that, where an investor is a taxpayer paying tax on all investment income at 40%, his actual return after tax will be reduced. The significance of this is not lost on investors, who always have full regard to their net-of-tax returns. When considering property investments, it is therefore necessary to consider whether valuations should also be based on net-of-tax incomes and yields.

For simplicity of illustration a tax rate of 50% is used in some of the examples.

Incomes in perpetuity

The formula for capitalising an income in perpetuity is Income ÷ i. If the gross income is £1,000 and the gross capitalisation rate is 10%, then $1,000 \div 0.10 = £10,000$.

If tax is payable at 50p in the £, then

$$1,000 \times \left(\frac{1-t}{1}\right) \div 0.10 \times \left(\frac{1-t}{1}\right)$$

$$= 500 \div 0.05 = \underline{£10,000}$$

Clearly, as the numerator and denominator are multiplied by a constant $\dfrac{1-t}{1}$ then they can be divided through by that constant.

Hence, $I \div i = \dfrac{I \times \dfrac{1-t}{1}}{i \times \dfrac{1-t}{1}}$

No difference in value estimate will occur, because the income is perpetual and is all return on capital.

Finite or terminable incomes

An income receivable for a fixed term of years may have a present worth which can be assessed on a single or dual rate basis, gross or net of tax. Consider an income of £1,000 receivable for five years on a 10% gross basis with tax at 50%.

A   Single rate

	Gross		Net of tax at 50p
	£1,000		£500
PV £1 p.a. for 5 years		PV £1 p.a. for 5 years	
@ 10%	3.7908	@ 5%	4.3295
	£3,790		£2,164

Here there is a clear difference between the two figures which can be seen to result from the tax adjustments that have been made.

$$I \times \frac{1 - \dfrac{1}{(I+i)^n}}{i}$$

cannot be equated with

$$I(1-t) \times \frac{1 - \dfrac{1}{(1+i(1-t))^n}}{i(1-t)}$$

Here, part of the £1,000 income is a return of capital. If tax is payable at 50p in the £, then only £500 is available to provide a return on capital and a return of capital. A purchase at £3,790 would be too high to allow for the returns implied if tax is at 50p. Where tax is payable, replacement of capital (purchase price) must be made out of taxed income.

In order to preserve the gross rate of 10% for investment comparison the valuation can be reworked, recognising that the return on capital is at 10% and the return of capital is at a net rate out of taxed income. i is therefore 0.10 and the ASF in the formula is at 5% adjusted for tax.

$$1,000 \times \frac{1}{0.10 + \left(0.1809 \times \dfrac{1}{1-t}\right)} = £2,165$$

or set out as a valuation:

	£1,000
YP for five years @ 10% and 5% adj. tax @ 50%*	2.165
	£2,165

*Formula $= \dfrac{1}{i + ASF}$ therefore becomes $\dfrac{1}{0.10 + \left(0.1809 \left(\dfrac{1}{1-t}\right)\right)}$

$= \dfrac{1}{0.10 + 0.3618} = 2.165$

The gross valuation has been adjusted to equate with the net valuation. Where there is a tax liability, the net valuation is deemed to be more correct because capital cost must be recovered out of taxed income.

Capital outstanding		10% gross	Capital recovered ($£1,000 - 10\% - 50$p in £) tax
1	2165.00	216.500	391.75
2	1773.25	177.325	411.3375
3	1361.91	136.190	431.90
4	930.01	93.000	453.50
5	476.50	47.650	476.175*
			£2,165

*Error due to rounding.

B Dual rate

The realisation that capital cost may have to be recovered out of taxed income has, for many years, been recognised in the valuation of leasehold property and has resulted in the compilation of dual rate tax-adjusted tables. Assuming that £1,000 is the profit rent produced by a leasehold interest, and adopting the same gross yield of 10%, a sinking fund at 3% and tax at 50%, the following gross and net valuations may be made.

	Gross
	£1,000
YP for 5 years @ 10% and 3% adj. tax @ 50%	2.098
	£2,098

	Net
	£500
YP for 5 years @ 5% and 3%	4.196
	£2,098

The net valuation is of an income of £1,000 less tax at 50%, namely £500. With a gross rate of return of 10%, the net rate must be 5% and, as the sinking fund rate is also assumed to be net, allowance has already ben made for tax on the sinking fund accumulations. As the whole income has been netted no further tax adjustment is needed (see Chapter 1).

The gross valuation becomes in effect a net valuation, because it assumes both a net accumulative rate and a grossing-up factor to allow for the incidence of tax on that part of the income representing capital recovery.

Thus in two cases – incomes receivable in perpetuity, and leasehold interests – the normal valuation approach has been shown to be equivalent to the true net approach, apparently obviating any dilemma. However, problems arise when considering deferred incomes, or cases where property is let below full rental value.

Deferred incomes

A deferred income is one due to commence at a given date in the future.

Example 5.2 Calculate the present worth of an income of £2,000 per annum in perpetuity due to commence in 5 years' time. A 10% gross return is required, and tax is payable at 50%.

	Gross		Net
	£2,000		£1,000
YP perp. @ 10%	10	YP perp. @ 5%	20
PV £1 in 5 years	£20,000	PV £1 in 5 years	£20,000
@ 10%	0.6209	@ 5%	0.7835
	£12,418		£15,670

Again, it can be seen that capitalisation in perpetuity gross and net each produce the same value of £20,000 in 5 years' time, but, by further discounting to allow for the 5 year deferment, the gross and net valuations produce different results clearly arising from the deferment factors of 0.6209 and 0.7835. Obviously a purchaser would wish to pay only £12,418, but what of the vendor?

Assuming initially that capital gains are not taxable, one can see that an investment purchased for £12,418 held for 5 years and sold for £20,000 is a 10% investment.

£12,418 × amount £1 for 5 years at 10% = £20,000

But if an investor were to deposit £12,418 in an income-producing investment, the 10% return of £1,241.80 in year one would be taxed. From a taxpayer's point of view, a 10% return, all in capital growth with no tax would be better than 10% all in income subject to taxation.

121

Taxation and valuation

If there was no CGT capital growth investments would be very attractive to high rate taxpayers, to such an extent that prices could be pushed up to the point of indifference, i.e. until the capital growth investment is equated with an income investment. In this example, if tax is at 50p in the £, a taxpayer would get the same return after tax from depositing £15,670 at 10% gross as from purchasing £2,000 p.a. in perpetuity deferred 5 years for £15,670.

The introduction of CGT in 1965 reduced the tax-free element of capital growth but did not lessen the belief held by some valuers that the net approach was still correct. It is recognised that the incidence of all taxes should be reflected in an investor's true return. Therefore, if tax is material to investors' decisions in the market place it should be allowed for in a valuation.

To explain a need for net valuation, a single question needs to be posed. 'If an investor is assured of a 10% gross return and pays tax at 50%, is he right to expect a 5% net-of-tax return?' To this one could add a supplementary question. 'Are investors interested in their return net of tax?' It cannot but be assumed that, as the Inland Revenue have a prior claim, then investors must have some regard to the net-of-tax income.

Rising freehold income

Combining the £1,000 income for 5 years with the £2,000 income commencing in 5 years and continuing in perpetuity, the result will be a normal term and reversion valuation.

Using the figures from the preceding examples, the gross and net valuations produce these results:

	Gross	Net
Value of £1,000 for 5 years	£3,790	£2,164
Value today of reversion to £20,000	£12,418	£15,670
	£16,208	£17,834

(In such cases, the net valuation will always be higher than its gross equivalent.)

The gross valuation of £16,208 may be analysed in two parts: an expenditure of £3,790 to acquire £1,000 for 5 years coupled with an expenditure of £12,418 for £20,000 in 5 years' time. In the absence of income tax, the investor readily achieves his 10% return: but what of his 5% net return? After tax on income, the investment will have the following cash flow:

Year	Cash flow
1	£500
2	£500
3	£500
4	£500
5	£20,500

This is the cash flow assumed for the 5% net valuation, and the investor would achieve a 5% return at an acquisition cost of £17,834. Therefore at £16,208 the investment must be showing a better return than 5%. If investors only expect a net return of 5%, valuing gross may result in vendors' interests being undersold.

Gross funds

The term 'gross funds' is used today to describe any investor exempt from income, corporation and/or capital gains tax. These are principally charities, local authorities, approved super-annuation funds, friendly societies and registered trade unions. Other institutions, such as insurance companies, enjoy partial relief by being assessed at a lower rate. Many first-class property invest-ments are now held by gross funds, which are an increasingly large part of the property market – so much so that co-ownership schemes in agricultural investment and in commercial investment have been carefully created to allow small and large funds to buy, as co-owners, substantial single investments in property while still preserving their tax-exempt status.

If the most probable purchaser in the market is a gross fund then the sub-market is one of gross funds. Because they pay neither income nor capital gains tax, the return to them will be both their gross and net return. Valuations within this sub-market must be based on analysis of comparable transactions, which suggests that no adjustments should be made for tax.

Net or gross?

Because a difference in the valuation may result when valuing net or gross of tax, the problem therefore remains. Should the valu-ation be net or gross? There is no categorical answer: a number of points may, however, be made.

1 In certain cases a net valuation will not produce an accurate estimate of market value, as every potential purchaser may have a different tax liability.

123

2   A net valuation should be carried out when advising a purchaser of his maximum bid for an investment when his required net-of-tax return is known.
3   In certain sub-markets the market is dominated by nontaxpayers. In these cases a gross valuation will produce the same valuation as a net valuation allowing for tax at 0%.

Capital gains tax (CGT)

The introduction of CGT in 1965 had an immediate impact on the property market. Initially it reduced the obvious benefit of investing in properties with high capital growth expectations such as freeholds with early substantial reversions. The market soon adapted to the changes but although there were pleas from a few to move to a net-of-tax approach to valuation the market responded with a simple adjustment to the ARY to account for this new risk element.

Reversionary properties still remained more attractive to individuals because of the differences between the CGT tax rate and the very high personal tax rates.

The introduction of indexation provisions in the Finance Act 1984 and the revision of those provisions in the Finance Act 1988, whereby only gains in excess of the indexed (retail price index) gains were to be taxed, increased the attractions of capital growth investments. The reduction in tax rates to two bands, 25% and 40% in 1988 coupled with the provision to tax gains at the same rate as that for taxing a taxpayer's income have eroded the advantages of growth investments over income investments. The remaining tax advantages are:

1   CGT is charged on net gains, i.e. after deduction of purchase and sale costs and allowable expenses.
2   CGT is charged on the gain after adjustment for indexation.
3   CGT is charged on the gain after deducting the taxpayer's tax free allowance.
4   The tax demand may be up to 2 years after the gain is realised.

For all these reasons individuals with a 40% tax liability may still favour the highly reversionary properties in preference to rack rented properties. But it is probably the ability of the right property to outpace inflation that attracts the private investor.

For the major investors the changes in indexation provisions have made it easier to take decisions to sell than previously. But because property is normally purchased as a long-term investment any gain is likely to be deferred many years and will not therefore have a significant bearing on purchase price. In addition, 'rollover-relief' may be possible, effectively postponing any CGT and, in any event for certain classes of investor their exemption from CGT makes them a market in their own right.

There may, however, be obvious cases where property is to be purchased with the intention of realising a capital gain at a specific date in the future. Where the purchasers in the market are likely to have the same intent or where investment advice is to be given to a specific client it might be necessary to reflect CGT in the valuation.

Before doing so the valuer should consider whether the gain will be treated as a capital gain or as income. Premiums, in particular, will pose a problem as they may be treated both as income and as capital.

Premiums are taxed under Income Tax Schedule A when the recipient is the landlord of the property and under Schedule D Case VI when the recipient is someone other than the landlord. In either case premiums for leases not exceeding 50 years will be treated partly as capital and partly as income.

The amount of the premium to be treated as capital is found by multiplying the amount of the premium by 0.02 and by the length of the lease less one year.

Example 5.3 A premium of £30,000 has been paid on the grant of a lease for 28 years. How much of this premium will be treated as income?

Premium	£30,000
$0.02 \times (28 - 1)$	0.54
Capital element =	£16,200

£16,200 will be treated as a capital receipt; the remaining £13,800 will be treated as income in the year in which the premium is paid.

The amount of capital gain is calculated by subtracting acquisition costs from disposal costs in the simple case, but, when a premium is received in return for the grant of a lease, only part of the asset has been sold.

In the case of part disposals a proportion of acquisition costs only is deducted from the capital receipt. This is calculated by multiplying the acquisition costs by

$$\frac{\text{the capital element of the premium } (P)}{P + \text{the value of the remainder}}$$

For instance, assume that in example 5.3 the value of the retained freehold reversion is £10,000 and the property was acquired in 1966 for £15,000. The capital gain would be calculated as follows:

Capital element of premium: £16,200
Purchase price of property: £15,000

Proportion of purchase price attributable to the part disposal:

$$= £15,000 \times \frac{£16,200}{£16,200 + £10,000} = £9,275.$$

Capital gain (£16,200 − £9,275) = £6,925

This gain will be charged at the CGT rate. How should CGT be incorporated in a valuation? The examples that follow illustrate a possible approach.

When a client needs to ascertain the price that should be paid for a property taking account of the future probable tax liability whilst achieving a specified required return then the valuer needs to work through the equation.

$$X_1 = [\, Y_1 - \{[\, Y_2 - (X_2 \times IA)] \times [TR]\} \times PV^n$$

where X_1 = value today, Y_1 = value in the future, X_2 = value today plus acquisition costs, Y_2 = value in the future less sale costs, IA = indexation adjustment based on expectation of RPI change over period n, TR = tax rate, PV^n = PV £1 in n years.

In the case of reversionary properties the assessment of X and Y are more complex but the theory is unaffected. The purpose is to derive that value for X, such that on sale in n years at Y_1, the investor will, after meeting any tax on gains, achieve the required return on capital. If the property is also income producing then further tax adjustments are needed. In practice such a valuation is rare, may be better handled by a DCF approach and will become an appraisal or valuation to a client. It will not be a market valuation because the discount rate is investor determined. If the discount rate is to be market determined then sales in the market place must be analysed on assumed income and capital gains tax rates, and assumed resale dates, none of which are obvious in the market place.

The examples that follow are illustrative and allow for CGT and income tax at 40% but are not adjusted for allowable expenses or for indexation.

Example 5.4 What price should an investor pay today for an investment in property producing no income for 5 years, expected to be worth £20,000 in 5 years' time? A return of 10% is required.

126

CGT is at 40% and the investment will be resold in 5 years' time. Then:

$X = (20,000 - (20,000 - X) \times 0.40) \times$ PV £1 in 5 years @ 10%

$= (20,000 - (8,000 - 0.4X)) \times 0.6209$

$= (20,000 - 8,000 + 0.4X) \times 0.6209$

$= (12,000 + 0.4X) \times 0.6209$

$= 7,450 + 0.2484X$

$X - 0.2484X = 7,450$

$0.7516X = 7,450$

$X = £9,912$

Proof: The investment should be purchased for £9,912, held for 5 years and resold for £20,000. After allowing for CGT at 40% a 10% return will have been achieved.

Future sum		£20,000
Less CGT:	£20,000	
Less acquisition	9,912	
Capital gain	10,088	
×40p in £	0.40	4,035
Net sum realised		£15,965
PV £1 in 5 years @ 10%		0.6209
		£9,912

A valuation incorporating a term and reversion is more complex, although the process of paying today a sum which after allowing for CGT leaves the investor with his desired return is again applicable.

Example 5.5 What sum should be paid for a freehold property producing an income of £1,000 for 5 years, rising to £2,000 thereafter? A gross return of 10% is required and the property is to be resold in 5 years. Income and CGT to be paid at 40%.

10% gross less tax at 40% = 6% net

Gross income	£1,000	
Less tax at 40p in £	£400	
Net of tax income	£600	
YP for 5 years @ 6%	4.2124	£2,527

127

Plus Reversion in 5 years to:

Gross income	£2,000	
Less tax @ 40p in £	£800	
	£1,200	
YP perp. @ 6%	16.67	£20,000 (value at reversion)

Normally, £20,000 would be deferred at 6% to find its present worth and added to £2,527, but it is necessary in this example to adjust the calculation for the potential CGT.

Therefore let X = the present worth.

Capital gains tax will effectively be charged at 40%.

Capital gain	$= £(20,000 - X)$
CGT	$= £(20,000 - X)0.4$
Net sum	$= £20,000 - (£8,000 + 0.4X)$
	$= £12,000 + 0.4X$
PV £1 in 5 years @ 6%	0.7472
	$£8,966 + 0.2988X$

If present worth $= X$, then

$$X = 8,966 + 0.2988X = £2,527$$
$$X = £11,493 + 0.2988X$$
$$0.7011\, X = £11,493$$
$$X = \underline{£16,392}$$

Here it will be seen that it is the future sum, net of CGT, that has been deferred for 5 years. This should provide the investor with his 6% net of tax return on the investment.

Check: if the company pays £16,392 and sells for £20,000, the gain will be (£20,000 − £16,392) = £3,608. On this sum CGT at 40% will be charged giving rise to a tax payment of £1,443 (3,608 × 0.4). The company is only therefore buying a future reversion, net of tax, of £20,000 less £1,443 (tax), which must be deferred 5 years at 6% giving a present worth of £13,865. To this is added the present worth of the income flow for the next 5 years of £2,527, giving the total net of tax present worth of £16,392.

CGT as it affects premiums has already been discussed. The approach used to reflect CGT in valuations to date may be adapted to cases where part of a premium will be treated as a capital gain.

The observant will recognise further points for consideration. In terms of investment analysis, i.e. advice to a specific client, a cash flow approach might be adopted. This arguably would be more accurate because the CGT would not be paid immediately upon sale, but will be deferred until agreement with the Inland Revenue has been reached. Nor has the calculation been completed in accordance with CGT rules as no adjustment has been made for fes or other permitted expenses.

The valuer must identify his market and, as far as possible, match his methods to parallel the behaviour of purchasers in that market.

The technique of discounting is relatively simple, but experience in the market is the only way the valuer can analyse, observe and thereby select a preferred approach. This may be gross or net, with or without allowance for CGT. The valuer who contends that he is estimating market value but who *cannot substantiate the approach adopted*, let alone his tax adjustment rates, is probably deceiving himself and his client. A market implies buyers and sellers; a valuation demands some assessment of the buyers. If their tax positions differ, then it is likely that the most probable purchaser will be found amongst that group of buyers enjoying the greatest tax advantage.

The valuer has the choice of expressing his assumptions explicitly or allowing the capitalisation rate to do it implicitly. The latter course is potentially dangerous if the property to be valued is not precisely comparable with the current market sales evidence.

Chapter six

Landlord and tenant valuations

The income approach to property valuation centres particularly on the relationship between landlord and tenant. This chapter examines several of the valuation problems raised by this relationship.

Premiums

A premium is a lump sum paid by a tenant to a landlord in consideration for a lease granted at a low rent, or for some other benefit. 'At a low rent' signifies a rent below full rental value, and the other benefits will be, as a rule, financial, having the same effect as a reduction in rent. Examples of this are the tenant paying for repairs that would normally be the landlord's responsibility, and the tenant financing the extension of the property without being charged an increase in rent.

A premium is often paid on the grant or renewal of a lease, but there may be more than one premium, payable at any time during the lease term. It entails a cash gain coupled with a loss of rent for the landlord because the usual result of charging a premium will be a letting at less than full rental value. The landlord is therefore selling part of his income.

The tenant will be paying a lump sum in return for a lease at a rent below full rental value, effectively buying a profit rent.

Why pay a premium?

The payment of a premium has many advantages to a landlord, and few to the tenant. It could be concluded that premiums will usually be paid where there is a seller's market, i.e. where there is competition among prospective tenants to secure an agreement with the prospective landlord.

The advantages to a landlord are several.

1   Although the amount of the premium will reflect the discount-ing of future income, an immediate lump sum receivable instead of a future flow of income is often more attractive due to the 'time value of money'. The landlord may prefer a lump sum in order to meet an immediate expense or to make any kind of cash investment.
2   Receipt of a lump sum immediately may reduce the diminish-ing effect that inflation has on the value of future income in real terms, especially if rent review periods are longer than is favourable to the landlord.
3   A premium may have tax advantages, but these are sub-stantially reduced now that income and capital gains are taxed at the same rate.
4   A premium should increase the landlord's security of income. Once the tenant has paid a premium, he has invested money in his occupation of the premises in expectation of making an actual or notional profit rent. As a result he is more likely to remain in occupation of the premises and should be a more reliable tenant. Some of the risk attached to the investment from the landlord's point of view may be reduced.

The advantages to a tenant are less well-defined.

1   A premium may be useful as a loss or deduction to be made from profits when being assessed for income tax or capital gains tax.
2   Paying a premium may be advantageous to a tenant when his financial circumstances are such that he prefers to part with capital in order to reduce his future recurring expenses.

However, the landlord will usually enjoy the greater benefits, and premiums will only usually be paid when the property in question attracts many prospective tenants.

Valuation technique

A premium entails a loss to the landlord of part of the income and a gain to the tenant of a profit rent. The amount of the premium should be calculated so that each party is in virtually the same position as if full rental value were to be paid and received.

The gain/loss of rent, capitalised over the period for which it is applicable, should be calculated to be equal to the amount of the premium. It is conventional practice to use full freehold rates to capitalise the landlord's loss of rent and full leasehold rates to capitalise the tenant's gain of profit rent, presumably on the basis that each party by definition is to be in the same position as if full rental value were being paid and received.

The following three examples assume a freehold rate of 10%, leasehold rates of 11% and 3% with tax @ 40p, a full rental value of £2,500, premiums payable at the start of the lease and no rent reviews.

Example 6.1 What premiums should A charge on the grant of a 21 year lease to B at a rent of £1,500?

Full rental value		£2,500
Rent agreed		£1,500
∴ A's loss of rent	=	£1,000
YP for 21 years @ 10%		8.6487 = £8,649

Example 6.2 A grants the above lease. What premium should B offer?

Full rental value		£2,500
Rent agreed		£1,500
B's gain of profit rent	=	£1,000
YP for 21 years @ 11% and 3% adj. tax @ 40%		5.9481 = £5,948

The problem of valuing freehold interests single rate and leasehold interests dual rate is here presented. In practice one would expect negotiation between parties to reach a compromise sum, which may be found by the following methods:

1 Average final offers: $\dfrac{£8,649 + £5,948}{2} = £7,298.5$ say £7,300

2 Average YPs: $\dfrac{8.6487 + 5.9481}{2} = 7.298$

× difference in full and agreed rents £1,000 = £7,298

In most cases the tenant is due to take occupation and the notional nature of the profit rent is not taxable and so some valuers will adopt a gross approach to the leasehold calculation bringing the figures much closer together (i.e. £10,000 × YP 21 years @ 11% and 3% = £10,000 × 6.9027 = £69,027).

Example 6.3 A grants B a lease for 28 years. A premium of £18,000 is to be paid. What rent should be fixed?

Again, a compromise must be reached. Taking the average of

two YP figures can save an unnecessary stage in the calculations, so this approach will be adopted.

	A	B
Full rental value	£2,500	£2,500
Agreed rent	x	x
YP 28 years	9.3066 (10%)	6.7194 (11% and 3% adj. tax @ 40%)

$$\text{Average YP} \quad \frac{9.3066 + 6.7194}{2}$$

$$= \underline{8.013}$$

Then 8.013 (£2,500 − x) = £18,000
£20,032.5 − 8.013x = £18,000
8.013x = £2,032.5
x = £253.65 p.a.

The gain or loss of rent is (£2,500 − x). When capitalised by using an average YP, this is the average capitalised gain or loss of rent and is thus the value of the premium. The unknown, x, can be easily calculated.

As has already been suggested, a tenant's repair, improvement or extension may be treated as a premium.

Example 6.4　A grants to B a 21 year lease at rent of £12,000 p.a. which is below full rental value. B has to repair the property at the commencement of the lease as part of the contract at a cost of £15,000. Estimate the full rental value.

	A	B
Full rental value	x	x
Agreed rent	£12,000	£12,000
YP 21 years	8.6487 (10%)	5.9481 (11% + 3% tax @ 40p)

$$\text{Average YP} \quad \frac{8.6487 + 5.9481}{2}$$

$$= 7.2984$$

Then: 7.2984 (x − £12,000) = £15,000

(The cost of repairs is in the nature of a premium for which B expects a reduced rent. (x − £12,000) is the gain/loss of rent, and multiplying this by the average YP gives the average capitalised gain or loss of rent.)

133

$$7.2984x - \pounds87,581 = \pounds15,000$$
$$7.2984x = \pounds102,581$$
$$x = \underline{\pounds14,055} \text{ p.a}$$

and this must be the full rental value of the premises. This was never a negotiated figure, as it was a known market fact borne in mind by both parties during the negotiations. But the use of the average YP is necessary as the rent of £12,000 would have been arrived at by negotiation.

The conventional investment method can give rise to answers that are hard to accept. In 6.1 and 6.2 A required £8,649 to compensate him for his loss of rent. B could only afford to offer £5,948, as this was all his gain of profit rent was worth to him. It would seem that an agreement at £7,300 would thus make both parties unhappy. We must remember that dual rate valuations using a remunerative rate 1% higher than for freehold valuations inevitably cause lower valuations of the interest, and that dual rate valuations are net in a gross form.

Another approach is the 'before and after valuation'. From the freeholder's point of view, whenever a lease at a low rent is granted the market value of the property may be depreciated by a sum greater than the initial premium calculation suggests. In example 6.1 £8,649 is the premium but the payment of £8,649 alters the nature of the investment from a growth income of £2,500 to a fixed income of £1,500 for 21 years with a reversion to FRV in 21 years' time. Thus the respective capitalisation rates may differ. If this is the case, a 'before and after valuation' is needed.

Before

FRV		£2,500
YP perp. @ 10%		10
		£25,000

After

Rent reserved	£1,500	
YP 21 years @ 12%*	7.562	£11,343
Reversion to	£2,500	
YP rev. perp. after 21 years @ 10%	1.35	£3,375
Estimated capital value		£14,718

£25,000 − £14,718 = Premium of £10,282

*Cost of capital or money rate as income is fixed for 21 years.

A further problem to be overcome is that the freeholder has indeed lost precisely £1,000 per annum but the tenant has gained a rising profit rent starting at £1,000 per annum. Traditional valuation methods do not fully reflect this factor. It seems reasonable to question the use of dual rate valuations in such problems and in the valuation of leasehold interests in general (see Chapter 4). A truer picture of real gain and real loss requires an explicit DCF approach.

Future costs and receipts

A study of conventional techniques of deferring future costs raises a number of further questions which are examined shortly.

The deferment of future receipts is relatively straightforward. Often an investment will provide a capital sum at some given time in the future. An example of this is a premium payable during the currency of a lease. This is part of the investment and could therefore be discounted at the remunerative rate.

Example 6.5 A lets 10 High Street to B for 21 years at £13,925 p.a. In addition, a premium of £15,000 is payable at the end of the lease. FRV is £15,000 p.a. Value A's interest.

Assuming a freehold rate 10%

Rent	£13,925	
YP for 21 years @ 9%	9.2922	£129,393
Rent	£15,000	
YP rev. perp. after 21 years @ 10%	1.35131	£20,269
Premium	£15,000	
PV £1 in 21 years @ 10%	0.13513	£2,027
Estimated capital value		£151,689

This approach implies that future fixed receipts should be discounted at the remunerative rate and added to the freehold value. In which case the premium of £15,000 varies in value according to the quality of the investment. This conventional approach cannot be accepted. The present worth of any known future sum must be found by reference to money market rates.

Future capital costs will often arise out of investment in property. Conventional valuation practice distinguishes two types of future capital cost.

1 *Liabilities.* These may have to be incurred for some reason and are a disadvantage to the investor, often being legally enforceable. They must therefore be provided for. Examples are

premiums to be paid in the future; a sum to be spent on dilapidations at the end of the lease; or work that must be carried out under fire regulations, etc. The investor must make certain that the cash required for the liability is available at the relevant time. Any accumulation must therefore be risk-free, and it follows that conventional practice recommends the discounting of liabilities at the accumulative rate. Rates of 2½% or 3½% are not acceptable per se but the rationale of using a reasonable net of tax safe rate is sound.

2 *Expenditure.* This is optional and will only be undertaken if it provides a sufficient return. This 'sufficient return' is taken for convenience to be the rate of return that the investment as a whole provides. Thus expenditure is discounted at the remunerative rate.

The distinction may be of vital importance to investment decisions.

Example 6.6   B offers £1,000 to A for his leasehold interest. A receives a profit rent of £380 p.a. with 14 years remaining and no rent reviews on head- or sub-lease. A has agreed to carry out repairs at a cost of £1,000 in 4 years' time. Should he accept B's offer?

Assuming a leashold rate 11% and 3% adj. tax @ 40%:

Profit rent	£380 p.a.	
YP for 14 years @ 11% and 3% adj. tax @ tax @ 40%	4.8183	£1,830
Less: Cost of repairs (1) Liability?	£1,000	
PV £1 in 4 years @ 3%	0.8884	£888.4
Estimated capital value (1)		£942
or: (2) Expenditure?	£1,000	
PV £1 in 4 years @ 11%	0.65873	£658.7
		£1,172
Estimated capital value (2)		

The distinction is obviously vital. If A treats the cost as a liability he should accept; on the other hand, if he treats the cost as an expenditure, he should decline the offer. In many cases the decision is an arbitrary one, the effect of which can be sizeably reduced by the ue of realistic 'safe' rates.

A further problem now emerges and that is the estimation of future expenditures and liabilities when they are not known or fixed in monetary terms at the date of valuation.

An expected major renewal in 4 years' time can only initially be estimated on the basis of cost today. But the deduction to be made from open market value in good condition must be an amount the market considers fairly reflects the current condition. Where the future sum is fixed in monetary terms then a present value calculation at a realistic monetary safe rate is satisfactory. Where it is a current estimate then the valuer must consider whether the costs will increase at a faster rate than that which can be safely earned on savings.

If the expenditure is likely to rise at 10% per annum and money can be saved to earn interest at 10% per annum, then the wisest solution is to deduct the full cost from today's value. If money can earn interest at a higher rate than the estimated inflationary increase in costs then a discounted sum can be deducted. If costs are rising faster than money rates then it would be logical to deduct the full cost now and indeed to have the repairs or renewals undertaken now. However, unless the work is essential as at the date of valuation, it may be as realistic to simply write down the value in sound condition by an appropriate factor.

Extensions and renewals of leases

The occupier or tenant of business premises will often be anxious to remain in ocupation because a business move might involve considerable expense, loss of trade and loss of goodwill, resulting in a large loss of profit. In these circumstances tenants will be keen to negotiate an extension of the lease, a renewal of the existing lease on similar terms, or the grant of a completely new lease on different terms.

The problem of a tenant who approaches the landlord as the lease draws to an end provides very little difficulty. The landlord will require a rent approaching, or at, full rental value, and the tenant will expect to pay it, because that is what it would cost to lease a comparable property. But finding alternative accommodation is not an easy operation, and business decisions are prudently taken well in advance. It is thus more usual for a tenant to approach the landlord well before the termination of the existing lease and when they do a valuation problem will arise. If the tenant approaches the landlord during the currency of the lease with a proposal to renew that lease immediately for an extended period, it will follow that the tenant is offering to surrender his current lease. (Such problems are often called 'surrender and renewals'.)

If, as is probably the case, a profit rent or a notional profit rent has arisen, then any surrender will be a surrender of valuable leasehold rights in the property. The tenant would be ill-advised to accept a new lease at full rental value.

The landlord, on the other hand, is not likely to agree to any indiscriminate extension of the tenant's profit rent because the anticipated reversion to full rental value will already be reflected in the open market value of the freehold. Negotiations must be conducted to see that following the surrender and lease renewal there is no diminution in the value of the landlord's or of the tenant's interests in the property.

Valuers acting for both parties will be checking the position from both sides on the basis that the present interest should equal the proposed interests. This will involve four or more valuations.

Example 6.7   T holds a lease from L at a rent of £1,500 p.a. FRI with 8 years unexpired. T wishes to remain in occupation of the premises and continue to pay the same rent by surrendering his current lease in return for a new 21 year term. The full rental value of the property is £2,200 p.a. FRI. Acting between the parties, advise what premium should immediately be paid.

Assuming a freehold rate 10% and a leasehold rate 11% and 3% adj. tax @ 40%.

A Landlord's present interest

Rent	£1,500 p.a.	
YP for 8 years @ 9%	5.5348	£8,302
Reversion to	£2,200 p.a.	
YP rev. perp. after 8 years @ 10%	4.665	£10,263
Estimated capital value		£18,565

B Landlord's proposed interest

Rent	£1,500 p.a.	
YP for 21 years @ 9%	9.2922	£13,938
Reversion to	£2,200 p.a.	
YP rev. perp. after 21 years @ 10%	1.35131	£2,972
Estimated capital value		£16,910

Present interest = Proposed interest
$$£18,565 = £16,910 + \text{Premium } (P)$$
$$P = £18,565 - £16,910$$
$$= \underline{£1,655}$$

C Tenant's present interest

Rent received	£2,200 p.a.	
Rent paid	£1,500 p.a.	
Profit rent	£700 p.a.	
YP for 8 years @ 11% and 3% adj. tax @ 40%	3.3622	
Estimated capital value		£2,353

D Tenant's proposed interest

Profit rent (as before)	£700 p.a.	
YP for 21 years @ 11% and 3% adj. tax @ 40%	5.9481	
Estimated capital value		£4,163

Present interest = Proposed interest
$$£2,353 = £4,163 - \text{Premium }(P)$$
$$P = £4,163 - £2,353$$
$$= £1,810$$

The landlord requires a minimum premium of £1,655, while the tenant can afford to offer £1,810. Negotiation between the parties will take place. A split at around £1,730 may be the result, or the parties may settle at a figure nearer the landlord's or tenant's figure depending upon their negotiating strength and the state of the market.

It must be pointed out that the above type of solution may result in a tenant's bid being lower than the landlord's minimum requirement. If the gap is sufficiently large, the proposals may be shelved. Considerable forces of inertia will, however, normally conspire to produce an agreement if the shortfall is of a minor nature: for example, the landlord, if satisfied with the tenant, may wish to save the advertising and legal fees involved in finding a new tenant. And the old tenant will have many reasons, already discussed, for being prepared to make a small loss in order to carry on in occupation of the premises.

Example 6.8 T occupies 6 High Street, holding a lease from L at a rent of £2,000 p.a. FRI with 8 years remaining. T requires a new 40 year lease, starting immediately, and proposes to carry out improvements to the premises in 3 years' time at an estimated cost of £12,000 which will increase full rental value by £2,500 p.a.

As a condition of the present lease, L requires that T pays a premium of £1,000 in 5 years' time. It is proposed that under the new lease T should pay a premium of £3,000 immediately and £5,000 after 20 years.

7 High Street is an identical property and has recently ben sold on a 10% basis. It had just been let on a 21 year lease at a rent of £6,000 p.a. FRI with a premium of £15,000 payable at the start of the lease by the lessee.

It is agreed that the rent for 6 High Street should increase by 50% halfway through the proposed term. Acting between the parties, assess what rent should be fixed under the proposals.

This problem is rather involved and includes examples of everything discussed in this chapter. It must be read and analysed extremely carefully before being attempted, and its implications must be fully realised. For example, if improvements costing £12,000 will increase FRV by £2,500 per annum, this is a fact that cannot be ignored when assessing the value of the landlord's present interest, because it might be possible for him to obtain possession in 8 years' time and carry out the said improvement.

It will be necessary to calculate the full rental value of 6 High Street from the information given concerning no. 7.

FRV of 7 High Street = £6,000 + annual equivalent of £15,000 premium. (£6,000 is a reduced rent to compensate for the premium. The full rental value will thus be £6,000 plus the value of the premium spread over the 21 year term.)

$$\text{From landlord's point of view} = £6,000 + \frac{£15,000}{\text{YP for 21 years @ 10\%*}}$$

$$\text{From tenant's point of view} = £6,000 + \frac{£15,000}{\substack{\text{YP for 21 years @ 11\%} \\ \text{and 3\% adj. tax @ 40\%}}}$$

*Property (freehold) sold on a 10% basis.

YP for 21 years @ 10%	= 8.6487
YP for 21 years @ 11% and 3% tax @ 40%	= 5.9481

$$\text{Average YP} = \frac{8.6487 + 5.9481}{2} = 7.2984$$

$$\frac{£15,000}{7.2984} = £2,055 \text{ p.a.} \qquad \therefore \text{FRV} = \underline{£8,055} \text{ FRI}$$

A Landlord's present interest

Rent	£2,000 p.a
YP for 8 years @ 9%	5.5348
	£11,070

Reversion (1): If landlord does *not* carry out the possible improvements.

Rent		£8,055 p.a.
YP rev. perp. after 8 years @ 10%*		4.665
		£37,577

Reversion (2): Assuming landlord does carry out the possible improvements, and assuming the delay is short enough to involve no appreciable loss of rent.

Rent		£10,555 p.a.
YP rev. perp. after 8 years @ 10%*		4.665
		£49,239

*Both rents are full rental values, although they differ in magnitude, the security of income is assumed unchanged.

The figure of £49,239 can only be achieved by an expenditure of £12,000 in 8 years' time and therefore value today must be reduced accordingly.

Cost of improvements	£12,000
PV £1 in 8 years @ 10%*	0.4665
	£5,600

*This is 'expenditure', and discounted at the remunerative rate.

This leaves a net present value for the reversion of £43,639 (£49,239 − £5,600).

Reversion (2) is more valuable so the landlord would improve, and the value of the interest is this increased sum.

Estimated capital value £11,070 + £43,639 =	£54,709

In addition, a premium is payable after 5 years:		
Premium	£1,000	
PV £1 in 5 years @ 10%	0.621	£621
Estimated capital value		£55,330

B Landlord's proposed interest

Rent	x	
YP for 20 years @ 9%	9.1285	$9.1285x$
Reversion to rent	1.5x*	

*Rent increased by 50%.

141

YP for 20 years @ 9.5%	8.8124		
PV £1 in 20 years @ 9.5%	0.1628	1.4348	2.1523x
Reversion to FRV		£10,555†	
YP rev. perp. after 40 years @ 10%		0.221	£2,333
Plus premiums: 1 Immediately			£3,000
2 In 20 years		£5,000	
PV £1 in 20 years @ 10%		0.14864	£743
			11.2808 x+£6,076

†Rent as increased by tenant's proposed improvements.

$$\text{Present interest} = \text{proposed interest}$$
$$£55,330 = £6,076 + 11.2808x$$
$$£49,354 = 11.2808x$$
$$£49,354 \div 11.2808 = x$$
$$£4,375 \text{ p.a.} = x$$

C Tenant's present interest

Rent received	£8,055	FRI
Rent paid	£2,000	FRI
Profit rent	£6,055	
YP for 8 years @ 11% and 3% adj. tax @ 40%	3.3622	
CV		£20,358
Less premium	£1,000	
PV £1 in 5 years @ 7%*	0.713	
		£713

*Liability: so use a realistic, low, safe, net accumulative rate. This rationale obviously raises a question mark about a dual rate YP using an accumulative rate of 3%; but to amend that would involve the re-appraisal suggested in Chapter 4.

Net CV	£19,645

D Tenant's proposed interest

Rent received	£8,055
Rent paid	x
Profit rent	£8,055 − x
YP for 3* years @ 11% and 3% adj. tax @ 40%	1.5403
CV	£12,407 − 1.5403x

*After 3 years T improves the premises and increases FRV.

142

Reversion to:	Rent received	£10,555
	Rent paid	*x*
	Profit rent	£10,555 − *x*

YP for 17 years @ 11% + 3% adj.
tax @ 40%   5.3594
PV £1 in 3 years @ 11%   × 0.7312 = 3.9188
CV   £41,363 − 3.9188*x*

Reversion to:	Rent received	£10,555
	Rent paid	1.5*x*
	Profit rent	£10,555 − 1.5*x*

YP for 20 years @ 11% + 3% adj.
tax @ 40%   5.8131
PV £1 in 20 years @ 11%   × 0.124 = 0.7208
CV   £7,608 − 1.0812*x*

Total   £61,378 − 6.5403*x*

Less   1   Improvements   £12,000
              PV £1 in 3 years @ 11%* 0.7312 = £8,774
*Expenditure.

          2   Premium now   £3,000
          3   Premium in 20 years   £5,000
              PV £1 in 20 years @ 7%*   0.2584   £1,292
*Liability   £13,066
New total CV: £48,312 − 6.5403*x*

Present interest = Proposed interest
$$£19,645 = £48,312 − 6.5403x$$
$$6.5403x = £28,667$$
$$x = £4,383 \text{ p.a.}$$

Minimum L will accept: £4,375 p.a.
Minimum T can offer: £4,383 p.a.
Agreement between parties of (say):   £4,380 p.a.

Examples 6.7 and 6.8 are as originally set out in the first edition and are included here in the same form to illustrate how the traditional or conventional valuer would approach this complex problem. It is obvious that the advice to landlord and tenant based on such calculations could be wrong. Provided the basis is supported by market evidence the valuers could argue that the figures are reasonable reflections of the current market. The reader's eyebrows should have risen over the last 5 pages and the red pen used frequently for marginal comment. The tutor need search no further for new problems; they are all here if the issues are reconsidered on an equated yield, modified cash flow approach, or on a full DCF basis.

The valuer must have regard to and take account of all the peculiarities of conventional valuation, the problems of future liabilities entered at current costs, the problems of long reversionary leases without rent reviews and the way in which a surrender and renewal can alter the market's perception of both the freehold and leasehold interests.

Marriage value

Where a property is split into multiple interests, either physically or legally, or both, each of the newly created interests will have a market value. The total of these values will not necessarily equate with the market value of the freehold in possession of the whole property. In such cases, an element of what is known as 'marriage value' might be shown to exist. The following example will serve to demonstrate this.

Example 6.9 A is the freeholder of an office block, the full rental value of which is £28,000 p.a. on FRI terms. Fourteen years ago A let the whole to B on a 40 year lease at a rent of £10,000 p.a. on FRI terms. B sub-let to C 6 years ago, at a rent of £18,000 p.a., FRI, for a term of 25 years. Value all interests. B wishes to become the freeholder in possession of the office block. Advise him how much he should offer for the interests of A and C. How much should they accept?

Valuation of current interests:		Freehold rate 10%	
1 A's interest:			
Rent	£10,000		
YP for 26 years @ 9%	9.929		
			£99,290
Reversion to FRV:	£28,000		
YP rev. perp. after 26 years @ 10%	0.839		£23,492
		Total	£122,782

2 B's interest:

Rent received:	£18,000	
Rent paid:	£10,000	
Profit rent:	£8,000	
YP for 19 years @ 10% and 3%		
adj. tax @ 40%	6.0112	£48,090
Reversion to rent received	£28,000	
− Rent paid	£10,000	
Profit rent	£18,000	
YP for 7 years @ 11% and 3%		
adj. tax @ 40%	3.0533	
PV £1 in 19 years @ 11%	0.1377	£7,567
Total		£55,657

3 C's interest

Rent received	£28,000	
− Rent paid	£18,000	
Profit rent	£10,000	
YP for 19 years @ 11% and 3%		
adj. tax @ 40%	5.6703	
Estimated value		£56,703

The total value of all interests at present is £122,782 + £55,657 + £56,703, i.e. £235,142.

B wishes to become freeholder in possession. How much will this be worth now that the full rental value can be received immediately and in perpetuity.

FRV	£28,000
YP perp. @ 10%	10
	£280,000

Notice that the total value of all interests at present is only £235,142: there will be what is called a *marriage value* created by the merger of interests of £44,858.

How is this marriage value created, and where does it arise?

Capital value is the product of two things: *income* and a *capitalisation factor*. It follows that the marriage value must arise from one or both of these.

1 *Income:* Does this change upon merger of the interests? In the case of the freehold in possession, the total income passing is

£28,000. When A, B and C have interests in the property A receives £10,000, B makes a profit rent of £8,000 and C makes a profit rent of £10,000. The total of rents and profit rents passing is therefore £28,000.

This holds for any year. The total of rents and profit rents will always be full rental value, because what the freeholder loses by way of rent, someone else gains as a profit rent.

2 *Capitalisaton factor:* Does this change? The freehold in possession is valued by applying a single rate YP to the whole £28,000. But when the interests are split, the profit rents earned by B and C are valued by dual rate YPs, adjusted for tax. This leads to a lower capital value:

YP for 10 years @ 10%   = 6.1446
YP for 10 years @ 10% and 3% adj. tax @ 40% = 4.0752

The effect of splitting the freehold in possession into three interests has been to reduce the total value of the block owing to the effect of valuing the leasehold interests dual rate. When leasehold and freehold interests are merged to create a freehold in possession, the total value is increased because the whole income is valued single rate.

This increase in value created by the merger is known as marriage value.

Marriage value	£44,856
C	£56,703
B	£55,658
A	£122,783

Unencumbered freehold: £280,000

The merger of interests will create additional value and so B can offer £224,342 for the interests of A and C. B's present interest is worth £55,658: the freehold in possession will be worth £280,000 and the gain £224,342 (£280,000 − £55,658).

But how much should B offer to A and to C? What price should A and C ask for their interests?

B's first move will be to buy either A's or C's interest. The maximum B will be able to offer to A is the gain to be made from the transaction. If A's interest is purchased the freeholder will only be subject to C's underlease.

146

Value of B + A

Rent	£18,000	
YP for 19 years @ 9%	8.9501	£161,101
Reversion to	£28,000	
YP rev. perp. after 19 years @ 10%	1.635	£45,780
Total		£206,881

B's present interest is worth £55,658: the gain will be £206,881 −
£55,658 = £151,223 and this is the maximum that can be offered
to A. The minimum that A will accept will be the market value of
£122,783. Assuming that A and B will employ valuers who will be
aware of both figures agreement will be reached between these two
boundaries.

The difference between these figures is: £151,223 − £122,783 =
£28,440 and is the marriage value between A and B.

It can also be found in the following way. A, before the transaction, had an interest worth £122,783: B had an interest worth
£55,658. This totals £178,441. The value of the combined interest
is £206,881; and the difference between these two figures is
£28,440, the marriage value.

B's next step will be to acquire the interest of C. It must be
noted that B now has an interest, as freeholder, worth £206,881.
By acquiring C's interest, B becomes the freeholder in possession
with an interest valued at £280,000. The gain that B stands to
make is therefore:

£280,000 − £206,881 = £73,119

This is therefore the maximum that B could offer to C. The minimum that C will accept will be the market value of £56,703. There
will again be negotiation between those two figures. The difference
between these two figures is £16,416, i.e. the marriage value
between B and C.

This may also be obtained by summating the present interest of
B and C (£206,881 and £56,702 = £263,584) and deducting this
from B's new interest worth £280,000. £280,000 − £263,584 =
£16,416.

Note that the total marriage value was found to be £44,856.
This is split between A and B and B and C:

Marriage value A + B:	£28,440
Marriage value B + C:	£16,416
Total marriage value:	£44,856

This term 'marriage value' usually refers to the above, the result of the merging of interests in the same property. It can also be used to describe the extra value created by a merger of two properties.

Example 6.10 B is the owner of a derelict house on a small site. On its own, the site is too small to be profitably developed, but could be used as a parking space. A is in a similar position next door. The area is zoned for shopping use and an indication has been given that planning permission would be given to construct a small shop covering both sites.

Assess the price that B could offer to A for the freehold interest in his property, and a reasonable sale price.

Value of B's present interest:	
Rent for parking, say	£50.00 p.a.
YP perp. @ 15%	6.67
CV	£333.50

Value of proposed merged site: this might be valued by using a 'residual valuation' (see Chapter 8) but market evidence indicates that similar sites have been selling for £3,000.

Maximum B can offer = £3,000 − £333.50	
=	£2,666.50
say	£2,650
Minimum A will accept	£333.50

A price will be reached by negotiation between these two figures. A marriage value of (£3,000 − £667) £2,333 has been created in this case, by a merger of sites.

Throughout this chapter, traditional approaches to valuation have been followed. Elsewhere, a number of these approaches have been questioned. It is therefore necessary to emphasise that it is the valuer's role to assess open market value. If the valuer feels confident that he can substantiate the particular approach adopted by reference to the market, then marriage value in multiple interest investments may well exist; but the valuer must be certain of this market fact. He must beware that it is not based on false assumptions and fortuitous mathematics.

For example, an approach adopted in the USA for valuing leasehold investments in property could be loosely described as the 'difference in value' method. The logic used is that if a property has a rental value of £28,000 a year, and on that basis has a market value of £280,000 but due to the grant of certain leases is currently worth only £122,782, then the value of the leasehold investments is £280,000 less £122,782. On this basis marriage value does not exist.

This, then, is one extreme. At the other, consider the value of a very short leasehold interest. The value is likely to be low owing to the short term and the problem of dilapidations. The freehold interest would however, reflect fully the loss of rental until review and in such a case genuine marriage value would exist.

It should be emphasised that the single rate valuation of lease-hold interests (see Chapter 4) will, in the absence of any significant adjustment of capitalisation rates, greatly reduce any apparent marriage value, and may produce valuations which have greater affinity with market realities. So too can the use of a real value or DCF equated yield approach.

A discussion of marriage value could not be complete without some mention of 'break-up' values. This in essence is the opposite of marriage value and recognises that different investors have different needs, objectives, risk preferences and tax positions. As one might purchase a company as a whole and then sell off separately the component parts to realise a higher total value so one might buy a freehold interest in a property and through careful sub-division of title realise a higher total value. The idea is really no more complex than that of lotting a large estate. This again emphasises the need to couple a thorough knowledge of the discounting technique with a thorough knowledge of the property market. A particular issue here is the whole question of unitisation of single property investments. The market will dictate whether 1,000 units in a £10 million property will be worth £10,000 per unit or more than £10,000 per unit or less than £10,000 per unit. The relationship need not remain constant so that under some market conditions greater value may be realised by buying out all the unit holders and reselling as a whole in the open market.

> The test is *not* – do the calculations suggest that marriage value
> exists?
> *but* – does the market evidence prove that marriage
> value exists?

Full rental value: non-standard reviews

How much rent should be paid under a lease with non-standard rent review periods so as to leave the two parties in the same financial position as if they had agreed on a standard term?

In times of rental increases or, indeed, decreases, the rent review pattern will affect the full rental value of a property, a concept so far regarded as being inflexible. It will be to the landlord's advantage in times of rental growth to insist upon regular rent reviews. Conversely, if he is burdened or presented with an arrangement whereby few, or no, rent reviews are provided for in the lease, then he may require a higher initial rent as compensation.

Two situations may arise where such compensation may be applicable. Firstly, a new lease may be arranged without the prevalent rent review pattern. For example, in a market where 3 yearly reviews are normally accepted, a new lease may be granted with 7 yearly reviews. In such a case the landlord might ask for a higher initial rent.

Secondly, the problem might arise at a rent review where the period between reviews is the result of previous negotiations. For example, a 42 year lease granted 21 years ago with a single midterm review will present problems if 3 yearly reviews are currently accepted, and again the landlord might ask for a higher reviewed rent as compensation.

Several methods have been devised to deal with this problem in a logical manner (see Andrew Baum, Full rental value). A single method is illustrated below, having been propounded in a letter by Jack Rose to the *Estates Gazette*, 3 March 1979, at page 824.

This method is designed to produce a single factor, k, which is applied to the full rental value on the usual pattern, to arrive at the compensatory rental value.

$$k = \frac{(1+r)^n - (1+g)^n}{(1+r)^n - 1} \times \frac{(1+r)^t - 1}{(1+r)^t - (1+g)^t}$$

where k = multiplier, r = equated yield (see p. 83), n = number of years to review in subject lease, g = annual rental growth expected, and t = number of years to review normally agreed.

Example 6.11 What rent should be fixed at a rent review for the remaining 7 years of a 21 year lease of shop property, when rents are expected to rise at 12% per annum and 3-yearly reviews are prevalent in the market? An equated yield of 15% based on the return provided by undated government stock with an adjustment for risk should be used, and the full rental value with 3-yearly reviews would be £15,000 p.a.

$$k = \frac{(1+0.15)^7 - (1+0.12)^7}{(1+0.15)^7 - 1} \times \frac{(1+0.15)^3 - 1}{(1+0.15)^3 - (1+0.12)^3}$$

$$= \frac{2.660 - 2.211}{1.66} \times \frac{0.521}{1.521 - 1.405}$$

$$= 0.2705 \times 4.4914$$

$$= \underline{1.2149}$$

Rent to be charged: £15,000 × 1.2149

$$= \underline{\underline{£18,224}} \text{ p.a.}$$

There is growing evidence in the property market that the rent review pattern in a lease has a considerable effect upon the rents required by landlords, and the above is an attempt to make such adjustments logically. This method, and the others suggested, are adaptations of discounted cash flow techniques to valuation problems. It must be concluded that the use of DCF in all valuations will remove all of the inconsistencies referred to in this chapter as well as those problems identified in Chapters 2, 3 and 4, and is the ultimate and logical refinement of 'the income approach'.

The logic behind the DCF approach is difficult to defeat but the market is reluctant to move into the uncharted area of market forecasting. The valuer is trying to establish on the basis of the market rental value for a specific fixed term what the rent should be for a longer or shorter fixed term. The first is assumed to equate with the actual annual rentals each year for the term discounted to their present worth and re-assessed as a fixed annual equivalent sum. The second is the projection or shortening of the actual expected annual sums re-expressed as an annual equivalent. This process can only be undertaken on the basis of an assumed (but hopefully research-supported growth rate) or on the basis of an implied growth rate (see Chapters 3 and 9).

The latter approach is more questionable in this exercise because the implied rental growth figures are long-term averages to be used for the purpose of valuing non-market rent review patterns. Either the landlord or the tenant would be concerned if the actual rental value rose at a higher or lower rate than the implied average growth rate. For an uplift rent the valuer is trying to determine the appropriate growth rate for that specific property. There is then, an argument in favour of using forecasted growth rates based on thorough research for assessing uplift rents rather than merely using implied rates.

In arbitration cases it is a question of presenting the strongest supportable case for or against the uplift, the arithmetical assessment is only a starting point.

In the case of non-normal rent reviews the courts have adopted a simple 10–15% increase for a longer review or increased the market rental by a factor for each additional year over the normal rent review evidence in preference to a DCF approach.

The examples in this chapter do not reflect the statutory rights of landlords and tenants which may have to be taken into account and are considered in chapter seven.

Chapter seven

Legislation and the income approach

In the examples shown in the text it has been assumed that land-lords and tenants are generally free to negotiate whatever lease terms they find acceptable for a particular tenancy of a property. In particular it has been assumed that they are free to agree the amount of rent to be charged for the premises and that in most cases the landlord can obtain vacant possession at the termination of the current lease. This is not the case in the UK and the valuer must have regard to the provisions of the Landlord and Tenant Acts and the various Rents Acts as they affect properties occupied for business and residential purposes. The Agricultural Holdings Acts are of similar importance in the case of agricultural property, but the valuation of agricultural property is considered to be outside the scope of this text.

The predominant feature of all landlord and tenant legislation is that it amends the normal law of contract as between landlord and tenant giving tenants substantial security of tenure (the right to remain in occupation following the termination of a contractual agreement) and setting out statutory procedures for determining and/or controlling the rents that a landlord can charge a tenant for the right to occupy a property. (The subject matter of this chapter is discussed in more detail in *Statutory Valuations*.)

Business premises

The most important statutes affecting business premises are the Landlord and Tenant Act 1927 Part I and the Landlord and Tenant Act 1954 Part II as amended by the Law of Property Act 1969 Part I.

These statutes primarily affect industrial and commercial property, but the expression 'business' includes a trade, profession or employment and includes any activity carried on by a body of persons whether corporate or unincorporate. This definition as set

153

out in Section 32, Landlord and Tenant Act 1954 Part II is sufficiently broad to include some types of occupation which would not normally be regarded as business occupations, such as a tennis club (see *Addiscombe Garden Estates Ltd and another* v. *Crabbe and others*, Queen's Bench Division [1958] 1 QB 513).

Compensation for improvements

Under the Landlord and Tenant Act 1927 Part I the tenant of business premises is entitled 'at the termination of the tenancy, on quitting his holding, to be paid by his landlord compensation in respect of any improvement (including the erection of any building) on his holding made by him or his predecessors in title, not being a trade or other fixture which the tenant is by law entitled to remove, which at the termination of the tenancy adds to the letting value of the holding' (Section 1, Landlord and Tenant Act 1927).

This right does not extend to improvements carried out before 25th March 1928, nor to improvements 'made in pursuance of a statutory obligation, nor to improvements which the tenant or his predecessors in title were under an obligation to make, such as would be the case where a tenant covenanted to carry out improvements as a condition of the lease when entered into' (Section 2, Landlord and Tenant Act 1927). Except that those made after the passing of the 1954 Act 'in pursuance of a statutory obligation' will qualify for compensation (Section 48, Landlord and Tenant Act 1954).

The tenant will normally require the consent of the landlord before carrying out alterations or improvements or alternatively he may apply to the court for a certificate to the effect that the improvement is a 'proper improvement' (Section 3, Landlord and Tenant Act 1927).

It should be noted under Section 19(2), Landlord and Tenant Act 1927 Part II that 'in all leases . . . containing a covenant, condition or agreement, against the making of improvements without licence or consent, such covenant . . . shall be deemed . . . to be subject to a proviso that such licence or consent is not to be unreasonably with-held . . .'. Section 49 of the 1954 Act renders void any agreement to contract out of the 1927 Act.

Compensation payable is limited under Scedule 1 of the Landlord and Tenant Act 1927 to the lesser of:

1 The net addition to the value of the holding as a whole as a result of the improvement; or
2 The reasonable cost of carrying out the improvement at the termination of the tenancy, subject to a deduction of an

amount equal to the cost (if any) of putting the works constituting the improvement into a reasonable state of repair, except as so far as such cost is covered by the tenant's repairing covenant.

Further, 'in determining the amount of such net addition regard shall be had to the purposes for which it is intended the premises shall be used after the termination of the tenancy' (Section 1(2), Landlord and Tenant Act 1927). For example, if the premises are to be demolished immediately then the improvements are of no value to the landlord and no compensation would be payable. But if the premises are to be demolished in, say, 6 months' time and there is a temporary user planned then compensation would be based on the net addition to value of the improvements for that 6 month period.

If the landlord and tenant fail to agree as to the amount of compensation, the matter can be referred to the county court. Where a new lease is granted on the termination of the current lease no compensation can be claimed at that point in time. Both the 1927 Act and the 1954 Act provide that the rent on a new lease shall exclude any amount attributable to the improvements in respect of which compensation would have been payable (see below).

Thus the initial problem to be solved by a valuer when instructed to value business premises is the extent to which they have been improved by the tenant and the extent to which these may become compensatable improvements under the provisions of the Landlord and Tenant Act 1927.

Example 7.1 Value the freehold interest in office premises currently let at £5,000 on full repairing and insuring terms with 6 years of the lease unexpired. The current full rental value on full repairing and insuring terms is £10,000. Improvements were carried out by the tenant and these have increased the market rental value by £1,000 and would cost today an estimated £8,000 to complete. Value the premises on the assumption that the tenant will vacate on the termination of the present lease and will be able to make a valid claim for compensation under the Landlord and Tenant Act 1927.

Current net income	£5,000	
YP for 6 years @ 8%	4.62	£23,100
Reversion in 6 years to	£10,000	
YP perp. deferred 6 years @ 8%	7.87	£78,700
		£101,800

Less compensation under Landlord and Tenant Act 1927 for improvements being the lesser of:

(a) Net addition to the value
Increase in rental attributable to improvements:

	£1,000
YP perp. @ 8%	12.5
	£12,500

(b) Cost of carrying out improvements   £8,000
∴ Compensation is   £8,000
PV £1 for 6 years @ 8%   0.63 − £5,040
                                         £96,760

Value of freehold allowing for payment of
compensation to tenant, say   £96,750

As shown elsewhere this traditional equivalent yield valuation raises some basic issues: first is the whole question of implicit versus explicit growth valuation models, the second is the validity of using current estimates of changes in rental value attributable to the improvements and of using current costs for assessing the compensations when the actual compensation will have to be based on figures applicable in 6 years' time. This is a further argument for at least checking the valuation by reference to a true DCF approach.

Security of tenure

In accordance with the provisions of Section 24(1) of the Landlord and Tenant Act 1954 tenants of business premises are granted security of tenure, however the parties may contract out of these provisions. Tenancies to which this part of the Act applies will not come to an end unless terminated in accordance with the provisions of Part II of the Act, so that some positive act by the landlord or tenant needs to be taken to terminate a tenancy. Where notice to terminate is served by the landlord he must give at least 6 months' notice and not more than 12 months' notice. Such notice cannot come into force before the expiration of an existing contractual tenancy. Thus in the case of most leases of business premises the earliest date a landlord can serve notice on a tenant is 12 months prior to the contractual termination date. If notice is not served the tenancy continues as a statutory tenancy until terminated by notice.

The Act further provides that a tenant has the right to the renewal of his lease. If the landlord wishes to obtain possession he may oppose the tenant's request for a new tenancy only on the grounds set out in the Act. Section 30(1) states the following grounds on which a landlord may oppose an application:

That is to say: (a) where under the current tenancy the tenant has any obligations as respects the repair and maintenance of the holding that the tenant ought not to be granted a new tenancy in view of the state of repair of the holding, being a state resulting from the tenant's failure to comply with the said obligations;

(b) that the tenant ought not to be granted a new tenancy in view of his persistent delay in paying rent which has become due;

(c) that the tenant ought not to be granted a new tenancy in view of other substantial breaches by him of his obligations under the current tenancy, or for any other reason connected with the tenant's use or management of the holding;

(d) that the landlord has offered and is willing to provide or secure the provision of alternative accommodation for the tenant, that the terms on which the alternative accommodation is available are reasonable having regard to the terms of the current tenancy and to all other relevant circumstances, and that the accommodation at the time at which it will be available is suitable for the tenant's requirements, including the requirement to preserve goodwill, having regard to the nature and class of his business and to the situation and extent of and facilities afforded by the holding;

(e) Where the current tenancy was created by the sub-letting of part only of the property comprised in a superior tenancy and the landlord is the owner of an interest in reversion expectant on the termination of that superior tenancy, that the estimate of the rents reasonably obtainable on separate lettings of the holding and the remainder of that property would be substantially less than the rent reasonably obtainable on a letting of that property as a whole, that on the termination of the current tenancy the landlord requires possession of the holding for the purpose of letting or otherwise disposing of the said property as a whole, and that in view thereof the tenant ought not to be granted a new tenancy;

(f) That on the termination of the current tenancy the landlord intends to demolish or reconstruct the premises comprising the holding or a substantial part of those premises or to carry

157

out substantial work of construction on the holding or part thereof, and that he could not reasonably do so without obtaining possession of the holding;

(g) Subject as hereinafter provided, that on the termination of the current tenancy the landlord intends to occupy the holding for the purposes, or partly for the purposes, of a business to be carried on by him therein, or as his residence.

To oppose an application under the last mentioned ground (g) the landlord must have been the owner of the said interest for at least 5 years prior to the termination of the current tenancy. Section 6 of the Law of Property Act 1969 extends Section 31(g) of the 1954 Act to companies controlled by the landlord and Section 7 of the Law of Property Act 1969 has altered the effects of 31(f) of the 1954 Act so that a landlord wishing to oppose the grant of a new tenancy under that ground must now not only prove his intent to carry out substantial works of alteration but also that it is necessary to obtain possession in order to complete such works. Thus if a landlord can demolish and rebuild without obtaining possession and if the tenant is agreeable or willing to co-operate then the courts will allow the tenant to remain in possession.

Section 32 of the Landlord and Tenant Act 1954 whilst requiring the new lease to be in respect of the whole of the building has now been amended by Section 7 of the Law of Property Act 1969, which adds Sections 31(A) and 32(1)(A) to allow a court to grant a new tenancy in respect of part of the original holding where the tenant is in agreement.

Compensation for loss of security

When a landlord is successful in obtaining possession the tenant may be entitled to compensation under Section 37 of the Landlord and Tenant Act 1954. 'Where the Court is precluded . . . from making an order for the grant of a new tenancy by reason of any of the grounds specified in paragraphs (e), (f) and (g) . . . the tenant shall be entitled on quitting the holding to recover from the landlord by way of compensation an amount determined in accordance with the following provisions of this section. . . .'

The amount of compensation payable will be 6 times the rateable value of the holding if for the whole of the 14 years immediately preceding the termination of the tenancy the premises have been occupied for the purposes of a business carried on by the occupier or if during those 14 years there had been a change in the occupation and the current occupier was the successor to the busi-

ness carried on by his predecessor. In all other cases the amount of
compensation shall be 3 times the rateable value of the holding
(these multipliers were revised in 1990, see page 178).

Terms of the new lease

Where a new lease is granted then the new rent payable will
normally be in accordance with the provisions of Section 34 of the
Act, particularly when the parties are in disagreement and the
matter is referred to the county court for settlement.

The Law of Property Act 1969 has amended Section 34 so that:

'the rent payable under a tenancy granted by order of the Court
under this part of this act shall be such as may be agreed
between the landlord and tenant or as, in default of such agreement, may be determined by the court to be that at which,
having regard to the terms of the tenancy (other than those
relating to rent), the holding might reasonably be expected to be
let in the open market by a willing lessor, there being disregarded:

(a) any effect on rent of the fact that the tenant has or his
predecessors in title have been in occupation of the holding;

(b) any goodwill attached to the holding by reason of the
carrying on thereat of the business of the tenant (whether by
him or by a predecessor of his in that business);

(c) any effect on rent of any improvement carried out by the
tenant or predecessor in title of his otherwise than in pursuance
of an obligation to his immediate landlord;

(d) in the case of a holding comprising licensed premises any
addition to its value attributable to the licence, if it appears to
the court that having regard to the terms of the current tenancy
and any other relevant circumstances the benefit of the licence
belongs to the tenant.'

Items (a), (b) and (c) are those that valuers have most
frequently to reflect in valuations of business premises. Items (a)
and (b) cause particular difficulty in assessment for, whilst it is
simple to explain the meaning of these requirements, it is often
extremely difficult to assess them in practice. Under item (a) the
valuer must demonstrate that, for example, premises have a rental
value as defined in the Act of £5,000, but in the absence of the
protective legislation the occupying tenant would bid £5,500, in
order that the overbid of £500 must be disregarded. Similarly
under item (b) if it can be demonstrated that the premises are

159

worth £5,000 but to any other tenant carrying on the same business are worth £5,500 then the £500 of business goodwill must be disregarded.

Section 1 of the Law of Property Act has extended the meaning of Section 34(c) to include tenants' improvements carried out at any time within 21 years of the renewal of the tenancy.

All the other terms and conditions of a new tenancy shall be as agreed between the parties, but if the parties cannot agree then Sections 33 and 34 of the Landlord and Tenant Act 1954 require the court to restrict the terms of the tenancy to 14 years with appropriate rent reviews (Law of Property Act 1969 Section 2 which adds sub-section 3 to Section 34 of the 1954 Act).

Example 7.2 Assuming the facts as stated in example 7.1, value the freehold interest and assume the tenant is granted a new 14 year lease with a rent review in the 7th year and that the improvements were completed 3 years ago.

The first step to resolve this problem requires the setting out of the income flow. Some valuers find it simpler to construct a cash-flow diagram (see Figure 7.1). In 6 years' time the lease is due for renewal, at a rental ignoring the worth of the improvements (Landlord and Tenant Act 1954). But there is some doubt as to the rent that could be charged at the rent review after 7 years. According to the Law of Property Act it would seem that no account should be taken of the value of the improvements for a period of 21 years. If this argument applies then the rent on the review must once more be at a figure excluding any value attributable to the improvements. This reasoning, coupled with the specific provisions in the Landlord and Tenant Act 1954, would effectively result in no account being taken of the improvements at any time during the whole of the new lease. Thus the cash flow will be as in Figure 7.1.

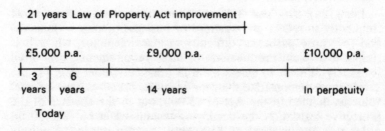

Figure 7.1

Solution, assuming cash flow as in Figure 7.1 (and see Notes following the valuation)

Current net income		£5,000	
YP for 6 years @ 7%		4.76	£23,800
First reversion to S.34 rent		£9,000	
YP for 14 years @ 7%	8.75		
PV £1 in 6 years @ 7%	0.67		£52,762
Second reversion to FRV		£10,000	
YP perp. def'd 20 years @ 7%		3.69	£36,900
			£113,462

Notes:
1 No specific allowance made for compensation for improvements as valuation assumes further renewals under Landlord and Tenant Act to current tenant or successor in title.
2 Conventional equivalent yield valuation assumptions underlie the valuation, the review pattern is such that an equated yield or DCF explicit valuation should be used as a check.

However, it is argued that if the Law of Property Act permits a review at 7 years this is virtually equivalent to the grant of 7 year leases with the right to renewal. Therefore if a 21 year period elapses prior to the rent review date there is a possibility that the full rental value of the improved premises could be charged on the review date.

This is contrary to the 1954 Act as originally drafted which clearly intended that the effects on rent of any improvements should be disregarded for the whole of the new tenancy of 14 years.

Whilst some confusion apparently exists, a number of points are becoming obvious from the decisions reached in a number of Landlord and Tenant cases.

First, the legislation relates quite clearly to the determination of 'rent payable under a tenancy granted by order of the Court', and this can only occur on renewal of a lease and not on a rent review.

Second, the Act uses the word 'reasonable' which suggests that the rent as determined need not be the maximum possible rent.

Third, the rent on any review will be determined in accordance with the appropriate clauses in the lease and, unless there is specific reference to Section 34 of the Landlord and Tenant Act 1954 or a specific statement that improvements carried out during an immediately preceding lease, or within 21 years of the review date, are to be disregarded, the review rent may fully reflect the current rental of the property as improved.

Professional advisers are therefore forewarned when acting for tenants to see that rent review clauses in leases are sufficiently worded to protect their clients.* When licences for improvements are granted they should also confirm that the effect on rental value of the improvements will be disregarded on review or renewal of the current lease.

If this advice is followed then tenants may avoid any repetition of *Ponsford and Others* v. *HMS Aerosols Ltd,* 1977, *Estates Gazette* 243: 743, where tenants of a factory rebuilt the premises which had been destroyed by fire at the same time substantially improving the property with the landlord's consent. Shortly after rebuilding, the rent was due for review. The wording of the lease and licence was such that the Court of Appeal held that the tenants would have to pay rent in respect of the improvements, the cost of which they had borne themselves. It therefore seems that the wording of the lease together with the wording of any licences will determine the factors to be taken into account when assessing the rent to be paid on review.

When valuing business premises, or advising tenants of business premises, the valuer must have careful regard to all the terms and conditions of the lease and to the relevant statutory provisions. (Readers are also referred to *English Exporters (London) Ltd* v. *Eldonwall Ltd.* [1973] Ch 415.)

In practice, negotiations and/or court proceedings may result in the new rent commencing many months after the termination of a current contractual lease. Section 64 of the 1954 Act further provides that any new terms, including those relating to rent, may only commence 3 months after the court application has been 'finally disposed of'. This can lead to a considerable loss of income for the landlord.

The Law of Property Act 1969 added a new section, 24A, to the 1954 Act.

(1) The landlord of a tenancy to which this part of this Act applies may:
  (a) if he has given notice under section 25 of this Act to terminate the tenancy; or
  (b) if the tenant has made a request for a new tenancy in accordance with section 26 of this Act;
  apply to the court to determine a rent which it would be

* See RICS/Law Society model rent review clauses.

    reasonable for the tenant to pay while the tenancy
    continues by virtue of section 24 of this Act, and the court
    may determine a rent accordingly.

(2) A rent determined in proceedings under this section shall
    be deemed to be the rent payable under the tenancy from
    the date on which the proceedings were commenced or the
    date specified in the landlord's notice or the tenant's
    request, whichever is the later.

From a valuer's viewpoint the interesting aspects of these provisions relate to the assessment of the amount of this interim rent.
Section 24A(3) contains the following direction:

In determining a rent under this section the court shall have
regard to the rent payable under the terms of the tenancy, but
otherwise subsections (1) and (2) of section 34 of this Act shall
apply to the determination as they would apply to the
determination of a rent under that section if a new tenancy
from year to year of the whole of the property comprised in the
tenancy were granted to the tenant by order of the court.

A number of principles were established in the Eldonwall case
and endorsed in *Fawke* v. *Chelsea (Viscount) (Estates Gazette
250:855).* The valuer is effectively urged to determine a rent for a
hypothetical yearly tenancy. *Ratners (Jewellers) Ltd* v. *Lemnoll
Ltd (Estates Gazette* 255:987) illustrates this point, emphasising
acceptance of the principle that, having determined a normal
market rent under the terms of Section 34, the valuer should
discount this rent to reflect the 'year-to-year' nature of the
tenancy. We doubt whether the debate is closed. Readers should
be aware that, due to the hypothetical year-to-year assumption,
the interim rent may be lower than the current rent passing, and
should be reminded that the formula employed in Chapter 6,
example 6.11, may be used to determine the annual equivalent
rent. Bowcock's *Property Valuation Tables* may also be employed
to this end, both methods being more rigorous than the crude
discount methods currently used. However, this general expectation may be contradicted by market evidence of annual rents
exceeding fixed term rents.

Landlord and tenant negotiations

It is important to appreciate that whilst the Landlord and Tenant
Acts are there to protect the tenant on termination of his lease,
many tenants will seek to negotiate new leases before their current

leases expire. The Landlord and Tenant Acts give the tenant increased bargaining strength and full regard should be had to these statutes when advising a landlord or tenant on the terms for a new lease.

Example 7.3 A tenant occupies shop premises on a lease having 2 years to run at £6,000 p.a. net. Ten years ago he substantially improved the property. The full rental value of the property today as originally demised would be £10,000 but as improved it is worth £14,000. The tenant wishes to surrender his present lease for a new 14 year lease without rent review; the landlord has agreed in principle and you have been appointed as independent valuer to assess a reasonable rent for the new lease.

As outlined in Chapter 6, this requires consideration from the tenant's and landlord's points of view on a 'before and after' basis.

Value of freeholder's present interest if he does not accept surrender of the lease:

Current income		£6,000	
YP for 2 years @ 7½%		1.79	£10,740
Reversion to FRV subject to S.34(c) L & T Act 1954 Part II and assuming a new 14 year lease without review is granted	£10,000		
YP for 14 years @ 7½%	8.49		
PV £1 in 2 years @ 7½%	0.86	7.30	£73,000
Reversion to FRV		£14,000	
YP perp. def'd 16 years @ 7½%		4.19	£58,660
Value of present interest			£142,400

(If the assumption here is that a review after 7 years would be permitted by the courts then one must further assume that professional advisers would see that the rent review clause fully reflected the intention of the L & T Act 1954 Part II as amended by the Law of Property Act 1969.)

Value of freeholder's proposed interest

Let rent to be reserved for new 14 year lease = £x per annum

Proposed rent	£x	
YP 14 years @ 7½%	8.49	£8.49x
Reversions to FRV	£14,000	
YP perp. def'd 14 years @ 7½	4.84	£67,760
Value of future interest		£67,760 + 8.49x

On the assumption that the freeholder should be no better off and no worse off the value of his present interest must be equated with the value of his future interest:

$$\text{Present interest} = \text{Proposed interest}$$
$$£142,400 = £67,760 + 8.49x$$
$$£142,400 - £67,760 = 8.49x$$
$$£74,640 = 8.49x$$
$$£8,791 = x$$

Value of tenant's present interest assuming no surrender:

FRV to tenant	£14,000	
Less rent reserved	£6,000	
Profit rent	£8,000	
YP for 2 years @ 8½% and 3% adj. tax @ 40%	1.10	£8,800
Reversion to	£14,000	
Less rent reserved	£10,000	
	£4,000	

YP for 14 years @ 8½% and 3% adj. tax 40p	5.48		
PV £1 in 2 years @ 8½%	0.85	4.66	£18,640
Value of present interest			£27,440

Value of tenant's proposed interest:

Let rent to be reserved for new 14 year lease = £x per annum, then new profit rent is:

FRV to tenant	£14,000
Less rent reserved	x
Profit rent	£14,000 − x
YP for 14 years @ 8½% and 3% adj. tax @ 40p	5.48
Value of proposed interest	£76,720 − 5.48x

$$\text{Present interest} = \text{Proposed interest}$$
$$£27,440 = £76,720 - 5.48x$$
$$5.48x = £76,720 - £27,440$$
$$x = £8,992$$

Here it would seem reasonable for the parties to accept a rent for a new 14 year lease, on surrender of the present 2 year term, of, say, £8,900 per annum. But these valuations should be cross-checked with a DCF approach.

Residential property

Over 65% of houses in England and Wales are now owner-occupied and the appropriate method for the valuation of such freehold residential property is that of direct capital comparison. However, there are still many individuals and families occupying tenanted property both on a furnished and an unfurnished basis. The capital value of such properties may be assessed by using the income approach.

The period since the Housing Act 1980 has seen a number of changes in political attitude towards the public and private sectors of the rented housing market. A large number of public sector tenants exercised their right to buy under the Act and are now home owners. But the hoped for stimulus for the private sector never materialised. The Housing Act 1988 makes further significant changes to the law relating to public and private sector housing, including Housing Associations.

The important changes in the private sector relate to the extension and amendment of the law concerning assured and shorthold tenancies. As from 15 January 1989 all existing and new assured tenancies come under the 1988 Act and the previous system of protected shorthold tenancies has been replaced by a new scheme of assured shorthold tenancies.

Private sector tenancies

Residential investment properties in the private sector can be grouped under the following heads:

1 Assured tenancies under the Housing Act 1988.
2 Assured shorthold tenancies under the Housing Act 1988.
3 Tenancies subject to protection under Part I of the Rent Act 1977 (the 1977 Act), generally referred to as regulated furnished or regulated unfurnished tenancies, including those tenancies previously known as controlled tenancies but automatically converted to regulated tenancies by Section 64 of the Housing Act 1980 (the 1980 Act). Tenancies in this category must have been 'entered into before, or pursuant to a contract made before the commencement of' the Housing Act 1988, i.e. 15 January 1989.
4 Tenancies of dwelling-houses with high rateable values (Schedule 1.2, 1988 Act).
5 Tenancies where the landlord remains resident in another part of the same building (Schedule 1(10), 1988 Act).
6 Tenancies at a low rent (Schedule 1(3), 1988 Act). Such

tenancies may be protected under the Landlord and Tenant Act 1954, Part I.

7 Tenancies with enfranchisement rights under the Leasehold Reform Act, 1967 as amended by the Housing Acts of 1969, 1974 and 1980.

(A further minor group of (formerly controlled) tenancies which are partially business lettings cannot become regulated tenancies (1977 Act, Section 24(3)) and will fall to be considered under Part II of the Landlord and Tenant Act 1954.)

Each is considered below in terms of the valuation implications of the legislation relating to each category. Those involved with the letting and management of residential property are referred specifically to the above legislation and to the Housing Act 1988 and the Landlord and Tenant Acts of 1985 and 1987.

Assured tenancies

The 1980 Act introduced a new class of tenancy in the private sector known as the assured tenancy. This was intended to encourage the institutional investor to build new homes to let on the open market.

Few tenancies were, in fact, created under the 1980 Act, largely due to the restriction of the provisions to new dwellings and to 'approved' landlords. Under the 1988 Act all new tenancies of residential property, other than those statutorily excepted by Schedule 1, will be assured tenancies.

The 1988 Act created a completely new scheme but borrows heavily from the 1977 Act and from the 1954 Landlord and Tenant Act. The working of the scheme broadly parallels that of the 1954 Act in terms of tenant protection, but grounds for possession as set out are very similar to those found in the 1977 Act. These tenancies may be granted at market rents.

It is too soon to judge how successful the new scheme will be in stimulating the private rented sector of the residential market, but the reaction of investors to the many business expansion schemes floated after the 1988 Finance Act provides hope for the government. If a new market is created then its success will depend upon the relationship between vacant possession values and the investment value of the same property subject to an assured tenancy.

The valuation of residential property subject to an assured tenancy is likely to be on an income approach, but it will be some time before there is sufficient confidence in the market for valuers to assess capitalisation rates and market rents. The income approach is likely to be the preferred approach because of the security of tenure provisions in the Act. Section 5 specifies that such tenancies can only be brought to an end with a court order and to obtain such an order the landlord(s) must follow the procedures set out in the Act and must specify the ground(s) for possession which must be one or more of those set out in Schedule 2 to the 1988 Act. In the case of grounds 1–8 inclusive, the court, if satisfied, must order possession; in all other cases the court may order possession.

The effect of these provisions is to create tenancies for residential property and hence residential investments of a continuing nature with strong similarities to business tenancy investments.

Assured shorthold tenancies

The 1980 Housing Act introduced the concept of shorthold tenancies but the 1980 provisions have been superseded by those set out in the 1988 Act.

An assured shorthold tenancy must be for a minimum period of 6 months. A prescribed notice must be served on the tenant prior to the grant of the tenancy stating that the tenancy is to be a shorthold tenancy. In addition to the grounds for possession specified in the 1988 Act for assured tenancies, the landlord is entitled to bring an immediate action for possession provided the tenancy has expired and provided all the correct notices have been served. The courts in such cases have to grant possession.

This added ability to recover possession suggests that such properties will be valued on the basis of capitalised term income plus a reversion to vacant possession capital value.

Tenancies created before 15 January 1989 and subject to the provisions of the Rent Act 1977

A regulated tenancy is one falling within the rateable value limits of £400 and £200 or £1,500 and £750, and since the Rent Act 1974 the same regulations now apply both to furnished and unfurnished tenancies, save where there is a resident landlord. No new regulated tenancies can now be created.

The main Act dealing with regulated tenancies is the Rent Act 1977. A regulated tenancy may be contractual or statutory. That is, a lease or an agreement for a lease may exist, or the tenant may be 'holding over' and exercising his statutory rights.

The 1965 Rent Act introduced the new concept of 'fair' rent and this is now consolidated in the 1977 Act. Section 70 of the

1977 Act sets out the rules for determining a 'fair' rent, the most important feature being that the effect on rental value of the scarcity of residential accommodation within an area must be ignored. A 'fair' rent will in areas of undersupply be lower than the rent one would expect if the premises were offered in the open market in the absence of the Rent Acts.

The Rent Act also requires that, in determining what is or would be a fair rent, regard shall be had to all the circumstances, and in particular to the age, character, locality and state of repair, of the dwellinghouse and, if any furniture is provided for use under the tenancy, the quantity, quality and condition of the furniture. But the following must be disregarded:

(a) any disrepair or defect attributable to a failure by the tenant to comply with the terms of the tenancy;
(b) any improvement carried out by the tenant otherwise than in pursuance of the terms of the tenancy (renewal of fixtures will be classed as improvements);
(c) any improvement to the furniture made by the tenant under the regulated tenancy or as the case may be any deterioration in the condition of the furniture due to any ill-treatment by the tenant.

The Rent Act requirement that the effect on rent of any provision improvement or deterioration of certain amenities in the locality shall be ignored was abolished by the 1980 Housing Act.

The 1968 Rent Act as amended by subsequent legislation provides for the appointment of Rent Officers in all local authority areas. Landlords and tenants both have the right to apply to the Rent Officer at any time, notwithstanding the existence of a contractual tenancy, for a rent to be registered. On receipt of an application for registration the Rent Officer inspects the premises, usually calls a meeting between landlord and tenant and subsequently notifies the parties of his intention to register a fair rent. Fair rents are registered exclusive of rates and on the assumption that the tenancy is subject to Sections 11–14 of the Landlord and Tenant Act 1985.* Either party may appeal to the Rent Assessment Committee.

Once a rent has been registered it remains the maximum recoverable rent for 2 years save for permitted variations to cover

---

*Under these sections landlords of residential premises let for terms of 7 years or less are responsible for structural repairs, exterior repairs and repairs to services, water, gas and electricity; this extends to certain fixtures such as WC, baths and basins. The liability of landlords has been further generally extended by the Defective Premises Act 1972 (see also S.116, Housing Act 1988).

extra rates borne by the landlord and increases where separate service charges exist. Re-application during the 2 years is only allowed on the grounds that there has been a change in the condition of the dwellinghouse or the terms of the tenancy. In all other cases the rent remains fixed for 2 years or until such later time that a rent is re-registered.

As far as the valuation of properties subject to regulated tenancies is concerned, the important points to note are as follows.

1 The recoverable rent is restricted to the level of a 'fair rent'.
2 The rent can only be increased after 2 years.
3 On the death of the original tenant the tenancy may be transferred twice. The second succession will be to an assured tenancy. The rules on succession have been amended by Schedule 4 of the 1988 Act.

There is still an active market for this type of investment, particularly where a portfolio of such properties is offered for sale. Those active in this market will be aware that a percentage of vacant possession value, between 25% and 50% in most cases, is used to assess market value when the income approach might only produce realistic market valuations by the use of very low capitalisation rates.

In a number of special cases the tenancy will be held to be outside the Rent Acts, or, provided the correct notices are served at the commencement of the tenancy, the courts have a mandatory power to grant repossession. Examples of such tenancies are: holiday lettings, lettings by educational establishments to students, lettings by absentee owners and lettings of properties purchased for retirement.†

In those cases where the tenancy is excepted by the Rent Act 1977 or where the court must order possession under that Act or the 1988 Act, and it is reasonable to assume that vacant possession can be obtained, the property should be valued by direct capital comparison.

Tenancies with high rateable values

The total number of tenanted houses and flats falling within this category represents a very small percentage of the whole, but still comprises an important sector of the market, particularly in central London. To be unprotected the rateable value of the tenancy as at 23 March 1965 must have exceeded £400 if situated in Greater

†Schedule 15, 1977 Act as amended by 1980 Act, see also Schedule 1, 1988 Act.

London or £200 if situated outside London. If the property was not tenanted prior to 1 April 1973, when the current valuation list came into force, or after 15 January 1989, then the figures are £1,500 and £750 respectively.

The valuation of such properties requires the capitalisation of the current contracted net income plus, the reversion to capital value, or the capitalisation of the reversionary net income, the latter and the capitalisation rate being assessed by reference to current market evidence. The capitalisation rate will therefore reflect the market's view regarding the possibility of such properties becoming assured tenancies.

As many of these properties will be in blocks of flats, special attention must be given to the calculation of landlord's outgoings and in terms of freehold valuations of blocks of flats to the Landlord and Tenant Act 1987, which gives tenants the collective right to buy under specific conditions.

Resident landlords

The Rent Act 1974 introduced a new special class of tenancy where the landlord resides in the same building. Such tenancies, whether of furnished or unfurnished premises, now fall under the 1977 Rent Act.

The important feature of a resident landlord letting, is that although the tenant enjoys limited protection from eviction (1977 Act, Protection from Eviction Act 1977 and the 1980 Act) the landlord, or, on the landlord's death, the landlord's personal representatives, can recover possession. Repossession may take 3 to 12 months through County Court procedures (1980 Act): the basis of valuation of such a property is therefore vacant possession value, deferred for 3 to 12 months, arguably the maximum period. The income approach is not, therefore, of particular relevance to this class of investment.

If created after 15 January 1989 it will be excluded from being an assured tenancy by Schedule 1 (similar provisions apply to circumstances where board and lodging is provided).

Tenancies at a low rent

A tenancy created after 15 January 1989 where no rent is payable or where the rent payable is less than two-thirds of the rateable value cannot be an assured tenancy (Schedule 1, 1988 Act).

A tenancy created before 15 January 1989 but satisfying the following conditions will be protected to some extent by the

171

Landlord and Tenant Act 1954 Part I, as too may a tenancy created after 15 January 1989:

1 The lease must be for 21 years or more.
2 The rent must be less than $^2/_3$ of the rateable value on 23 March 1965.
3 The rateable value on 23 March 1965 must have been £400 or less in Greater London, or £200 or less elsewhere.
4 The tenant must be in occupation of the dwelling.

Protection under this Act comes into operation on the expiration of a contractual tenancy. In many cases the tenant will have far more valuable rights under the Leasehold Reform Act 1967 but where this is not the case Part I of the 1954 Act will apply to tenancies terminated prior to 15 January 1999 and the tenancy will continue as a statutory tenancy under the 1977 Rent Act. Where the tenancy is terminated after 15 January 1999 it will continue by virtue of Schedule 186 Local Government and Housing Act 1989 as an assured monthly periodic tenancy (Housing Act 1988). A landlord may also request an interim monthly rent.

An income approach would appear to be the correct approach but the right to buy provisions of the 1987 Act need to be referred to when advising on the sale of properties in this category.

Tenancies subject to the Leasehold Reform Act 1967

Under the Leasehold Reform Act 1967 (as amended by the Housing Acts of 1969, 1974 and 1980) certain lessees of residential property now enjoy the right to acquire the freehold title to their home (enfranchise) or to obtain a 50 year extension to their original lease. The following conditions must be satisfied for the Act to apply:

1 The tenancy must be a long tenancy, that is for a term of years certainly exceeding 21 years.
2 The rent reserved must be low, that is less than $^2/_3$ of the rateable value of the property on 23 March 1965 or on the first rating assessment if the property is rated after that date.
3 The tenant must occupy the house as his residence, 'house' including any building designed for living in. Houses divided vertically into maisonettes may comprise several units for the purposes of the Act; houses divided horizontally into flats may comprise one unit only.
4 Under the 1967 Act the rateable value must not exceed £400 in Greater London or £200 elsewhere (Section 1(1)a). Section

118 of the 1974 Housing Act added three further rateable value tests.

(a) Premises first appearing in the valuation list after 1 April 1973, in respect of which qualifying leases were created on or before 18 February 1966: the rateable value limit is £1,500 in Greater London and £750 elsewhere.

(b) Premises first appearing in the valuation list after 1 April 1973, in respect of which qualifying leases were created after 18 February 1966: the rateable value limit is £1,000 in Greater London and £500 elsewhere.

(b) Premises included in the valuation list before 1 April 1973 at assessments in excess of the original limits: the rateable value limit is now £1,500 in Greater London and £750 elsewhere.

Provisions are contained in Schedule 8 of the 1974 Act to allow for reductions in rateable values which have been increased by tenants' improvements, so that certain cases might be brought within the Act when otherwise they would have been excluded.

5 The tenant must have occupied the property for the last 3 years before serving notice or for periods amounting to 3 years in the last 10 years.

Equity sharing leases granted by certain public authorities are specifically excluded by the 1980 Act.

A qualifying tenant may enfranchise under the Act by giving the landlord notice of his intention to do so, negotiating for the acquisition of the landlord's interest and paying all costs incurred. The landlord may only resist enfranchisement by using Section 18, on the ground that the property or part of it, which was acquired by the landlord before 18 February 1966, is or will be reasonably required for occupation as the only or main residence of the landlord or an adult member of the landlord's family. In this case the landlord will be liable to pay compensation to the tenant based on the loss of the right to a 50 year extension to his lease.

Alternatively the tenant may wish to obtain a new 50 year lease at the expiration of his current tenancy. The landlord may resist this application on the same ground, or under Section 17 by applying to the court within one year before the original tenancy expires for an order that he may resume possession for the purposes of redevelopment. In either case the landlord must pay compensation assessed as before. (It should be noted that redevelopment proposals do not defeat an application for enfranchisement.) An extended tenancy shall be granted on the same terms as the original tenancy, at a ground rent representing the letting value of the site which is designed to be a continuation of the type of rent (often a ground rent) paid under the original lease.

The most typical problem likely to present itself to the valuer is to assess the price payable by a tenant on enfranchisement. Two methods of valuation may be applicable: the 'original method' based on the 1967 Act and used in, for example, *Miller* v. *St John Baptist's College*, 1977; and the 'new method' based upon Section 118 of the 1974 Act applying where the rateable value of the property exceeds £1,000 in Greater London and £500 elsewhere (but is, of course, subject to the upper limits of £1,500 and £750). The 'new method' was used in *Norfolk* v. *Trinity College, Cambridge*, 1976.

1 'Original method'

The price to be paid on enfranchisement under Section 9 of the 1967 Act shall be the market value of the landlord's interest on the assumption that the tenant had acquired a 50 year extension of his lease under the Act. Section 82 of the 1969 Housing Act amends Section 9 so that the tenant's own bid for the freehold is to be disregarded.

Example 7.4 A holds a ground lease of a London house at a ground rent of £20 per annum with 25 years unexpired. The fair rental value of the house is £2,000 p.a. Freehold houses of a similar type have sold for £25,000. By comparison the bare site would appear to be worth £10,000. The current rateable value is £450. Advise A on the price he would have to pay to enfranchise.

Landlord's interest:

Ground rent	£20 p.a.	
YP for 25 years @ 8%*	10.675	£213.50

Reversion to modern ground rent:

Site value: £10,000 ('cleared site' approach)

$$\text{Modern ground rent} = \frac{£10,000}{\text{YP perp. @ 8\%}} = \frac{£10,000}{12.5}$$

$$= £800 \text{ p.a.}$$

or Freehold value £25,000. Value of site say 40% = £10,000 ('standing house' approach).

---

*The Lands Tribunal has always accepted yields of 6–9% on ground rents.

Modern ground rent as before = £800 p.a.
YP perp. @ 8%*   12.5
PV £1 in 25 years @ 8%   0.146   £1,460

Estimated value   £1,673.50

Example 7.5 Using the facts of example 7.4 advise A if the site were worth £40,000 for redevelopment purposes.

Landlord's interest (as before):   £1,673.50

Plus: Marginal development value
       £40,000 − £10,000   =   £30,000
       PV £1 in 25 years @ 8%   0.146   £4,380

                                      £6,053.50

Less: Compensation to tenant for loss
      of notional extended lease:
      Rent received   £2,000 p.a.
      minus modern ground rent   £800 p.a.

      Profit rent   £1,200 p.a.
      YP for 50 years @ 13% and 3%
      adj. tax @ 40%   6.9072
      PV £1 in 25 years @ 13% 0.047102 £390.42

Estimated value   £5,663.08

2 'New method'

Section 9 of the 1967 Act has been supplemented by provisions contained in Section 118 of the 1974 Act, governing the price to be paid on enfranchisement where the rateable value falls between £1,000 and £1,500 in London and £500 and £750 elsewhere. From *Norfolk* v. *Trinity College* it appears that Section 82 of the 1969 Act does not apply to these cases, so the tenant's bid may be taken into account. Also, in these cases the valuation should not reflect the right to a 50 year extended lease, but the tenant's right to remain in possession under Part 1 of the 1954 Landlord and Tenant Act.

Example 7.6 B holds a ground lease with 20 years unexpired at a ground rent of £35 per annum. The current fair rent is £1,500 per annum. The rateable value in 1965 was £425 and on 1 April 1973 was £1,250. The market value of the property in possession

---

*Although the reversion is to a 50 year lease, followed by a reversion to a fair rent, the Tribunal has always accepted the assumption of a perpetual ground rent.

is £35,000, and the market value of the leasehold interest is £20,000. Advise B on the price he should pay on enfranchisement.

Landlord's interest:

Ground rent	£35 p.a.	
YP for 20 years @ 8%	8.8042	£308
Reversion to fair rent*	£1,500 p.a.	
YP rev. perp. after 20 years @ 12%	0.8639	£1,296
Estimated value		£1,604

*Where the lease is due to expire after 15 January 1999, a reversion to a market rent under assured tenancy terms might be valid (Schedule 11 Local Government and Housing Act 1989).

From *Norfolk* v. *Trinity College, Cambridge*, the tenant's bid should be reflected by apportioning the marriage value which he or she would realise on enfranchisement (see Chapter 7).

Value of freehold in possession	£35,000
Value of freehold subject to lease	£1,604
Value of leasehold:	£20,000

(From the Norfolk case it seems that the value of the leasehold interest is best assessed by comparison and should reflect the attractiveness of the right to enfranchise.)

Marriage value = £35,000 − (£1,604 + £20,000)
= £13,396

Assuming that the parties are of equal bargaining power, take 50%:

		£6,698
Total enfranchisement price:	£6,698 +	£1,604
	=	£8,302

An additional modification brought in by the 1974 Act concerns improvements: the price paid on enfranchisement should be diminished by the extent to which the value of the house and premises has been increased by any improvement carried out by the tenant or his predecessors in title.

In November 1977 a question was raised in Parliament concerning the Norfolk case. Written answers indicated that Section 118 of the Housing Act 1974 was likely to be amended at an early date.

The Housing Act 1980 made a number of changes to the legislation concerning leasehold enfranchisement but did not amend Section 118 of the 1974 Act. Thus the enfranchisement price can vary considerably, depending upon whether 'new' or 'old' approaches are appropriate. Because of this, an application for a reduction in rateable value may save a tenant many thousands of pounds in the event of enfranchisement.

Of the amendements introduced by the 1980 Act, the following are of general interest. Those concerned in practice with Leasehold enfranchisement are referred to Sections 141 and 142 and Schedules 21 and 22 of the 1980 Act.

Leasehold Valuation Tribunals (similar to Rent Assessment committees) have taken over leasehold reform matters from the Lands Tribunal, although there is a right of appeal to that body. While all Lands Tribunal costs formerly had to be borne by tenants, each party's Leasehold Valuation Tribunal costs are to be borne by that party.

A formula is laid down for assessing the price to be paid for a 'minor superior tenancy' (reversions of not more than one month). The price to be paid is found from:

$$P = £ \frac{R}{Y} - \frac{R}{Y(1 + Y)^n}$$

where P = price payable, R = profit rent (improved ground rent less ground rent), Y = yield (decimal fraction, derived from market price of $2\frac{1}{2}\%$ consolidated stock), n = period in years (with part years taken as whole years) of the unexpired term of the minor superior tenancy prior to the enfranchisement notice.

References
Miller v. St John Baptist's College (1977): *EG* 243:535.
Norfolk v Trinity College, Cambridge (1976): *EG* 238:421.

Also note:
Delaforce v Evans: *EG* 215:315.
Farr v. Millersons Investments: *EG* 218:1177.
Goldridge v. Official Custodian for Charities: *EG* 222:1672.
EG 227:1467.

The following list of additional statutes is not comprehensive, but the valuer may need to refer to them when valuing residential and commercial property:

Public Health Acts 1936, 1961	Dangerous structures and public health nuisances.

Housing Acts 1957, 1961, 1969, 1974	Housing standards, grants, etc.
Defective Premises Act 1972 } Occupier's Liability Act 1957 }	Landlords' duties of care, where liable for repair and maintenance, extended to all persons likely to use the premises, not only the tenant.
Factory Act 1961 Offices, Shops and Railway } Premises Act 1963 }	May require expenditure by owners to bring premises up to standard in respect of fire precautions, heating, sanitary conveniences, etc.

A number of changes to the law relating to residential and business tenancies were introduced by the Local Government and Housing Act 1989 and are briefly referred to in this chapter. In particular, Schedule 7 deals with compensation for business tenancies and the Landlord and Tenant Act 1954 (Appropriate Multipliers) Order 1990 has amended the multipliers. The multiplier under Schedule 37 (2) is still three if the relevant date is before 1 April 1990. It is one if the relevant date is after 1 April 1990. These are doubled in appropriate cases. In some cases removal expenses will be paid if part of the property is domestic. Transitional arrangements provide for a multiplier of eight where the landlord's notice is given after 31 March 1990 but before 1 April 2000 and the tenancy was in existence or was contracted before 1 April 1990 and the tenant has exercised an option for compensation to be based on the Rateable Value as at 31 March 1990. The discontinuance of the domestic rating system has produced the References to Rating (Housing) Regulations 1990. These amend the Landlord and Tenant Act 1954, the Leasehold Reform Act 1967, Rent (Agriculture) Act 1976, Rent Act 1977, Housing Acts 1985 and 1988, Local Government and Housing Act 1989 by providing for alternative measures for assessing qualifying conditions, etc. where reference to rateable values is not possible.

Chapter eight

Development appraisal

A property may be said to have development potential whenever an element of latent value may be released by the expenditure of capital upon that property. There are three general cases where such latent value might exist:

1 In the case of a bare or underdeveloped site where planning permission for development has been, or is likely to be, obtained.
2 In the case of an existing building where planning permission has been, or is likely to be, obtained for a change of use, or where general upgrading of the building is intended.
3 In the case of an existing building where planning permission has been, or is likely to be, granted for its demolition and replacement.

In all three cases the preferred valuation approach is, as in all other cases, by direct capital comparison. However, as stated in the introduction to Chapter 2, directly comparable sales are often difficult to find, and it is in the market for property with development potential that the most difficulty in finding good comparable evidence is experienced. In the investment market, the income approach is the most suitable and widely used alternative to direct capital comparison. In the market for property with development potential an adaptation of the income approach known as the *residual valuation* is the most widely used method of valuation.

The residual method

The conventional approach to a residual valuation is based upon a simple equation:

Gross development value − (costs + profit) = Residual value.

The gross development value of a property is the capital value of the developed or improved site. What remains after the deduction of all costs incurred in the development or improvement is the residual value which includes the value of the bare site or of the site and building, where the building is to be improved or demolished.

Example 8.1a   A plot of land has planning permission for the erection of 7,000 m² (gross) of office space on five floors. The development will be completed in 2 years from now and rents are expected to average £120 per m² (net). Building costs are expected to average £400 per m², excluding fees.

Prepare a valuation to advise a prospective developer of his maximum bid for the site. Comparable evidence of prices obtained for similar sites is not available.

Gross development value:
7,000 m² (gross) × 85%* = (say) 6,000 m² (net)

6,000 m² @ £120 per m² p.a.	£720,000 p. a.	
YP perp. @ 7%	14.29	£10,285,714
Less Purchaser's costs @ 2.750%		275,287
		£10,010,427

*Reduction for non-usable space of 15%

Less costs:

(a) Building costs: 7,000 m² @ £400 per m²	£2,800,000	
(b) Architects' and quantity surveyors' fees @ 12½% of building costs	£350,000	
Total building costs:	£3,150,000	
(c) Finance costs: 15% p.a. for 2 years on 50% of total building costs [£1,575,000 × (1.15)²] − £1,575,000 =	£507,937	
(d) Legal fees, estate agents' fees and advertising upon disposal: @ 2% GDV + promotion, say:	£253,239	
(e) Developer's profit: @ 15% GDV	£1,501,564	
Total costs:		£5,412,740
Residual:		£4,597,687

Let site value = x
Legal and valuation fees on site purchase @ 3% = $0.03x$
Total accumulated debt after 2 years @ 15% p.a. = $1.03x(1.15)^2$

$$1.03\ x(1.15)^2 = £4,597,637$$
$$1.362x = £4,597,687 \qquad \text{Site value} = £3,375,254$$

This, the conventional residual method of valuation, has been the subject of fierce criticism in recent years, often by no less influential a body than the Lands Tribunal, whose members denounced the method as 'far from a certain guide to values' (*Cuckmere Brick Co. Ltd. and Fawke* v. *Mutual Finance Ltd.* (1971) *EG* 218:1571) and have suggested that 'once valuers are let loose upon residual valuations, however honest the valuers and however reasoned their arguments, they can prove almost anything' (*First Garden City Ltd.* v. *Letchworth Garden City Corporation (1968) EG* 200:123).

Part of the problem facing valuers has been the dificulty of handling an increasing number of variables such as VAT , fees, etc. in the valuation exercise when carried out manually. Currently many development surveyors use spreadsheets or computer software packages. These do not remove the basic criticism but the flexibility of such programs and their speed of operation enable valuers to check each appraisal for sensitivity and so derive greater confidence in their opinions of value.

Example 8.1a has been reappraised using a package prepared and marketed by Michael Gilbert FRICS of Kel Computing Limited, Marlow, Buckinghamshire. It is but one of many such programs now available to valuers.

Example 8.1b Development study summary (valued on 10 November 1988).

Freehold

Income: 6,000 m² at	£120.00	£720,000 p.a.	
Net value at 7.000%		£10,010,427	
Gross sum available			£10,010,427
Purchase price		£2,988,583	
Acquisition costs	3.00%	£89,656	£3,078,239
Construction (24 months)			
7,000.0 m² at	£400.00	£2,800,000	£2,800,000
Associated costs			
Professional fees at	12.50%	£350,000	
Post-construction costs		£20,000	
Letting fees	15.00%	£108,000	
Costs of sale	2.00%	£200,209	
Non-recoverable VAT		£530,697	£1,208,906

Development appraisal

Finance – compounded quarterly
Interest on site at	15.000%	£1,054,207	
Interest on development			
at 15.000%		£563,365	£1,617,572

Total project cost		£8,704,719
Project surplus	15.00%	£1,305,708
		£10,010,427

Return on cost	8.27%

Rental cover 22 months   Finance cover 11 months

Project timetable
Start date 09/11/1988	0 months planning
End date 11/1990	0 months demolition
	24 months construction
	0 months sales/letting
	24 months total

Tenure   Freehold

Income & capitalisation
Rental value at	£120.00 pnm	£720,000 p.a.	
Capitalised at	7.000%	£10,285,714	
less Purchaser's costs	2.750%	£275,287	£10,010,427
*Gross sum available			£10,010,427

Development summary
Net floor area (m²)		6,000.0
Gross floor area (m²)		7,000.0
Base construction cost		£400.00 pgm
*Site purchase		£2,988,583
*Total project cost		£8,704,719
*Project surplus	15.00%	£1,305,708
Yield on project cost		8.271%
Void cover (finance)		11 months
Void cover (rental)		22 months
Net/gross ratio		85.71%

Costs

Acquisition
Purchase price		£2,988,583		
Agents	1.25%	£37,357 v		
Legal costs	0.75%	£22,414 v		
Stamp duty	1.00%	£29,885	£3,078,239	£439.75 pgm

Construction
    Gross Floor Area – Sq Mtr   7,000.0
    Total Construction Cost   £2,800,000   £400.00 pgm

Professional fees
    Architect   12.50%   £350,000 v   £350,000   £50.00 pgm

Post Construction Costs
    Promotion   £20,000 v
    Letting Fees 15.00%   £108,000 v
    Costs of Sale 2.00%   £200,209 v   £328,209   £46.89 pgm

Non-Recoverable VAT   £530,697   £75.81 pgm

Finance – compounded quarterly
    Interest on Development
        Costs at 15.000%   £563,365   £80.48 pgm
    Interest on Site Purchase at 15.000%   £1,054,207   £150.60 pgm

Total project cost   £8,704,719   £1,243.53 pgm

Project surplus   15.00%   £1,305,708   £186.53 pgm

                           £10,010,427   £1,430.06 pgm

v = vatable item, pnm = per net metre, pgm = per gross metre

Schedules

Areas in square metres

Entire building	Area		Rental		Construction	
	Gross	Net	Rate	Value	Rate	Cost
	7,000.0	6,000.0	120.0	720,000	400.0	2,800,000
	7,000.0	6,000.0	120.0	720,000	400.0	2,800,000

Net value at 7.000%, less costs: 2.75%   10,010,427

VAT Schedule	Cost	VAT Rate%	Total VAT	Recover %	Net VAT
Purchase price	2,988,583	0.00	0	0	0
Construction	2,800,000	15.00	420,000	0	420,000
Professional fees	350,000	15.00	52,500	0	52,500
Acquisition & funding	89,656	15.00	8,966	0	8,966
Ancillary	0	15.00	0	0	0
Post-construction	328,209	15.00	49,231	0	49,231
	6,556,448		530,697		530,697

Development appraisal

Finance: Interest rate on site purchase   15.000%
Interest rate on development costs 15.000%
Builders' retention   0.00%

Costs	Amount	Months	Weight %	Interest	Total
Acquisition	3,078,239	24		1,054,207	4,132,446
Demolition	0	24	50	0	0
Construction	2,800,000	24	50	428,566	3,228,566
Professional fees	350,000	24	50	53,571	403,571
Non-recoverable VAT	530,697	24	50	81,228	611,925
Post-construction	20,000	0	50		20,000
Letting & sale costs	308,209				308,209
	7,087,147			1,617,572	8,704,719

Interest is compounded quarterly in arrears.
It is assumed that construction related payments are made monthly.

Notes on 8.1a and 8.1b

1 Building costs will be incurred in stages throughout the building programme. If appropriate, compensation to the tenant under the Landlord and Tenant Acts and demolition and site clearance works should be included.

2 Architects' and quantity surveyors' fees are also incurred during the building programme, often similarly to building costs. These are usually charged as a percentage of building costs. VAT is generally payable on fees and should be added.

3 Finance costs are incurred as interest charges levied by the lender, probably on a daily basis, on the accumulated debt. Building costs and fees will be borrowed in stages as they are needed to meet architects' certificates which, as here (8.1b) effectively means payments monthly in arrears. As a matter of expediency it may be assumed that, on average, half of the total accumulated debt is outstanding over the development period, as prior to the halfway stage less than half will be owed, while after the halfway stage more than half will be owed.

4 Upon completion of the development, the building will almost certainly be let or sold, unless built for the developer's own occupation. Upon letting or sale, both estate agents and solicitors will be employed. Estate agents often pass on the cost of advertising to clients. Both fees are usually charged as a percentage of the first year's rent or of the sale price in the cases of letting and sale respectively.

5 The developer's profit, often regarded as an allowance which caters for risk and contingencies such as falling values and rising costs, is usually expressed as a percentage of the gross development value or of total building costs. As a third gauge, particularly where the developer does not intend to sell the completed development, his initial yield may be calculated. This is the relationship between the initial income produced by the

completed development and the developer's total outlay (excluding profit). The figures for rental cover and finance cover indicate the period for profit erosion in the event of not letting on completion.

6 The residual figure includes the site value, or, more accurately, the developer's maximum bid for the site. This will be expended immediately at, or prior to, the outset of the building programme. Legal fees upon conveyance of the site title and valuer's fees for advising upon the site bid will be incurred and charged as a percentage of the site cost. Thus an immediate debt comprising the site cost and fees will be incurred, and will accumulate interest until it is paid off 2 years later. The site value being £2,988,583, costs £89,656 and interest of £1,054,207 to give a total £4,132,446 (8.1b).

7 The EC rulings on VAT can readily be incorporated into the program.

The computed results suggest a residual site value net of all fees and other expenses of £2,988,583 (compared to £3,375,254). Part of the reason for this difference lies in the greater arithmetical accuracy and part due to the allowance for VAT. The advantage of the fuller analysis lies in the additional information given and the breakdown of items such as interest and VAT. Further information could be incorporated such as planning application costs. Of equal importance is the ability to gauge the sensitivity of the appraisal; the results of such a sensitivity analysis are printed below.

Given this added information, the valuer could go back to the main program and re-run the calculation on the basis of the most pessimistic, most optimistic and most probable scenarios.

Development study sensitivity analysis (10 November 1988)

Base values:

Purchase price £2,988,583   Average cost of finance 15.00%

Section	1	2	3	4	5
ERV	120.00	0.00	0.00	0.00	0.00
Construction	400.00	0.00	0.00	0.00	0.00
Capitalisation	7.00	7.00	7.00	7.00	7.00

Tables:

showing the effect that changes have on the purchase price (in thousands)

ERV (£ per m)		115.00	117.50	120.00	122.50	125.00
Cost (£ per m)	420.00	2,587	2,713	2,838	2,963	3,089
	410.00	2,663	2,788	2,913	3,039	3,164
	400.00	2,738	2,863	2,989	3,114	3,239
	390.00	2,813	2,939	3,064	3,189	3,315
	380.00	2,888	3,014	3,139	3,265	3,390

Yield %		6.50	6.75	7.00	7.25	7.50
Finance %	16.00	3,364	3,125	2,903	2,697	2,504
	15.50	3,411	3,170	2,946	2,737	2,542
	15.00	3,459	3,215	2,989	2,778	2,581
	14.50	3,507	3,260	3,032	2,819	2,621
	14.00	3,555	3,307	3,076	2,861	2,661

Relative sensitivity of purchase price (in thousands) to a 2.5% variation in:

ERV	5.03%
Construction cost	2.52%
Yield	4.99%
Finance rate	1.08%

The residual method can only be of limited accuracy because of the crude estimates made of the timing of costs and benefits. For example, most models apportion costs very crudely over the construction period and as many other costs such as fees and finance are directly linked to construction costs the result must be less than perfect. For example, the development of modern office buildings and shopping centres involve very high finishing costs, i.e. the project will be end loaded; assuming finance on half the cost for the full period cannot produce an accurate picture of the financing involved.

In a residual valuation it is very difficult to reflect accurately on phased developments as is found in the case of business parks and large residential schemes. The residual cannot cope accurately with positive/negative cash flows.

Cash flow models have been developed to counter these difficulties and criticisms (see Andrew Baum, *Residual Valuations: A Cash Flow Approach*). Testing the residual results against cash flow models suggests that the greater variability ocurs with phased developments such as low-rise residential schemes where cash inflows coincide with cash out-flows. The variation in result is less pronounced with the relatively simple one-off development, especially those with a project term of 12 months or less.

The cash flow approach

In the absence of alternative development schemes, it is almost certain that the cost of borrowing money will be at least as high as the rate of interest that the developer could earn on excess funds. It is therefore reasonable to conclude that the developer should pay off debts as soon as income is produced by the development.

The developer will pay considerable attention to his likely cash flow and his likely maximum borrowing requirement over the building period. A cash-flow table will provide full information concerning these two points, and will allow for the accurate estimation of finance charges. In addition, the timing of costs and benefits may be accurately reflected and 'phasing' may be taken into account. Also, changes in costs and values may be built into the cash-flow table.

Example 8.2 A site has the benefit of planning permission for the erection of a block of 20 flats, totalling 1,100 square metres of space. The value of each completed flat on current values[4] is £10,000, but flat prices are expected to continue to rise at 5% per annum. Building costs are estimated at £80 per m^2 and are expected to rise at 0.5% per month. It is expected that 5 flats will be sold in each of months 9–12 and that building costs will be evenly distributed over a 12 month building period. Architects' and quantity surveyors' fees will be payable in two instalments in months 6 and 12 at 10% of building costs. Agents' and solicitors' fees will be charged on sale at 1% of the sale price of each flat, and the developer will require a profit of 15% of the sale price. Advise him as to his maximum bid for the site.

1 Flat prices are increasing at 5% per annum or 0.4% per month.

In month 9, 5 flats will sell for £10,366 each;	(£51,830)
In month 10, 5 flats will sell for £10,407 each;	(£52,035)
In month 11, 5 flats will sell for £10,450 each; and	(£52,250)
In month 12, 5 flats will sell for £10,491 each.	(£52,455)

2 Building costs are estimated at £80 per m^2, spread evenly over 12 months, rising at 0.5% per month. Total costs of £88,000

187

divided by 12 gives a cost of £7,333 in month 1, which will increase by 0.5% in month 2, etc. The results:

£7,370 in month 2;
£7,406 in month 3;
£7,444 in month 4;
£7,481 in month 5;
£7,518 in month 6;   Plus arch/QS fees @ 10% of cost to date: £4,455

£7,556 in month 7;
£7,594 in month 8;
£7,632 in month 9;   Plus fees @ 1% and profit @ 15% of sale price: £518 + £7,775
£7,670 in month 10; As above: £520 + £7,805
£7,708 in month 11; As above: £523 + £7,237
and £7,747 in month 12; As above: £525 + £7,868 plus Arch/QS fees @ 10% cost months 7–12: £4,590

From this information a cash-flow table can be constructed incorporating the effects of interest charges at 1% per month.

Month	Benefits (£)	Costs (£)	Net (£)	Cap O.S. (£)	Interest (£)
1	–	7,333	– 7,333	7,333	73
2	–	7,370	– 7,370	14,776[1]	148
3	–	7,406	– 7,406	22,330	223
4	–	7,444	– 7,444	29,997	299
5	–	7,481	– 7,481	37,778	377
6	–	11,973	–11,973	50,129	501
7	–	7,556	– 7,556	58,186	582
8	–	7,594	– 7,594	66,362	663
9	51,830	15,925	+35,905	31,112	311
10	52,035	15,995	+36,040	4,608[2]	+ 46
11	52,250	16,068	+36,182	+40,836	+408
12	52,445	20,731	+31,724	+72,968[3]	

Residual   = £72,968.

Let site value = x; let fees on site purchase = 3% = $0.03x$.
Then   1.03x + interest for 12 months at 1% per month
= £72,968

$$1.03x(1.01)^{12} = £72,968$$
$$1.03x(1.1268) = £72,968$$
$$1.1606x = £72,968$$
$$x = £62,869$$

Notes:

1 Already outstanding from month 1 is a debt of £7,333, and an interest charge of £73. Added to these is a new loan of £7,370, the total being £14,776 on which the interest charge for month 2 will be levied.

2 This figure is positive, as the total debt of £31,112 plus £311 interest is more than repaid by the receipt in month 10 of £36,040. Hence a surplus of £4,608 remains. This can be invested to earn interest at 1% per month.

3 This final surplus remains after paying all costs except the cost of the site itself, and fees and finance on its purchase. Calculated as before, the developer's maximum site bid is £62,869.

4 The estimates in this illustration have been left at their 1979 levels for historic reasons. Equivalent sale price for flats in 1989 would be in the region of £100,000, and costs would be substantially higher.

In this form the cash flow has been undertaken on a terminal value basis. The same calculation can be presented in a present value form.

Month	Benefits (£)	Costs (£)	Net (£)	PV £1@ 1%	PV
1	–	7,333	– 7,333	0.9900	– 7,259
2	–	7,370	– 7,370	0.9803	– 7,225
3	–	7,406	– 7,406	0.7706	– 7,188
4	–	7,444	– 7,444	0.9609	– 7,153
5	–	7,481	– 7,481	0.9515	– 7,118
6	–	11,973	–11,973	0.9420	–11,278
7	–	7,556	– 7,556	0.9327	– 7,047
8	–	7,594	– 7,594	0.9235	– 7,013
9	51,830	15,925	+35,905	0.9143	32,828
10	52,035	15,995	+36,040	0.9053	32,627
11	52,250	16,068	+36,182	0.8963	32,430
12	52,445	20,731	+31,724	0.8874	28,153
				NPV	£64,757

Let site value = x; let fees on site purchase = 3% = $0.03x$
Then

$$1.03x = £64,757$$
$$x = £62,870 \text{ (variation due to rounding).}$$

An important prerequisite for a cash flow approach is an accurate scheduling of construction activities. This uses network analysis, or critical path analysis whereby critical sequential events become the critical path, and other non-sequential events can be scheduled to run in parallel, in turn some of the parallel costs may also be sequential. The end result is the production of a project network with a start and finish date with all the intermediate critical dates. The actual costs can then be estimated and transferred to a cash flow. The two together will then become part of the project manager's management tools for monitoring the development programme.

Such an approach, if applied to example 8.1, would highlight the need to reduce the construction period in order to reduce the high finance costs. The need to reduce finance costs in periods of high interest rates has played its part in developing innovative construction techniques including the concept of off-site construction of 'pods' such as complete toilet and washroom facilities which are swung into position as the development rises floor by floor.

Cash flows and residuals can be calculated on a current cost basis, or on a future cost basis building in variations in rents as well as variations in labour and materials. None of the computerised sophistications can, however, overcome the problem that the acceptability of residual and cash flow development appraisal methods rests not with their rationale, which is irrefutable, but with the quality of the evidence used by the appraisal team to estimate costs and benefits.

Viability studies

Early in this chapter it was stated that the residual method of valuation is based upon a simple equation:

Gross development value − (costs + profit) = Residual value

The aim of the residual valuation is to find the unknown in this equation, the residual value. Often, however, a prospective developer will be aware of the likely site cost and consequently of the cost of fees and finance, either because the vendor has stated an asking price, or because negotiations have revealed the minimum figure which the vendor will accept. This is particularly likely in the case of an existing building which is to be improved or replaced.

In such a case the single unknown in the equation can now become the developer's profit. The aim of viability study is to assess the profit likely to be made from a development scheme, given the cost or asking price of the subject site.

The cash-flow table is particularly adaptable as a viability study.

Example 8.3 Using the facts of example 8.2, advise the developer of his likely profit if the total cost of the site, including fees, is £50,000.

The cash flow is almost identical to that used in example 8.2, but the total outlay on site and fees of £50,000 should be built in as a cost, while developer's profit is omitted as a cost and instead becomes the residual figure. Interest and cumulative figures are rounded to the nearest pound.

Month	Benefits (£)	Costs (£)	Net (£)	Cap O.S. (£)	Interest (£)
1	–	57,333	−57,333	57,333	573
2	–	7,370	− 7,370	65,276	653
3	–	7,406	− 7,406	73,335	733
4	–	7,444	− 7,444	81,512	815
5	–	7,481	− 7,481	89,808	898
6	–	11,973	−11,973	102,679	1,027
7	–	7,556	− 7,556	111,262	1,113
8	–	7,594	− 7,594	119,969	1,200
9	51,830	8,150	+43,680	77,489	775
10	52,035	8,190	+43,845	34,419	344
11	52,250	8,231	+44,019	+ 9,256	+ 93
12	52,455	8,272	+44,183	+53,532	

£53,532 represents the developer's profit. This can be expressed as

$$\frac{£\ 53,532}{£208,570} = 25.6\% \text{ of GDV,}$$

or as $\quad \dfrac{£\ 53,532}{£\ 99,504} = 54\%$ of total building costs.

The residual method has become a straightforward DCF exercise. Nevertheless, there will still be areas of variability, and the criticism that the result is sensitive to changes in inputs remains. The next stage is therefore to incorporate probability measures in the analysis (see Chapter 9). Rents, costs and interest charges may be weighted according to the valuer's expectation of possible changes, such an approach being eminently suited to computer analysis.

Part three

Chapter nine

Analysis

The other side of the valuation coin is the analysis of property investment opportunities. This requires the careful consideration of the relationship between the known and expected returns and costs. Expected returns can only be estimated by a forecast of the future. This necessarily introduces the valuer to the concepts of risk.

Risk and uncertainty in valuation

A property investment is an exchange of capital today (current purchasing power) for future benefits. These future benefits may be in the form of income or capital growth, or a combination of both. As indicated earlier in the text, this requires the valuer to have some regard for the future and, as has so frequently been said before, the only certain thing about the future is its lack of certainty. When an investor purchases future rights he has accepted 'risk'.

Risk and uncertainty in everyday usage are taken to be one and the same, but for our purposes there is an essential difference. Risk is used in those cases where a probability or weight can be assigned to alternative expectations and uncertainty is used to mean that no measure of certainty (probability) can be assigned to any of the alternative expectations.

When a valuer describes a property investment as being 'risky', he is implying some relative measure; further, that by such comparison:

1 The rents expected in the future may not be realised, i.e. the rental growth will be less than anticipated.
2 Increase in rent will not occur at the time expected, e.g. property may become vacant and take some time to re-let.
3 The principal sum involved may not be realisable, may not increase with time or may fall with time.

4 Some market money rates may move against the property, i.e. an increase in rates will result in a fall in value, *ceteris paribus.*

5 Other property investments will out-perform the subject property.

6 The long-term property investment may be out-performed by short-term investments.

For one or more reasons a valuer may wish to reflect this greater risk in his valuation. A common approach is to increase the discount rate.

Such an adjustment is inevitably arbitrary and by adding to the discount rate one is implying that the risk itself grows over time. For example, a property producing an income of £100 per annum might be valued in perpetuity at 10%, giving a total present value of £1,000. Assume a similar property is to be valued but certain risks suggest an increase in the rate to 20%. The present worth is £500. Initially this may seem perfectly acceptable but any present value of any income stream can be considered to be the sum of the present values of each year's income.

This means that the PV of £100 after 1 year at 10% and 20% is respectively £90 and £83, a reduction of 7.78%; but after 40 years the £100 becomes worth £2.2 and £0.06, a reduction of 97.27%. Thus by comparison, between the investments, it is being inferred that the risk attached to each £100 is increasing at an increasing rate.

To overcome this problem one approach adopted is to make three estimates of the future – the best estimate, the most likely, and the worst – and to estimate the probability of each occurring. This approach, however, ignores all the other possible outcomes. In fact, estimates should be attempted for all the probable outcomes.

The following section is reprinted with amendments from an article which first appeared in the *Estates Gazette,* 234: 29–31, entitled 'The investment method – an objective approach' by P.J. Byrne and D.H. Mackmin.*

You are instructed by a banking organisation to prepare a valuation for mortgage purposes of a new owner-occupied office building.

Having measured and surveyed the building and checked your findings with the architect's plans, you are satisfied that the building contains a total lettable area of 12,000 sq. ft. It is your considered opinion, having regard to all the relevant factors, that the

*Reproduced by kind permission of the Estates Gazette Ltd., and without any updating of figures.

property would let at a figure between £2.50 and £3.00 per sq. ft and would sell as an investment on the basis of a 5–6.5% rate. (These figures have no implications beyond this particular example.)

After further deliberation a premiminary valuation is prepared:

Area: 12,000 sq. ft
Full rental value: £31,000 (approx £2.60 per sq. ft)
Yield: 6%

Income   £31,000
YP perp. @ 6%   16.67
                     £516,770

In time, this may be demonstrated to be a valid solution.

An experienced valuer may well be able to reduce the range of rents and yields, but in the absence of absolute levels for either of these factors, any valuation must entail some consideration of the variability which is possible over the range within which the eventual selection will be made.

The range suggested for rents is £2.50 to £3.00 per sq. ft, and for yields 5–6.5%. Given these limits, and taking steps of, say, 5p per sq. ft and 0.25% on the yield, Table 9.1 shows the variations in final valuation obtained by altering these two variables within their respective ranges.

Table 9.1

Rental (£ sq. ft)	Yield (%)						
	5.0	5.25	5.50	5.75	6.0	6.25	6.50
2.50	600000	571429	545455	521739	500000	480000	461539
2.55	612000	582857	556364	532174	510000	489600	470769
2.60	624000	594286	567273	542609	520000	499200	480000
2.65	636000	605714	578182	553044	530000	508800	489231
2.70	648000	617143	589091	564378	540000	518400	498462
2.75	660000	628572	600000	573913	550000	528000	507693
2.80	672000	640000	610909	584348	560000	537600	516923
2.85	684000	651429	621819	594783	570000	547200	526154
2.90	696000	662858	632728	605218	580000	556800	535385
2.95	708000	674286	643637	615653	590000	560400	544616
3.00	720000	685715	654546	626087	600000	576000	553847

There are 77 possible 'outcomes' in Table 9.1. Which one is correct? Are *any* of them correct? Can the valuer justify his best assessment – which is clearly only one of a much larger number of possible solutions – because this selection also implies the conscious rejection of, in this case, at least 76 other values?

Is it possible to use the information at our disposal to arrive at a closer estimate of the likely value of this property?

Initially, a range of value between £461,539 and £720,000 may be noted. The valuer in his best assessment has subjectively and/or objectively endeavoured to reduce this range. The approach suggested here merely formalises this process.

If an analysis of file data is made it may be possible to determine the relative frequency of occurrence for the various rental levels between the minimum £2.50 and maximum £3.00.

Let us suppose that for this example such an analysis is possible for 50 comparable transactions: the results can then be tabulated, as in Table 9.2. This gives a good indication of the probability of occurrence of the various possible rentals, presupposing, of course, that the 50 transactions are truly comparable. If insufficient data are available it may be necessary to use other methods, as described below.

Table 9.2

Rental (£ sq. ft)	Frequency	% Occurrence	Probability
2.50	1	2.0	0.02
2.55	2	4.0	0.04
2.60	5	10.0	0.10
2.65	6	12.0	0.12
2.70	7	14.0	0.14
2.75	9	18.0	0.18
2.80	7	14.0	0.14
2.85	6	12.0	0.12
2.90	5	10.0	0.10
2.95	1	2.0	0.02
3.00	1	2.0	0.02
Total	50	100.0	1.00

Each rental may now be 'weighted' by multiplying it by its probability of occurrence and summated to give one overall *expected* rental value, each element being included in proportion to the probability of its occurrence (i.e. the total of the individual answers to these calculations gives the rent that can be expected on the basis of the available data).

All possible rental values have been built into the result; none are actually discarded at this stage, but their importance is now related to the *known frequency of occurrence* of each rental level. Since the distribution of probabilities in Table 9.2 is almost symmetric, then the expected rental will be in the centre of the distribution. In this case it is £2,746 (£2.75).

The expected rental obtained here is specific to the distribution shown in Table 9.2 other shapes of probability distribution can occur, and when this happens the expected value will be different. An analysis of transactions, for example, might show a different frequency and probability pattern, as in Table 9.3.

It is not unreasonable to argue that in each of these distributions the 'modal value' – that rental having the largest observed frequency of occurrence – could be taken as representative, since it is the most likely value. The application of this average measure would at least imply that a full analysis had been carried out.

Table 9.3

Rental (£ sq. ft)	Frequency	% Occurrence	Probability
2.50	2	4.0	0.04
2.55	5	10.0	0.10
2.60	20	40.0	0.40
2.65	10	20.0	0.20
2.70	4	8.0	0.08
2.75	2	4.0	0.04
2.80	3	6.0	0.06
2.85	2	4.0	0.04
2.90	1	2.0	0.02
2.95	1	2.0	0.02
3.00	0	0.0	0.00
Total	50	100.0	1.00

However, in the second case (Table 9.3), the relative frequency of other classes shows that some rentals are quite probable, £2.65 for example. The use of the expected value – the weighted mean – reflects the possibility that these other results might occur. The expected rental value in this case is £2.65, showing this in spite of the evidence that 40% of observed rentals are at £2.60, 46% are above £2.60, and 14% below.

The different results from these two sample distributions of rents are compared in Table 9.4 for the seven possible yields used before. This range of values may be acceptable if the number of alternatives remains relatively small. The range of *possible* alternatives may be very large, however – and, more important, it may be possible to determine how likely they are to occur by means of

Analysis

Table 9.4

Yield (%)	Rental (£ sq. ft)	
	£2.75	£2.65
5.00	660000	636000
5.25	628572	605714
5.50	600000	578182
5.75	573913	553044
6.00	550000	530000
6.25	528000	508800
6.50	507693	489231

an analysis of observed frequencies. There are three possible ways of dealing with this problem:

1 Ignore it.
2 Use a computer to calculate and display the results for *all* possible alternatives. (Such an exercise is called 'simulation'.)
3 Make use of available experience to determine *subjective* probabilities for the occurrence of 'likely' values for these variables. These probabilities can then be built into the consideration of alternatives. This method is usually more likely to appeal to the financial advisers of investing organisations, because it is conceptually closest to the procedures currently in use. We shall therefore amplify these comments on it.

In the example above, Tables 9.2 and 9.3, the various yields were all suggested as equally possible. Clearly the valuer should be able to say from his knowledge that all are not equally possible, but that some are most unlikely and, more important, that some are very likely. This view is based upon the *considered* opinion of the valuer.

There are standard and easily learned rules to enable such considered opinions to be converted to subjective probabilities recognised to be just as valid and formalised as the objective assessments derived from long-run frequencies, as in Tables 9.2 and 9.3. A complete probability distribution can be built up for any variable using these methods. As has been seen (see p. 197) yields are just as likely to vary as rentals in this example, and after consideration the following subjective probabilities have been placed against the possible yields (see Table 9.5).

Table 9.5

Yield (%)	Probability
5.00	0.02
5.25	0.03
5.50	0.05
5.75	0.15
6.00	0.45
6.25	0.20
6.50	0.10
	Total 1.00

The distribution of probabilities is such that only a few yields are considered likely to occur. From this distribution the expected value for the yield may be obtained by weighting each yield by its probability: in this case the value is 5.995% (6.00).

The implication of the subjective selection of a high probability of occurrence for a particular yield is that it is considered relatively risk-free. It is also possible, therefore, to use such assessments as indicators of individuals' attitudes to risk in their investment.

The years' purchase may then be calculated, and the capital value arrived at in the usual way.

Distribution 1 (Table 9.2)
Estimated yield 6%
Estimated full rental value 12,000 × 2.75   £33,000
YP perp. @ 6%   16.67

£550,110

Distribution 2 (Table 9.3)
Estimated yield 6%
Estimated full rental value 12,000 × 2.65   £31,800
YP perp. @ 6%   16.67

£530,106

Note that these valuations are not comparable with one another, but may be compared individually with the original best estimate, or preliminary valuation.

Any solution derived in this way must be understood to be an estimate. The use of a statistical analysis of this type can only produce estimates. But – and this is more important – it produces a more consistent approach to uncertain situations, highlighting the stages in the appraisal process and pointing to any inconsistencies requiring correction or modification. As such, the method outlined *is* part of a more scientific approach to valuation. It must be emphasised that in this illustration many questions of market data collection, storage and analysis which are integral to the rigorous statistical consideration of the variables the valuer needs to use have been by-passed.

This approach emphasises the role of the valuer. Every input – variable or otherwise – is dependent upon the strength of the valuer's file evidence, his rental and value analysis, and his understanding and assessment of current market conditions. The approach differs in that the valuer is enjoined to consider ranges of uncertain variables much more carefully, any single 'figure' arrived at *always* being recognised as an estimate based on a proper analysis of the market.

Using a method such as this, a valuer may quite reasonably derive a series of results for any valuation. In that case, great care must be taken in presenting such findings to the client. The complete findings should be incorporated into valuation reports as appendices, as they are a full summary of the valuer's views of the investment.

Naturally the method should not be applied automatically. It requires a clear understanding of the statistical methodology and its implications; it could also be inappropriate in some situations.

Many valuers see little need for the explicit use of probability in their valuations. In this book it has been indicated that on many occasions there is a lack of certainty. One cannot be certain what the rent of a vacant building really is until it is actually let, one cannot be certain what rent will be achieved on review (indeed, it is possible to miss the review date or for legislation to be introduced freezing rents), one cannot be certain of the capitalisation rates to be used, and one cannot be certain about future costs on repairs and refurbishment. There is risk; why not reflect it?

Risk and uncertainty in analysis

The phenomenal growth in institutional investment in land and buildings has turned the attention of the valuer to investment analysis. The violent boom and slump of the property prices in the early 1970s went a long way to accelerate the rate at which techniques used in other investment areas have come to be used in property investment analysis.

When property is purchased as an investment it is purchased for its present and future income and for capital growth. Occasionally other factors (such as prestige) enter into the decision, but for the rational investor such factors should not override decisions based on sound appraisal.

The following information may be required by investors, and is usually presented in a written report (see Appendix B).

1 Location. Here the valuer provides a description of the town, its geographical location in relation to other major towns and cities, details the population and road, rail and air communications, and comments upon the town's economic base. The position of the property within the town or city is then outlined.

2 Description of the property. This section of the report deals with the age, design, construction and condition of the building(s) comprising the subject property. A comment may also be made concerning running costs.

3 Town planning. A full report of the result of enquiries made with the local planning authority should be included.

4 Rating assessment, rates payable, etc.

5 Tenure: freehold or leasehold, with details.

6 Details of occupation tenancies, including comments on the tenants' covenants following investigation of the companies' accounts, etc.

7 Fire insurance: extent of coverage required and premiums payable.

8 Management problems.

9 Terms of the transaction, including the valuer's recommendations.

The investor requires full details of the street, town and the region in which the property is located. This part of the report must include details of the current operating expenses, income and future rental growth prospects, the latter being substantiated with economic projections of the town and region's growth. Future rental growth will in part be influenced by the quality and/or suitability of the building for its permitted user. The tenant's covenant is relevant, but provided the building is readily lettable it may not be a crucial factor. To some investors a good covenant is a bonus rather than a prerequisite. As far as management is concerned most investors wish to see that the burden of management is minimised.

The different types of property available for investment funds can be readily sub-divided in terms of their suitability as investments into prime, secondary and other. But as more statistical information on performance becomes available traditional distinctions between, say, prime and secondary shop properties may disappear. Greenwells in their October 1976 report on property, whilst emphasising rental growth, covenant, fashion, marketability and volatility as the five main reasons for many institutions pursuing a policy of investing only in prime properties, indicated that in terms of income growth and long-term return secondary property could turn out to be a better investment.

In addition to the foregoing, investors require some information on the rate of return or yield that they can expect from the investment. As indicated in Chapter 1, DCF techniques have been developed for analysing investments. Where a valuer is asked to advise on a specific property investment for a specific client the prospective purchase price is generally a known factor. For analysis purposes all acquisition costs such as solicitors' fees, survey and valuation fees, stamp duty, etc., must be added to the estimated purchase price before the yield is calculated.

Yields

Some reference has already been made to problems of the terminology relating to yields (Chapter 2). In the following paragraphs we outline the type of information required by investors and the methods of calculation used by valuers, adhering to what we consider to be currently acceptable and accurate terms.

In the case of most investments it is possible to calculate the 'initial yield'. This is the simple relationship between the first year's income from an investment and the purchase price.

$$\frac{\text{Income or dividend}}{\text{Purchase price}} \times 100 = \text{Initial yield}$$

In the case of stocks this is frequently called the interest-only yield, and it may also be called the flat or running yield.

When, in the case of property, the first year's income is the full rack rental on net-of-outgoing terms this measure of return becomes the capitalisation rate for conventional valuations of comparable properties.

Another measure in the case of Government Stocks is the 'Redemption Yield' which may be gross or net after allowing for tax on income and/or capital gain. Information on stock yields may appear in the press as follows (*The Times*, 1977):

		Int. only yield	Gross red. yield
Treasury 15¼% 1996	110	14.384%	14.314%
Treasury 9½% 1999	74¼	12.931%	13.233%

It is not possible to check these figures exactly because certain information is missing. In particular, there is no information as to when and how frequently dividends are to be paid, nor precisely when in 1996–9 the stocks will be redeemed. For the calculations to be exact one would also need to know whether they were cum- or ex-dividend.

If the Treasury 15¼% were selling for £100 today then the 'nominal yield' would be 15¼%.

The 'initial yield' is $\dfrac{15.25}{100} \times 100 = 15\frac{1}{4}\%$.

The 'gross redemption yield' is also 15¼% because there will be no capital gain or loss on the redemption date, the purchase price of £100 for £100 par value being fully redeemed in 1996.

But when the purchase price differs from the face value the initial or interest-only yield will differ from the nominal yield.

It cannot be assessed precisely because the cum- or ex-dividend factor will have a bearing on the interest-only yield.

It can also be noted that in 1996 a purchaser of the stock today will receive back £100, so there will in effect be a capital loss of £10 over the intervening years. With the 9½% Treasury stock there is a capital gain of £100 − £74.25 = £25.75.

This capital gain or capital loss is generally taken into account by investors, hence the use of the Gross Redemption Yield as a measure.

In these examples the redemption yield is in effect the Internal Rate of Return for the investment. It is that rate which will discount all the benefits to equate with the purchase price. Trial and error with PV factors could be used provided the dividend and redemption date were known precisely but here it has been precisely assessed by computer.

When property is purchased the initial yield may be very low. This will be true where the property is let at less than FRV with an early reversion to FRV.

Institutional investors have long recognised this factor and have generally requested details of 'initial yield', 'reversionary yield', 'equivalent yield' and sometimes 'equated yield'. The latter are today relatively easy to calculate, but valuers might care to reflect upon the lengthy reiterative processes that had to be followed by the investment valuer before the age of programmable calculators and computers, in order to calculate such a yield to at least two decimal places.

Up until the mid-1960s the investment valuer would always base his yield calculations on current rental estimates. Thus a freehold property worth £1,000 per annum producing £500 per annum for the next 3 years and offered at £8,500 would be analysed to give an initial yield of:

$$\frac{500}{8,500} \times 100 = 5.8\%;$$

a yield on reversion of $\frac{1,000}{8,500} \times 100 = 11.76\%;$

and an equivalent yield of 10.26%.

The latter is similar in this instance to an internal rate of return and represents the rate of interest which will discount 3 receipts of £500 and £1,000 in perpetuity starting in 3 years to equal £8,500.

Redemption yields as such cannot be calculated for property investments because, unlike Government Stock, the future benefits of income are not fixed and the redemption figure is the resale value, which again is not fixed. However, there may be cases where an expected redemption yield will be calculated. To do this some assumption must be made as to future sale date or dates, following which estimates of projected rent and resale value need to be made. It will then be possible to calculate the expected redemption yield either on a gross basis or net-of-tax basis.

It is a basic assumption that property is purchased for its expected rental growth as well as its current yield (initial yield) and that the expected growth in conjunction with the current yield will match long-dated gilt yields. The growth necessary in respect of a specific set of assumptions can be calculated. This is generally called the 'implied growth rate'.

A common starting point for this type of analysis is the gross redemption yield from British Funds or the interest-only yield on undated stock. For example on 5 January 1977 3% Treasury were selling at $20^5/_8\%$ per £100 face value to show 15.105%; 4% Consols were selling at $26^3/_4$ per £100 face value to show 14.794% and 1995 $12^3/_4\%$ Treasury at $87^1/_4$ to show a gross redemption yield of 15.089%. At that time minimum lending rate was $14^1/_2\%$, and the clearing banks' base rate 14%. In November 1988 the yields were respectively 9.23%, 9% and 9.96%.

These rates represent nil growth in income, nil risk to income and nil risk to capital if held to redemption. Any other investment can only be worth while if its comparable return is in excess of these yields. There is much truth in this statement; but the selection of the appropriate yield requires some care, as these vary from day to day and property is a less volatile long term investment.* A stock may go up or down 1% in 24 hours but this does not imply an immediate comparable movement in property yields.

Logically an investor would not purchase equity investments at less than the safe return from Government Stock unless the expected growth income was sufficient to cover the yield gap.

Thus on 5 November 1988 ICI shares were selling at £10.25 per share yielding 5.3% and BP at £2.47 yielding 6.7%. These shares one trusts will have, *ceteris paribus,* a continuous annual or semi-annual growth expectation. This may well fluctuate from year to year, but assuming that a 10% growth in dividends can be expected a comparison can be made with Government Stock.

For ICI the return could be more realistically expressed by substituting in the formula for a growth stock. This formula is given as

$$D = \frac{D_o(1+b)}{(r-b)}$$

where b is the per cent increase on previous years' dividends (the expected growth rate per annum), D_o is the last dividend paid, D is the current price and r is the redemption yield. Hence:

$$1,025 = \frac{54.32(1+0.10)}{(r-0.10)}$$

$$1,025 = \frac{54.32(1.1)}{(r-0.10)}$$

$$r = 0.15829$$

---

*In the text the opportunity cost of capital for property investors has been taken to be 2% above the rate earned on Government Stock, but this is subject to argument. The Economic Development Institute in its Compounding and Discounting Tables for Project Evaluation states: 'For private enterprise the opportunity cost of capital will be a weighted average of the borrowing rate for funds and an acceptable price-earnings ratio for equity shares. For the society as a whole, the opportunity cost of capital is the return on the last (that is, marginal) investment which could be made were all the available capital fully invested in the most remunerative alternative manner' (World Bank, 1973).

Thus a purchase of ICI shares at £10.25 represents an anticipated 15.83% return on the assumption of an expected 10% growth in dividends. BP on the same assumption would have given 17.37%.

Again this comparison has been made by making a forecast as to future dividends. Clearly it would be reasonable to incorporate some probability assessment in the forecast.

Property on the other hand can rarely be considered to produce a continuous annual growth in income. But if an owner-occupied freehold property was under consideration producing an imputed income of £100 per annum and selling for £1,250 a similar calculation would be possible. Thus:

$$\frac{100}{1,250} \times 100 = 8\% \text{ initial yield}$$

Assuming a 10% growth in rent per annum then

$$1,250 = \frac{100(1 + 0.10)}{(r - 0.10)}$$

$$1,250r - 125 = 110$$

$$= 0.188$$

i.e. a return of 18.8%

Reconsidering the formula and rephrasing one can state that when initial yield $= i$, growth rate $= b$ and discount rate $= r$, then

$$i = \frac{1 + r}{1 + b} - 1$$

$$b = \frac{(1 + r)}{(1 + i)} - 1$$

$$r = (1 + i)(1 + b) - 1$$

Thus in the example given where $i = 8\%$ and $b = 10\%$

$$r = (1.08)(1.1) - 1 = 0.188 = 18.8\%$$

Property let at rack rental with rent reviews restricts the potential receipt of any increase in rent to the rent review date. Although rents may rise continuously at some long run average compound rate, for property investments to equate with yields from stocks and shares the growth between reviews must be sufficient to compensate for the contracted fixed income between reviews.

Hence the purchase of a property let at £100 per annum for 5 years with reviews assumed to be every 5 years for the sum of

£1,250 must, if the discount rate is 18.8%, reflect a rate of growth in income greater than 10% per annum compound.

The problem can be phrased as

$$£1,250 = £100 \times \frac{(1 - PV)}{r} + \left[x \times \frac{1}{i} \times \frac{1}{(1 + r)^n} \right]$$

where $r = 18.8\%$ and $i = 8\%$ and $x = $ rent on review.

$$1,250 = 100 \times \frac{\left(1 - \dfrac{1}{(1 + 0.188)^5}\right)}{0.188}$$

$$+ \left[x \times \frac{1}{0.08} \times \frac{1}{(1 + 0.188)^5} \right]$$

$$1,250 - \left[100 \times \frac{1 - \dfrac{1}{(1 + 0.188)^5}}{0.188} \right) \right]$$

$$= x \times \frac{1}{0.08} \times \frac{1}{(1 + 0.188)^5}$$

$$1,250 - [100 \times 3.074] = x \times 12.5 \times \frac{1}{(2.366)}$$

$$1,250 - 307.40 = x \times 12.5 \times 0.422$$

$$942.60 = 5.275x$$

$$£178.69 = x$$

Thus the rent on review in 5 years' time must be (say) £179 in order that the investment can be considered to be acceptable as a continuous growth income of £100 compounding at 10% per annum.

$$£100 \times \text{amount of } £1 = £179$$

$$\text{Amount of } £1 \text{ in 5 years} = \frac{£179}{100}$$

$$\text{Amount of } £1 \text{ in 5 years} = 1.79$$

$$\text{rate of growth} = \text{approx } 12\tfrac{1}{2}\% \ ((1.225)^5 = 1.7821)$$

Analysis

Clearly, given any initial yield, cost of capital rate and rent review pattern, the growth yield can be calculated. Formulae (see Chapter 3) and tables have been produced for certain rates, years, etc., but most valuers will be better advised to consider the ideas rather than memorise the formulae. It is always preferable to consider the expectation (probability) of a particular income on reversion than to become lost in tables yet again.

An alternative approach is to consider the appropriate yield gap between property investments and comparable equity shares. If equities are moving from 6% to 7% property should perhaps move from $6^1/2$% to $7^1/2$%. It is, after all, logical to state that if first class industrial and commercial organisations are increasing dividends by 10% p.a., presumably they can increase their rent payments by a comparable amount; thus first class factory rents should rise in line with the performance of the leading industrialists and if retail sales are rising by 30% p.a. then retail rents can increase by a similar percentage.

In summary, most investors will require to know the initial yield on total acquisition costs, the reversionary yield (yield on reversion), the equivalent yield, and the equated yield, i.e. the internal rate of return on specific assumptions (see post).

All of these calculations can be carried out on a before or after tax basis, but from the point of view of a specific client or investor it is suggested that if the client is subject to tax of any form on income or capital gains from property then net of tax returns should be provided.

But in order to calculate these yields an assumption of certainty has been made. The more sophisticated investor will wish to take the analysis a stage further, because the advice as it stands gives no indication of the probability of achieving the stated yield. Consider example 9.1.

Example 9.1 Your clients are contemplating the acquisition of a property investment. The property is fully let producing a net cash flow from contracted rents of £1,000 per annum for the next 2 years. These rents are considered to be certain. In 2 years' time the rents are due for review. You have considered the likely level of rents in 2 years' time and expect the rent roll to be in the region of £3,000; expressing this in capital terms you have prepared the following table of cash flows together with a probability measure for the capital reversions in 2 years' time. The asking price plus acquisition cost gives a total purchase price of £32,640. Advise your client.

End year	Net sum	Probability	Expectation	
One	£1,000	1	£1,000	
Two	£1,000	1	£1,000	
	£30,000	0.20	£6,000⎞	£36,500
	£37,500	0.60	£22,500⎬	(Expected return
	£40,000	0.20	£8,000⎠	in 2 years' time)

To assess the internal rate of return the generalised formula

$$PV = \frac{I_1}{(1 + i)} + \frac{I_2}{(1 + i)^2} + \cdots \frac{I_n}{(1 + i)^n}$$

must be solved for i, in this case in terms of:

$$£32,640 = \frac{1,000}{(1 + i)} + \frac{1,000 + 36,500}{(1 + i)^2}$$
$$i = 0.08$$

The internal rate of return is virtually 8%. If this calculation involved more inputs and more probability factors it could only be solved quickly by using a computer.

If the client's target rate is 7% the valuer would reconsider the NPV on this basis given his expectations.

Year	Sum	PV at 7%	
One	£1,000	0.9346	£934.60
Two	£37,000	0.8734	£32,752.50
			£33,687.10
	Less purchase costs		£32,640.00
	Positive NPV say		£1,047

The investment on this basis is worthwhile.

Such calculations should of course be carried out on a true net basis from the specific client's viewpoint.

Here it has been recognised that the position in 2 years' time is not certain, as there is a rent review. In this example the rent on review has been assumed to be certain at £3,000, but the future benefit of £3,000 in perpetuity may have a present worth between £30,000 and £40,000 depending upon the analyst's assumptions as to the discount rate. The 'expected value' in 2 years' time has therefore been calculated before considering the internal rate of return on his basis. The normal analysis would have opted for the most probable figure of £37,500 and would have ignored the other possible outcomes.

It is essential for the prudent investor to pause and consider the other possible outcomes and the effect that a change in the reversionary value might have on expected return. In this example it has been stated that the rent will be £3,000 but that the market capitalisation rate of 8% could, under certain circumstances, fall as low as 7½% and, under others rise as high as 10%. These forecasts, which are for only 2 years hence, could be fairly accurate and would of course be based on a reasonable interpretation of the state of the economy and the extent to which national and local economic factors might affect future capitalisation rates for this type of investment. It will therefore be desirable in some instances to consider not only the possible rates of return but also their probability, and hence the variance of the return and the standard deviation.

Table 9.6

Possible rate %	Probability of occurrence	Expected rate of return %	Deviation of possible from expected	Deviation squared	Deviation squared × probability
7.5	0.2	1.5	−0.8	0.64	0.128
8.0	0.6	4.8	−0.3	0.09	0.054
10.0	0.2	2.0	1.7	2.89	0.578
	1.0	8.3			0.760%

Table 9.6 indicates that the expected rate of return is 8.3%, this being the weighted average of all possible outcomes which, in relation to an income of £3,000, would give an expected value of £36,144 (YP × income). The variation of return in this case is 0.76%, which can be converted into a standard deviation by taking the square root, giving a standard deviation of 0.87%. These latter two measures are measures of the risk involved. The smaller the standard deviation the smaller is the probability of the actual return deviating from the expected rate of return. In certain cases such a measure is extremely useful, particularly if one has an extreme case of two projects both with an expected rate of 8.3%, but one with a standard deviation of say 0.87% and the other with a standard deviation of 3%, for it is clear, in these terms, that the former is a far less risky investment.

An alternative is to consider the probability distribution of present values for alternative investments. For example, given distributions as in Figure 9.1 the less speculative investment is investment A. The client is therefore in a position to make a better decision between investments than he would have been if the only information he had received was the figure of present value. He can also judge whether the added return from the more speculative investment is likely to compensate for the added risk.

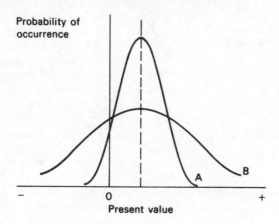

Figure 9.1

Probability distributions as in Figure 9.1 help to emphasise the possibility of a negative present value. Different investors have different attitudes towards risk and some cannot afford to make an investment if there is the slightest possibility of a loss. So to advise on the purchase of a property merely because it shows a positive NPV at the investor's target rate of discount is inadequate advice, because it again ignores the other possible outcomes which could occur with a change in income forecasts. Some indication of this possibility should be given to the investor.

A further alternative for considering uncertainties in investment decision-taking is the decision tree. Here again informed guesses as to probable outcomes need to be made. In example 9.1, whilst a number of probability factors were incorporated, these were based on a specific assumption as to a future event at the end of year 2, namely that the income would be £3,000 per annum. In reality this will be uncertain. Thus at the end of year 2 the tenant could renew the lease or he could vacate the property, and in the latter case it might either be re-let immediately, or there might be some probability that it would take a year to find a new tenant.

Provided probability factors can be assessed for each of the alternative outcomes a decision tree can be constructed. With this information the valuer is able to assess the present value of the entire tree.

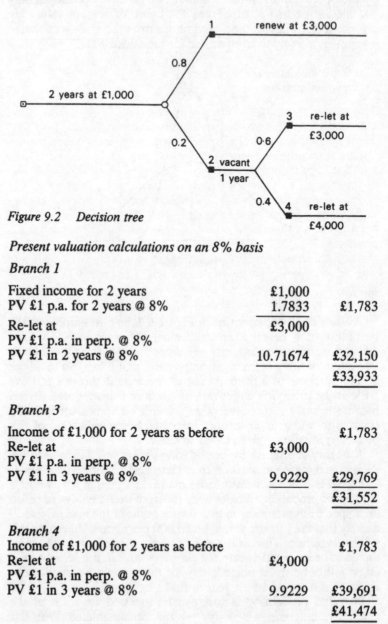

Figure 9.2   Decision tree

Present valuation calculations on an 8% basis

Branch 1

Fixed income for 2 years	£1,000	
PV £1 p.a. for 2 years @ 8%	1.7833	£1,783
Re-let at	£3,000	
PV £1 p.a. in perp. @ 8%		
PV £1 in 2 years @ 8%	10.71674	£32,150
		£33,933

Branch 3

Income of £1,000 for 2 years as before		£1,783
Re-let at	£3,000	
PV £1 p.a. in perp. @ 8%		
PV £1 in 3 years @ 8%	9.9229	£29,769
		£31,552

Branch 4

Income of £1,000 for 2 years as before		£1,783
Re-let at	£4,000	
PV £1 p.a. in perp. @ 8%		
PV £1 in 3 years @ 8%	9.9229	£39,691
		£41,474

214

Depending on the actual outcome, this investment has a present value at 8% of £33,933, or £31,552, or £41,474. Allowing for the probabilities and conditional probabilities we have:

$$£33,933 \times 0.8 = £27,146$$
$$£31,552 \times 0.2 \times 0.6 = £3,786$$
$$£41,474 \times 0.2 \times 0.4 = \underline{£3,317}$$

Weighted present value: £34,249

This can be compared to the asking price of £32,640. This figure could also be calculated by working back down the decision tree. These techniques have long been used in business management, but are still in their infancy in the valuation profession, and valuers who use such techniques will need to have a thorough knowledge of statistics.

Provided there is good market evidence, and the valuer uses that evidence with sound judgment, then the best defensible valuation is likely to be based on a best-estimate income capitalisation approach.

The problems of how to fully reflect risk in analysis increases with the complexity of the problem itself. The simplest decision is in respect of the single investment opportunity and the yes/no decision. From that one moves to the decisions which involve choices between alternative investments, after which one becomes inevitably involved in portfolio risk analysis. An investor must concern himself not only with the risks of a proposed new investment, but also he must consider the impact of that new investment on any existing investments held within a portfolio. Thus a valuer advising on a property might view it as a high risk and advise against the purchase, but in terms of the addition of that investment to an existing portfolio and in terms of the investor's overall aims it might be a perfectly acceptable risk. The subject of portfolio analysis has to be treated in a rigorous mathematical format, and for that reason it is felt to be outside the scope of this book.

However, almost all valuers are now agreed that in the property development world one cannot make any assumption as to certainty, and for long this has been held by the Lands Tribunal to be one reason for rejecting the traditional developers' or residual valuation (see Chapter 8).

Future uncertainty continues to be the reason given by most valuers for restricting the amount of detail provided for investors to a minimum. However, a number of investors currently expect their investment surveyors to provide them with more information on yields and more supportive data on market rents, market

215

Analysis

analysis and market performance. This information is used by the investors in their own assessment of the probability of achieving their investment aims.

In Chapter 3 the valuation of a property let at £10,000 per annum for 2 years with a current market rental value of £20,000 per annum, was considered in some depth. The relationship between the all risks yield (or market capitalisation rate) of 5% and the expected or equated yield requirement of 12% was examined and on a 5 year rent review pattern an implied annual rental growth of 7.6355% was calculated. This produced an implied rent in 2 years of £23,170 and a capital value on a modified DCF basis of £386,323. These figures would be rounded in the market but are used here to indicate the kind of information that an investor might require.

Acquisition costs

The majority of investors require yield calculations to be based on total acquisition cost. Solicitor's fees, surveyor's fees and stamp duty are the usual costs that need to be added to purchase price. In special cases it may be necessary to take account of immediate capital costs such as repairs, or in the case of a vacant building, refurbishment and letting expenses. In other cases it may be sensible to take account of rental apportionment and/or outstanding arrears of rents.

e.g.	Purchasing at the valuation of		£386,323
	Add for Legal fees	say 3½%*	
	Surveyor's fees	inclusive	
	Stamp duty	of VAT	13,521
	Total acquisition cost		£399,844

Initial yield

The initial yield may mean the relationship between the before tax net rents receivable during the first 12 months of ownership and total acquisition cost; the return expected during the investor's current financial year or the relationship between current contracted rents and total acquisition cost. In the absence of specific direction from the client it would be normal to assess the

*In 1989 competition had reduced the cost of professional fees to an inclusive average of 2.75%.

relationship between current contracted rent and total acquisition costs.

e.g. Current rents   £10,000
Less landlord's expected
non-recoverable management
expenses inclusive of VAT
    Minimum fee, say   500
                                                                £9,500

$$\frac{9,500}{399,844} \times 100 = 2.376\%$$

This yield can be crucial to some investors. Actuarial calculations of the relationship between expected repayments or claims on a fund and that fund's current income may dictate an absolute cut-off rate. Thus a fund may be operating on a 3.5% cut-off or target rate and be forced to reject this property.

Other funds whilst having regard to the initial yield and its implication for their whole portfolio will be aware that a low initial property yield can be balanced by high yielding stocks to achieve a total return for the fund above the target rate.

Yield on reversion

It is normal in an investment report to include an assessment of the yield at reversion calculated on the basis of current estimates of open market rentals.

e.g. Estimated rental value   £20,000
Non-recoverable management fees say   750
                                                              £19,250

$$\frac{19,250}{399,844} \times 100 = 4.814\%$$

Equivalent yield

The amount of additional information provided depends upon the client. Most will require advice on the internal rate of return based on current rentals and values.

Analysis

e.g. Value in 2 years' time on basis
      of open market rental of   £20,000
      × YP perp. at 5%   20
                                                            _____
                                                             £400,000

Then the IRR on annual in arrears assumption is found from

    0 − (£386,323 + £13,521) − £399,844
    1   + £   9,500
    2   + £409,400

and is 2.395%.

*5% is taken to be an ARY based on gross rents.

It should be clear that further adjustments could be made for
quarterly in advance and for sale fees. Such sophistication is not
going to explain to an investor that this could be a good investment. The potential for the investment can only be indicated by
making some assessment of the future.

Equated yield

Not all investors will require an equated yield analysis but it is a
useful measure and one which can help the investment valuer in
formulating his or her investment purchase advice.

e.g. Implied rent in 2 years as previously   £23,170
      × YP perp. at 5%   20
                                                            _____
                                                             £463,400

Here the IRR on an annual in arrears assumption is found from

    0 − £399,844
    1 + £   9,500
    2 + £463,400

and is 8.849%.

In Chapter 3 it was suggested that the real return might be
expected to be 12% and yet this analysis suggests 8.849% which
may not be sufficient to persuade an investor to buy. This variation

highlights some very important but as yet unresolved issues in the professional areas of valuation and investment advice. In the Chapter 3 valuation it was assumed that the 5% all risks yield was accounting for the non-recoverable management costs, and no account was taken of acquisition costs. The profession is still divided over the correct approach. A strongly held view is that (a) management costs should always be deducted in all valuations other than true net situations and that (b) acquisition costs should be deducted from the valuation figure bfore expressing an opinion on value. Note the effect this has in the following amended valuation and analysis.

e.g. *Revised valuation:*

Next 2 years	£10,000	
Less management, say	£500	
	£9,500	
YP 2 years at 12%	1.6901	£16,056
Reversion to	£23,170	
Less management, say	£750	
	£22,320	
YP perp. at 5%		
× PV 2 years at 12%	15.944	£357,464
		£373,520

Let x = purchase price and acquisition costs at $3\frac{1}{2}$% = $0.35x$
Then $x + 0.035x$ = £373,520
$\quad$ 1.035x $\quad$ = £373,520
$\quad\;\; x$ $\qquad\quad$ = £360,889, the corrected valuation figure.

Revised equated yield analysis:

0 − £373,520 (£360,889 + 3.5%)
1 + £ 9,500
2 + £457,900 (£22,420 × 20 YP + £9,500)

which gives an IRR of 12%.

In the property market valuations are prepared for vendors and investment advice given to buyers. The parties are different, the valuers are different and neither side actually knows why the other decided the price was acceptable and a bargain struck. It should, however, be clear that the investor will be interested in the expected returns, and in the actual returns; they are not interested in the rates per cent used in the valuation.

How much information the valuer provides the investor will depend upon the investor's requirements. The assessment of implied rental growth rates allows the valuer to compare historic growth patterns in the specific market with current market expectations with the growth needed to achieve an overall acceptable return for the investor. That detailed analysis coupled with detailed market analysis provides the valuer with the knowledge to advise if only in the general form of saying, 'Our records indicate that over the last 15 years rents in the High Street have risen on average by 12% per annum. The population of the area is rising and is expected to continue to rise. There are no plans at the moment before the planning authority for any increase in retail space. If the current growth in rentals continues then a purchase at £*x* should produce a return over the next *n* years in excess of medium term redemption yields of 10%.'

A number of writers believe that investment advice needs to be based on a more rigorous cash flow approach. If undertaken by computer the process can be very simple as well as being very sophisticated and providing the analyst with the opportunity to test the sensitivity of the investment. The additional data that can be handled could include: adjustments for rent review costs and lease renewal costs; adjustments for voids and refurbishment; more accurate allowance for other non-recoverable service or repair costs; adjustment for sale costs; adjustment for income and capital gains tax; adjustment for depreciation. Such modelling also allows the valuer to test the effect of different rental growth factors either on an average long-term basis or by adopting different rates of growth over different time periods.

It has already been indicated that the complexities of certain geared leaseholds can only effectively be handled in this way. The complexities of current development funding schemes also suggest that the valuation and analysis of these kinds of property investment will also have to be handled by computer.

Regression analysis

Regression analysis is currently being discussed by valuers as a potential tool for valuation and analysis. In its simplest form, the statistical technique of regression analysis enables the analyst to predict the value of one variable from the known value of another. Valuation would be an extremely simple science if, for example, the valuer could predict the sale price of a property from its total floor area. This would indicate that a linear relationship between value and size existed which, if plotted on a graph, would produce a straight line the slope of which would be dependent upon the value of the variable factor, *b*. Where *a* is a constant, the standard formula for a linear relationship is

$$y = a + bx$$

where in the simple case selected above *y* represents house value and *x* represents total floor area. For example, it might be noted that in a given locality the price of houses was always equal to £5,000 plus the floor area multiplied by 5. Then:

$$y = £5,000 + 5x$$

It is a usual presumption that value is a function of a number of variables. Multiple linear regression enables the analyst to bring into play as many variables as may be considered to be likely to affect the value or likely selling price of the subject property, such as parking facilities, outlook, location, size, specific facilities such as central heating and garage space and other factors such as the age and condition of the building.

Though little used in the UK, linear and multiple linear regression has been extensively used and developed in appraisal work in the USA, primarily because of the greater acceptance in America of the computer. Most multiple regression computer packages are of the step-wise form. The program input consists of a list of property characteristics for the type of property under analysis, together with details of the actual sale prices or rentals achieved, or repair costs incurred. The computer correlates each feature with the known factor, sale price, selects that feature with the highest correlation, produces a regression equation and estimates the sale prices on that basis. The computer then calculates the difference between actual price and the estimated price, and then proceeds to select from the remaining features the next highest correlation, and proceeds until all the features have been used.

The end result is an equation which can, with care, be used to estimate sale price, or whatever other factor is required in respect of another property. As more data become available these are added to the existing store and the program re-run to check for any significant changes in preferences by purchases such as for natural gas in preference to oil-fired central heating.

Any predicted figure must not be regarded as an absolute, and the valuer requires some indication of accuracy or acceptability.

The statistical measure used is generally R (the correlation co-efficient) and R^2 (the coefficient of determination).

When the data produce a value for R as close as posible to 1 (1^2 = 1) this would imply that the variation of the dependent variable (sale price, rental value) is explained fully by the independent variable(s). If R falls below 0.9 then only about 80% of the variation of the dependent variable is explained by the inde-pendent variable(s) and the smaller R becomes the less meaningful is the whole analysis.

The use of multiple regression analysis has been limited to mass valuation problems, particularly for land-tax purposes. Its use is fairly widespread in America, but it has also been used in Japan, Australia, Canada and South Africa, and in the UK studies have been carried out by the Inland Revenue.

Users of this technique need no reminder of the old motto 'garbage in – garbage out', but for others the warning needs to be made. The results can only be as good as the raw data permit.

The majority of reported examples concern house prices, but it is sugested that regression and multiple regression could be used for:

1　Testing the relationship between size and price or rent (for example, the rate at which land price per hectare decreases with the increase in the size of the holding being sold, or the extent to which rents per square metre for office or industrial space decrease with the size of the letting).
2　Time/value trend analysis.
3　Determining the rental value of all types of premises (as rent is a function of size, location, facilities, running costs, etc. it should be possible to produce a regression equation).
4　Predicting gross trading income from licensed premises, theatres, restaurants, etc., from the number of persons using the premises.
5　Predicting petrol throughput for service stations based on traffic counts and other variables.
6　Estimating repair expenses based on property maintenance records.

Clearly valuations and analyses of the type outlined in this chapter are only likely to be undertaken by the larger national valuation practices, government and institutional investors. For these reasons the description of the alternative techniques used has been kept to a minimum to give the average reader and student valuer a general idea of the developing techniques. Readers requir-ing a more detailed approach to the techniques are referred to the recommended reading at the end of the book.

We began by suggesting that valuers should keep their minds open to new techniques. A major development in appraisal techniques in the near future will be the use of statistics, and Norman Benedict aptly summarised our own feelings in an article published in the *Appraisal Journal* as long ago as October 1972:

Statistical analysis can significantly broaden the role of the appraiser and substantially increase his effectiveness, providing him with the tools to attain greater sophistication and expertise in the areas of marketability, feasibility and investment analysis.

Correspondingly, the appraiser who clings to yesterday's tools to meet tomorrow's challenges will become progressively less effective and less involved in his work, while the appraiser who seeks constantly to acquire new skills will develop both personally and professionally. In summation, then, statistics represents a golden opportunity for an appraiser to experience both personal and professional growth.

Appendix A

The valuation of commercial and industrial property*

This leaflet sets out general guidance and incorporates the terms on which a Chartered Surveyor will normally undertake the valuation of commercial and industrial property in England and Wales. It does not cover every aspect of valuation nor does it deal with special problems.

1. What is a valuation?

A valuation is the individual opinion of a valuer based on the relevant facts known to him.

The most common bases of valuation required are 'open market value' and 'open market rental value'. These may be defined as the best price or the best rent which might reasonably be expected to be obtained for the interest in the property at the date of valuation assuming:

(a) a willing seller or lessor;
(b) a reasonable period in which to negotiate the sale or letting taking into account the nature of the property and the state of the market;
(c) that values will remain static during that period;
(d) that the property will be freely exposed to the open market; and
(e) that no account will be taken of any higher price or rent that might be paid by a purchaser or lessee with a special interest.

Whilst 'open market value' is usually required there are cases where a client will need a different basis of assessment. For example, an owner may be under pressure to realise certain of his assets, in which case a 'forced sale value' would be appropriate. Another basis of value is depreciated replacement cost which may

*RICS copyright reserved.

be adopted in certain instances in relation to the value of company assets. The valuation of certain classes of property, such as hotels, licensed property and petrol filling stations, may have regard to trading potential.

Additionally, a valuation for the purposes of, say, Capital Gains Tax, Development Land Tax or compensation following compulsory acquisition will be subject to statutory rules.

The range of purposes for which a valuation may be required is substantial and includes sale, purchase, letting, obtaining finance, accounting, rating, compulsory purchase, and tax reasons. Even apparently minor differences in the purpose for which a valuation is to be used (for example, one tax calculation rather than another) can produce significantly different figures. The interest to be valued may be freehold or leasehold or some incorporeal estate or interest, such as an easement or a restrictive covenant, and may be subject to other interests. It is pertinent to note that what may appear to a client to be relatively minor variations in lease terms or small variations in planning assumptions can dramatically alter the final figure.

2. The valuer

In most cases there are no legal restrictions as to who can undertake a valuation, but in his own interests the client should instruct someone with the necessary skill, knowledge and experience. Chartered Surveyors in general practice are qualified in these skills, both by training and experience, although some surveyors specialise in certain types of valuation.

In certain cases, such as a valuation for insurance company solvency purposes, there is a statutory requirement that the task must be carried out by a qualified valuer, such as a Chartered Surveyor, whilst in the case of a valuation for Stock Exchange purposes that body requires the work to be done only by those with appropriate professional qualifications.

3. Confidentiality

A valuation is a confidential report for a particular client and for the special purposes of that client. The purpose for which a valuation is prepared is fundamentally important. An obvious example is that of a fire insurance assessment based on the cost of rebuilding, which may bear no relation to the open market value of the property. It must be stressed that the valuation should only be used within the context of the instructions under which it is prepared.

There will be cases where the valuation will be specifically prepared for more than just the instructing party, as, for example, a bank providing a loan facility. Generally, however, the valuer will accept a liability only to the person or company instructing him, and will accordingly make his report confidential to that client.

Usually a valuation report will contain a reminder of this point by including a paragraph on the following lines:

'The report is provided for the stated purpose and for the sole use of the named client. It is confidential to the client and his professional advisers. The Valuer accepts responsibility to the client alone that the report will be prepared with the skill, care and dilligence reasonably to be expected of a competent Chartered Surveyor, but accepts no responsibility whatsoever to any person other than the client himself. Any such person relies upon the report at his own risk. Neither the whole or any part of this report or any reference to it may be included in any published document, circular or statement nor published in any way without the Valuer's written approval of the form and context in which it may appear.'

4. Extent of inspection and investigations

The quantity and nature of information available to the valuer in preparing his report will depend on his instructions and the time and conditions under which he is allowed to carry out his work. For example, a client may require a valuation based only on an external inspection, in which case the valuer must rely on information provided in relation to floor space and other matters.

Normally, however, the valuer will carry out an inspection of the premises and make such enquiries and investigations as he deems necessary. These may entail informal enquiries of the Local Planning Authority and other authorities. Although the valuer may sometimes obtain written confirmation of details provided informally by such authorities, it will usually be necessary for the client's solicitor to make formal enquiries.

The valuer will often have to rely upon information provided by the client, his solicitor or accountant, as, for example, in the case of legal restrictions or tenancy agreements or where the valuation is by reference to accounts. There will also be instances where the valuer will need personally to examine copies of appropriate legal documents, such as leases, and where these are not available his report will refer to the assumptions he has made or the information with which he has been provided.

It is important to appreciate that a valuation is not a structural survey. The valuer will have regard to all apparent defects and wants of repair in making his assessment of value and will take into account the age of the property. He will not, however, carry out the detailed search for defects which is undertaken as part of a structural survey, nor will he necessarily set out the various defects when making his report.

There are various defects which can influence the value of a property significantly but which are undetectable unless a detailed investigation of the structure is undertaken, which might also require an additional specialist inspection. A paragraph on the following lines may therefore be included in the report:

'We have not carried out a structural survey nor have we inspected woodwork or other parts of the property which are covered, unexposed or inaccessible and such parts will be assumed to be in good repair and condition. The report will not purport to express an opinion about or to advise upon the condition of uninspected parts and should not be taken as making any implied representation or statement about such parts.'

Similarly, it is extremely difficult without chemical analysis or an inspection by a Chartered Building Surveyor or structural engineer to check whether potentially deleterious materials have been used in the construction of the building or have since been incorporated. Accordingly a paragraph on the following lines may be included in the report:

'We have not arranged for any investigation to be carried out to determine whether or not any deleterious or hazardous material has been used in the construction of this property or has since been incorporated and we are therefore unable to report that the property is free from risk in this respect. For the purpose of this valuation we have assumed that such investigation would not disclose the presence of any such material in any adverse conditions.'

If the client requires not just a valuation but also a structural survey many Chartered Surveyors will be prepared to undertake such a survey and will be able to arrange for specialist investigations if the client so wishes. Such additional work and responsibility will normally involve a higher fee.

5. Instructions

It is essential that a client clearly defines the terms of reference within which he wishes a valuation to be carried out. Often a preliminary discussion with the valuer will be of benefit so that areas of potential uncertainty may be resolved prior to any work being undertaken.

6. Valuation fees

The fees for a valuation will vary according to the nature of the work and a Chartered Surveyor will quote the appropriate fee for the particular valuation requested. In addition, out-of-pocket expenses and VAT are usually payable.

7. Terms of appointment

In the absence of express agreement to the contrary, the terms on which the valuer will undertake the valuation are set out in the Conditions of Engagement.

Conditions of engagement

1. The Valuer should advise the Client as to his opinion of the value of the relevant interest in the property, as specified by the Client.
2. The purpose for which the valuation is required shall be as agreed between the Client and the Valuer.
3. Unless otherwise specifically agreed, the value advised by the Valuer shall be the open market value current at the date of valuation.
4. Subject as hereinafter provided, the Valuer shall carry out such inspections and investigations as are, in his professional judgement, appropriate and possible in the particular circumstances.
5. The Valuer shall unless otherwise expressly agreed rely upon information provided to him by the Client or the Client's legal or other professional advisers relating to tenure, tenancies and other relevant matters.
6. The Valuer shall have regard to the apparent state of repair and condition of the property but shall be under no duty to carry out a structural survey of the property nor to inspect woodwork or other parts of the structure which are covered, unexposed or inaccessible; neither shall he have a duty to arrange for the testing of electrical, heating or other services.

7. In making the report, the following assumptions will be made:
   (a) that no deleterious or hazardous material was used in the construction of the property or has since been incorporated;
   (b) that the property is not subject to any unusual or especially onerous restrictions, encumbrances or outgoings and that good title can be shown;
   (c) that the property and its value are unaffected by any matters which would be revealed by a local search and replies to the usual enquiries, or by any statutory notice, and that neither the property, nor its condition, nor its use, nor its intended use, is or will be unlawful; and
   (d) that inspection of those parts which have not been inspected would neither reveal material defects nor cause the Valuer to alter the valuation materially.
   The Valuer shall be under no duty to verify these assumptions.
8. The Valuer shall provide to the client a report setting out his opinion of the value of the relevant interest in the property. The report will be provided for the stated purposes and for the sole use of the named Client. It will be confidential to the Client and his professional advisers. The Valuer accepts responsibility to the Client alone that the report will be prepared with the skill, care and dilligence reasonably to be expected of a competent Chartered Surveyor, but accepts no responsibility whatsoever to any person other than the Client himself. Any such person relies upon the report at his own risk. Neither the whole nor any part of the report or any reference to it may be included in any published document, circular or statement nor published in any way without the Valuer's written approval of the form and context in which it may appear.
9. The Client shall pay to the Valuer in respect of the said professional advice a fee to be agreed between the Client and the Valuer. In addition, the Client will reimburse the Valuer the cost of all reasonable out-of-pocket expenses which he may incur and pay the amount of any Value Added Tax on the fee and expenses.

Contracts for services – explanatory notes

1. In general practice it has been usual for instructions from clients for valuations to be accepted with the minimum of formality as to the terms and conditions on which the service is to be provided.

2. Many member firms have adopted the practice of incorporating in their valuation reports standard forms of caveat which are used within the profession or in their own offices. Among the various clauses defining, restricting or excluding liability which members use from time to time, the most important and commonly used are:

(a) A clause indicating that a valuation is not a structural survey.

(b) A 'latent defects' clause.

(c) A clause relating to deleterious and hazardous materials.

(d) A clause excluding liability to third parties under the principles of *Hedley Byrne v Heller**

(e) A restriction on publication clause.

(f) General assumptions as to title.

Recent legal decisions have emphasised the need for such caveats and in particular the need to state whether or not the surveyor is prepared to accept liability to third parties.

3. Over the years the institution has received legal advice that unless the caveats included in surveyors' reports are agreed at the time of accepting instructions, and thereby included in the contract for services between the client and the surveyor, they may not provide any defence for the surveyor in any subsequent action in relation to his advise.

4. To assist members in formalising their contracts for services with their clients (where members think it appropriate), the Institution has prepared a leaflet incorporating conditions of engagement for the valuation of commercial and industrial property). This is intended to help the client understand the position. Counsel's advice on the leaflet has been obtained.

5. It is strongly recommended that on a request for a valuation a member should write to the client identifying the property concerned, the purpose of the valuation and the basis of his charges. With his letter to the client he should send a copy of the leaflet and indicate that any instructions he accepts will be subject to those terms unless otherwise agreed. Written confirmation by the client of his acceptance is also recommended.

6. Counsel has advised that the report to the client should also reiterate:

(a) the purpose of the valuation;

(b) any qualifications to which it is subject; and

(c) the form of caveats used by the member.

**Hedley Byrne & Co Ltd* v. *Heller & Partners Ltd* [1964] AC 465.

Appendix B

Illustrative investment property purchase report

Prepared by Gooch and Wagstaff, Chartered Surveyors. The property is fictional and the valuation date was November 1988. [Appendixes 1–5 referred to in the report are not included here.)

Contents

Summary
Instructions
Location
Site
Description and construction
Accommodation
Services
Rating
Town planning
Tenure
Occupation and letting
Covenant
Rental value
Valuation
Recommendation
Limitations

Appendix B

Address of property

Summary

Terms have been agreed on behalf of XYZ Limited to purchase this freehold shop investment.

Purchase Price:	£450,000 (FOUR HUNDRED AND FIFTY THOUSAND POUNDS).
Tenure:	Freehold
Approximate Area:	1,713 sq.ft.
User:	High-class retail shop.
Letting:	Let to and trading as Bakers on assignment from XXXX (UK) Ltd. 25 years from 23 August 1979, FRI terms at £11,750 p.a.
Reviews:	23rd August 1989 and every 5 years upwards only.
Estimated Rental Value:	£21,350 p.a.
Estimated Yields:	2.54% net initial rising to 4.61% on reversion in August 1989. Net equivalent yield 4.53%.

We conclude that the price agreed reflects the current market and we recommend the acquisition to XYZ Limited.

This summary should only be read in conjunction with the detailed comments which follow.

Address of property

Instructions

We are instructed to prepare a Report and Valuation on the freehold shop investment located at XXXX on behalf of XYZ Ltd. It should be noted that whilst we have inspected the property and briefly describe its structure, we are not instructed to report on its structual condition and we understand that you have carried out your own structural survey and are satisfied with the result.

This report is subject to the Limitations set out in the extract from the Guidance Notes on the Valuation of Assets produced by the Royal Institution of Chartered Surveyors which is attached as *Appendix 1.*

232

Location

XXXX, is a historic City with a population in the region of 50,000 persons (1981) which is substantially increased by visiting tourists and by students. The estimated shopping catchment is some 120,000 persons. The City is situated close to the junction of the X(M) and the A111 thus providing good access to London (200 miles), XXX (23 miles) and XXXX (16 miles). The A222 to Z, the A333 to B and C and the A444 to D all radiate from the Town thus providing good communications to the surrounding centres and to the X(M).

A British Rail main line service connects XXXX to London Kings Cross (the fastest journey time being 2 hrs and 55 mins) and X Airport is approximately 25 miles to the North by road. A location map is attached as *Appendix 2*.

The property is located within the established shopping area in the City Centre on the South side of XXXX at the top of XXXX Street and is close to the Town's main car parks. A Street Map is attached as *Appendix 3*. The City Centre is well represented in terms of national multiples and includes such occupiers as Next, Boots, Marks & Spencer, F.W. Woolworth, Burtons and W.H. Smith. A market is held in XXXX Place on Saturdays and this is a busy pedestrian thoroughfare linking the Town's main car park with the principal shopping area of Market Place and Street. An extract from the traders plan is attached as *Appendix 4*.

Site

The site which slopes up to the rear is roughly rectangular in shape and has a frontage to XXXX of 15′ 4″ and a depth of 72′ 0″. The site extends to an area of approximately 1,110 sq.ft. (0.0255 acres) and is outlined in red on the attached Ordnance Survey Extract (*Appendix 5*).

Description and construction

The property is an attractive Grade II Listed Building constructed circa 1850 comprising a ground floor shop unit with rear storage and 3 floors of disused residential space above having access from the rear yard. Access to the yard is provided via a passageway to the side of the shop. The shop has a somewhat limited internal width averaging 9′ 7″.

The building is constructed of brick and sandstone quoin blocks and eaves cornice under a pitched slate roof. The windows are single glazed wooden sash.

The shop has no central heating. The upper floors are heated by a coke burning boiler in need of replacement, serving radiators.

Accommodation

We have measured the property in accordance with the RICS Code of Measuring Practice and the building has the following approximate floor areas and dimensions:–

3rd Floor	— residential	432 sq.ft.	
2nd Floor	— residential	370 sq.ft.	
1st Floor	— residential	411 sq.ft.	
Ground Floor	— Sales	398 sq.ft.	(287 sq.ft. ITZA)
	— Rear Store	102 sq.ft.	
Total		1,713 sq.ft.	

Overall frontage (including passageway)	15' 4"
Gross frontage	11' 0"
Net frontage	9' 7"
Internal Width (Average)	9' 7"
Shop Depth	41' 11"
Built Depth	72' 0"

Services

We understand that the property is supplied with mains water, electricity and drainage.

Rating

We have made verbal enquiries of XYZ Council and are informed that the property is included within the current Valuation List having the following description and assessments:-

Description	Gross Value	Rateable Value
Shop, House and Premises	£1,530	£1,247

The current commercial rate in the pound is 294p.

Town planning

We have made verbal enquiries of the Local Planning Authority,
XYZ Council, and understand that the property is a Grade II
Listed Building situated within the City Centre Conservation Area
as defined by the City of XYZ Local Plan dated March 1988 but
not yet adopted. The listing is recorded as:

'House now shop. Mid 19th century, circa 1900 shop front grey
(yellow) brick; flemish bond, ashlar dressings. Welsh slate roof. Six
panel door at right and recessed shop door at left have fan lights
with glazing bars. Rounded top light to shop window with similar
glazing bars. Shop door has bevelled glass in patterned glazing
bars. Tuscan pillasters and bracketed cornice frame shop. Upper
floors have sashes with glazing bars. Projecting stone sills cut back
underneath at forty five degrees. Chamfered stone quoins support
similar cutback in cornice with paved brackets and finishing in
pyramidal coped blocks. Low pitched roof with tall banded chim-
ney on left.'

Policy E18 in the Local Plan generally aims to protect and
enhance the character, appearance and setting of the City's conservation areas. Policy E19 sets out a number of restrictions and
guidelines relating to the City Centre Conservation Area itself,
covering the visual historical and architectural importance of the
buildings.

Under the section headed 'Land Use Policies' in the Local Plan
it is stated that no major development or re-development for
shopping will be allowed in the City Centre except in the shopping
and business centre as allocated in the XYZ Zone (Policy CC1).
Policies CC2 and CC3 stipulate that in the Shopping and Business
Centre commercial and community purposes will take precedence
over other uses except where upper floor space is to be converted
to residential use. Furthermore, XXXX is included in the area in
which changes of use of ground floors to office use (as covered by
Class II of the Town and Country Planning (Use Classes Order)
1972), betting offices and amusement arcades will not be permitted. Elsewhere in the Shopping and Business Centre office
users will be given consideration by the Local Planning Authority
provided they do not exceed more than 10% of the net frontage
length of ground floor properties in retail and commercial uses.

We are informed that there are plans to review traffic management in the XXXX Place area to restrict service vehicle access
during shopping hours.

We have traced the planning history through the local planners.
It has been assumed that the property has planning consent for use

as a shop and we are aware of a planning consent dated 11th February 1982 permitting change of use from residential to office of the 1st, 2nd and 3rd floors which expired in 1987. We are informed that this is the only planning consent given since 1974.

A new development is planned for the site on XXXX between Boots and No. 10 XXXX which will span the slip road and the through-road off XXXX Bridge. The development will comprise 12 shop units extending to some 40,000 sq.ft. and work is due to begin by Christmas 1989. The developers are ABC Ltd and the landowners are the City Council. We anticipate that this development will improve XXXX as a shopping location and increase the pedestrian flow past the subject property.

CDE Ltd and the City Council are planning a joint development of a scheme incorporating an hotel, 270,000 sq.ft. of retail, 1,000 space car park, an ice-rink and a swimming pool, on the site of the existing ice rink and car park north of A Road by the river. It is anticipated that an application for planning permission will be submitted in 1989 but this proposal is very much in its early stages. However its location should serve to enhance XXXX.

In B Street XXXX Estates are currently refurbishing Nos. 68–70 and the ABC Centre on the other side of the river has recently been extended with only one remaining unit unlet. North of the City a mixed development of shops, industrial and residential units is to be constructed near XXXX. The planning consent is still subject to a Section 52 Agreement relating to infrastructure works but it is not anticipated that this should hinder the works. An application has been made on a site to the east of the City for an industrial estate incorporating bulky goods retail warehouses.

We are of the opinion that none of the developments or policies described are likely to adversely affect the subject property and we are not aware of any other relevant current policies or proposals.

Tenure

The property is freehold with a right-of-way in Fee Simple granted to the occupiers of the adjoining premises over the passageway along the side of the subject property. This gives access to the upper floors of the adjoining building.

Occupating and letting

The entire property was let to XXXX Ltd by virtue of a lease dated 30 August 1979 for a term of 25 years from 23 August 1979 subject to five yearly upward only rent reviews at a current rent of

£11,750 p.a. The lease is drawn on full repairing and insuring terms with the landlord effecting insurance and recovering the premium direct from the tenant.

The lease was recently assigned to   and The tenant is prohibited from assigning or underletting the whole or part of the demised premises without prior written consent from the landlord which is not to be unreasonably withheld.

The tenant covenants 'not without consent in writing of the lessor first obtained to use the demised premises or any part thereof or suffer the same to be used otherwise than as a high-class retail shop only'. Although the upper floors are fitted out for residential use and such a use would be acceptable in planning terms, we have valued the upper parts as storage ancillary to the retail in accordance with the terms of the lease.

Covenant

We have no information on the covenant of the tenant and have assumed that you are satisfied with the covenant status.

We understand from your solicitors that the assignment does not appear to be documented and they should satisfy themselves as to the legal position in this regard, particularly as we understand that a schedule of repairs dated 31st May 1988 is still outstanding and should have been completed within six months of the date of the licence to assign.

Rental value

XXXX is a Cathedral City with a substantial catchment area and is much sought after by national multiple retailers. The main shopping area in the City Centre is centred around A Street and XXXX with B Street being relatively secondary in terms of rental value and location.

The XXXX Centre on the other side of the river, was opened in 1976 and commands rents equating to between £40 and £45 Zone A. A second phase was opened in 1986 extending the original 70,000 sq.ft. by a further 100,000 sq.ft. where rents equating to between £35 and £37 Zone A have been achieved. A Street and XXXX command higher rental values, the highest rent achieved on review is reported as equating to £92 Zone A at No. 10 A Street. However we understand that this was not an arms length deal in that the landlords were reluctant to grand permission for the tenant to assign his lease until the review was settled and the tenants consequently accepted the landlords quoting figure without further negotiation. We have therefore attached little relevance to this deal. The XXXX Shop unit at No. 20 A Street was let recently at a rent equating to £65 Zone A although this is generally regarded as having been underlet.

We understand that the proposed ABC Ltd's scheme on XXXX was appraised on the basis of shop rents equating to £70 Zone A at today's rents and that CDE's scheme is being appraised on rents in excess of £70 Zone A.

No. 15 A Street was reviewed in September 1987 to a rent equating to £64 Zone A and Nos. 4/5 A Street were reviewed to a rent equating to £55 Zone A in 1985. At the botom of A Street, No. 18 was reviewed in August 1988 to a rent equating to over £63 Zone A. However it was agreed between the respective parties that the restrictive user had the effect of discounting the rent by 15%. On this basis the Zone A open market rental equates to over £72 Zone A. We believe similar rents are being achieved in A Street on premium deals but are unable to obtain precise information in this respect.

The current rent reserved under the lease is £11,750 p.a. exclusive, which equates to £34 Zone A.

We are of the opinion that the current open market rental value of Address is approximately £21,350 p.a. equating to £66 Zone A.

Valuation

Terms have been agreed to purchase this freehold shop investment in the sum of £450,000 (FOUR HUNDRED AND FIFTY THOUSAND POUNDS), subject to contract.

We therefore estimate that the agreed acquisition price reflects a net initial yield of 2.54%, rising to 4.61% on reversion in August 1989 to produce a net equivalent yield of 4.53%. These yields are after allowance for acquisition costs of 2.75% to cover fees and Stamp Duty.

Recommendation

We draw attention to the fact that at the time of valuation there was a limited amount of directly comparable rental evidence available on which to base our valuation particularly taking account of the limited shop width. It is relevant that we were aware of other parties bidding for the investment and indeed, having submitted an offer for this property we were informed that two other offers had been received by the vendor at the same level and are subsequently informed of a further offer of £475,000. We are of the opinion that the agreed purchase price of £450,000 (FOUR HUNDRED AND FIFTY THOUSAND POUNDS) for this freehold shop investment is appropriate in the current market and recommend the purchase to   Limited.

REF/DATE

Limitations

Extracts from the RICS guidance notes on the valuation of assets – 2nd edition

'The Valuer shall have regard to the apparent state of repair and condition of the property but shall be under no duty to carry out a structural survey of the property nor to inspect woodwork or other parts of the structure of the property which are covered, unexposed or inaccessible; neither shall he have a duty to arrange for the testing of electrical heating or other services.

Unless otherwise expressly agreed the Valuer shall, in arriving at his valuation of the property, assume that:

(a) good freehold or leasehold title (as the case may be) can be shown that the property is not subject to any unusual or onerous restrictions, encumbrances or outgoings;

(b) the property is unaffected by any statutory notice and that neither the property nor its use or its intended use gives rise to a contravention of any statutory requirement; and

(c) the property is free from dry rot, woodworm and latent defects and that no deleterious materials have been used in the construction of the property.

The Valuer shall be under no duty to verify these assumptions.'

'This report is confidential to the client for the specific purpose to which it refers. It may be disclosed to other professional advisers assisting the client in respect of that purpose, but the client shall not disclose the report to any other person.'

'Neither the whole nor any part of this report or any reference thereto may be included in any published document, circular or statement nor published in any way without the Valuer's written approval of the form and context in which it may appear.'

Further reading

Chapter 1 Valuation mathematics

A.E. Baum, 'Discounted Cash Flow: the Internal Rate of Return and the Cost of Borrowing', *EG* 244:28.

P. Bowcock, 'High Speed NPV', *EG* 242:443.

P. Bowcock, 'High Speed IRR', *EG* 243:739.

P. Bowcock, 'High Speed Quarterly in Advance', *EG* 245:551.

P. Bowcock (1978) *Property Valuation Tables*, Macmillan.

G.R. Brown, 'NPV/IR: Some Qualifying Comments on Mutual Exclusivity', *EG* 244:533.

Compounding and Discounting Tables for Project Evaluation, World Bank, 1973.

A.W. Davidson (compiler), *Parry's Valuation and Conversion Tables*, 10th edn, Estates Gazette, 1978.

G.H. Lawson and D.W. Windle (1977) *Tables for Discounted Cash Flow*, Longmans.

'Mainly for Students', *EG* 252:724.

N.H. Noton, 'Valuation Tables: a New Look', *EG* 252:999.

C.F. Raper, 'Internal Rate of Return – Handle With Care', *Appraisal Journal*, July 1976.

J.J. Rose (1977) *Rose's Property Valuation Tables*, The Freeland Press.

Chapter 2 The income approach

P.J. Byrne and D.H. Mackmin, 'The Investment Method: an Objective Approach', *EG* 234:29.

N. Enever, 'The Valuation of Investments – Which Tables?', *EG* 238:864.

V. Fieldgrass, 'Valuations or Guesstimates? A Reply', *EG* 233:997.

W.D. Fraser (1984) *Principles of Property Investment and Pricing*, Macmillan.

D.H. Mackmin, 'Valuations or Guesstimates?' *EG* 233:663.

D.H. Mackmin, 'The Appraisal Process', *EG* 244:123.

'New Standards for Sale, Purchase and Mortgage of Land and Buildings',
  Chartered Surveyor, June 1980.
J. Ratcliffe and A. Trott, 'Valuation: Demands and Techniques', *EG*
  255:435 and 529.
A. Trott, *Property Valuation Methods: Interim Report*, Polytechnic of the
  South Bank, RICS, 1980.
P. White, 'Taking a View of Valuations', *EG* 242:799.

Chapter 3 The income approach to freeholds

A. Baum (1984) 'The Valuation of Reversionary Freeholds: A Review',
  Journal of Valuation 3:157–67, 230–47.
A. Baum (1984) 'The All Risks Yield: Exposing the Implicit', *Journal of
  Valuation* 2:229–37.
A. Baum and N. Crosby (1988) *Property Investment Appraisal*, Routledge.
D. Bornand (1988) 'Accrual illusion', *Journal of Valuation* 6:4.
D. Bornand (1985) 'Conveyancing of Commercial Property Investments',
  Solicitors Journal, August 9 and 16.
P. Bowcock (1983) 'The Valuation of Varying Incomes', *Journal of
  Valuation* 1:366–71, 72–6.
N. Crosby (1982) 'The Investment Method of Valuation: A Real Value
  Approach', Ryde Memorial Prizewinning Paper, RICS (unpublished).
N. Crosby (1983) 'The Investment Method of Valuation: A Real Value
  Approach', *Journal of Valuation* 1:341–50, 2:48–59.
N. Crosby (1984) 'Investment Valuation Techniques: The Shape of
  Things to Come?' *The Valuer* 53/7:196–7.
N. Crosby (1985) 'The Application of Equated Yield and Real Value
  Approaches to the Market Valuation of Commercial Property
  Investments', unpublished PhD thesis, University of Reading.
N. Crosby (1986) 'The Application of Equated Yield and Real Value
  Approaches to Market Valuation', *Journal of Valuation* 4:158–69,
  261–74.
N. Crosby (1987) *A Critical Examination of the Rational Model*,
  Department of Land Management and Development, University of
  Reading.
M.J. Greaves, 'Discounted Cash Flow Techniques and Current Methods
  of Income Valuation', *EG* 223:2147 and 2339.
M.J. Greaves (1985) 'The Valuation of Reversionary Freeholds: A
  Reply', *Journal of Valuation* 3:248–52.
W. Greenwell *et al.*, 'A Call for New Valuation Methods', *EG* 238:481.
N. Harker (1983) 'The Valuation of Varying Incomes: 1', *Journal of
  Valuation* 1:363–5.
I.G. Jones (1983) 'Equivalent Yield Analysis', *Journal of Valuation*
  1:246–52.
W.A. Leach, 'Hardcore Method of Valuation', *EG* 246:475.
D.H. Mackmin, 'Current Valuation Practice', *Valuer*, 49, (3):74.

Further Reading

P. Marshall, 'Equated Yield Analysis: A Valuation Method of the Future?', *EG* 239:493.

P. Marshall, *Donaldons Investment Tables*, 2nd edn, Donaldsons, 1979.

S.G. Sykes (1981), 'Property Valuation: A Rational Model', *The Investment Analyst* 61:20–6.

S.G. Sykes and A.P.J. McIntosh (1982) 'Towards a Standard Property Income Valuation Model: Rationalisation or Stagnation', *Journal of Valuation* 1:117–35.

P.H. White, 'Questions of Investment Valuation', *EG* 241:669.

P. White (1977) 'The Two Faces of Janus', *Occasional Paper in Estate Management* (9), Reading, College of Estate Management.

E. Wood (1972) 'Property Investment – A Real Value Approach', unpublished PhD thesis, University of Reading.

E. Wood (1973) 'Positive Valuations: A Real Value Approach to Property Investment', *EG* 226:923–5, 115–17, 1311–13.

Chapter 4 The income approach to leaseholds

A. Baum (1982) 'The Enigma of the Short Leasehold', *Journal of Valuation* 1:5–9.

A. Baum and D. Butler (1986) 'The Valuation of Short Leasehold Investments', *Journal of Valuation* 4:342–53.

A. Baum and D. Mackmin, *The Income Approach to Property Valuation*, 2nd edn, Routledge & Kegan Paul, 1981.

A. Baum and S.M. Yu (1985) 'The Valuation of Leaseholds: A Review', *Journal of Valuation* 3:157–67, 230–57.

P. Bowcock, 'The Valuation of Varying Incomes', *Journal of Valuation*, 1:4.

M. Colam, 'A More Modern Method', *EG* 251:1054.

M. Colam (1983) 'The Single Rate Valuation of Leaseholds', *Journal of Valuation* 2:14–18.

A.W. Davidson (1968) 'The Deferment of Terminable Incomes', *Chartered Surveyor*, July.

W.D. Fraser, 'The Valuation and Analysis of Leasehold Investments in Times of Inflation', *EG* 244:197.

W.D. Fraser (1977) 'The Valuation and Analysis of Leasehold Investments in Times of Inflation', *EG* 244:197–201.

M.J. Greaves (1969) 'The Valuation of Varying Profit Rents', *Chartered Surveyor*, March.

N. Harker *et al.* (1988) 'Double Sinking Fund Correction Methods', University of Aberdeen discussion paper.

A.P.J. McIntosh (1983) 'Valuing Leasehold Interests', *EG* 265:939–41.

A.P.J. McIntosh, 'The Rational Approach to Reversionary Leasehold property Investment Valuations', in *Land Management: New Directions* (D. Chiddick and A. Millington, eds), Spon, 1983.

D.H. Mackmin, 'Dual Rate for Leaseholds?', *EG* 234:663.

D.H. Mackmin, 'The Analysis of Leasehold Transactions', *Valuer* 48(9):287.
D.H. Mackmin, 'A Matter of Amortisation', *EG* 245:289.
'Mainly for Students', *EG* 206:1166.
A. Millington (1983) 'Sinking Fund Theory', *EG* 266:595–9.
E. Wood (1974) 'Valuations in an Inflationary Economy', *Estatesman*, January.

Chapter 5 Taxation and valuation

A. Baum (1985) 'Premiums on Acquiring Leases', *Rent Review and Lease Renewal* 5:212–22.
A. Baum and D. Butler, 'The Valuation of Short Leasehold Investments', *Journal of Valuation* 4:4.
P. Bowcock, 'Capital Gains: The Tax Equation', *EG* 241:823.
A.W. Davidson (1973) 'Valuation and Taxation: A Question of Convention', *Valuer*, January/February.
M.J. Greaves, 'The Effects of Taxation on the Investment Method of Valuation – Capital Gains Tax', *EG* 203:603.
T.A. Johnson, 'Valuation Allowance for Capital Gains Tax', *EG* 201:871.
A. Macleary, 'Irregularities in the Capital Taxation of "Short" Leaseholds', *Journal of Valuation* 6:4.
'Mainly for Students', *EG* 237:128.
J.J. Rose, 'Reversionary Valuation Allowing for Capital Gains Tax', *EG* 202:873.

Chapter 6 Landlord and tenant valuations

A.E. Baum, 'Rent Reviews: Full Rental Value', *EG* 254:717.
R. Bernstein, 'Rent Reviews: Valuing the Incomparable', *EG* 251:147.
P. Bowcock, 'Lease Rents and the Hypothetical Tenancy', *EG* 227:1271.
P. Bowcock, letter in *Rating and Valuation Reporter*, July 1975.
P.H. Clarke (1980) 'Rent Reviews: A Framework for Valuers', *JPEL*.
A. Colborne, 'Premiums', *EG* 247:1065.
N. Harker, 'Inflation-Proof Rent Reviews', *EG* 250:233.
J. Hill, 'Rent Reviews: Valuing the Comparable', *EG* 251:245.
M. Lister, 'Three-Year Rent Reviews', *EG* 254:383.
D.H. Mackmin (1975) 'Valuation Commentary', *Rating and Valuation Reporter*, June.
'Mainly for Students', *EG* 256:406.
A.D. Nicholls (1975) 'Valuation Commentary', *Rating and Valuation Reporter*, March.
J.J. Rose (1979) *Tables of the Constant Rent*, The Freeland Press.
J.J. Rose, 'Inflation-Proof Rents', *EG* 249:531.
C. Ward, 'Negotiation of Rents', *EG* 255:769.

Further Reading

Chapter 7 Legislation and the income approach

J.E. Adams, 'Business Tenancies: Statutory Renewal Terms', *EG* 251:1045.

T.M. Aldridge, *Rent Control and Leasehold Enfranchisement*, 7th edn, Oyez, 1978.

C.C. Hubbard, 'Leasehold Enfranchisement: the Problem of Development Value', *EG* 223:1753.

Letter re above, *EG* 223:2041.

C.C. Hubbard, 'Leasehold Enfranchisement: Qualification and Valuations Under the Housing Act 1974', *EG* 234:729.

C.C. Hubbard, 'Leasehold Enfranchisement: A Review', *EG* 256:809 and 908.

W.A. Leach, 'Valuations Under the Leasehold Reform Act 1967', *EG* 220:509.

'Mainly for Students', *EG* 245:768.

'Mainly for Students', *EG* 256:296 and 406.

P. Marshall, 'Techniques for Applied Valuation Examinations', *EG* 241:751.

Chapter 8 Development appraisal

A.E. Baum, 'Residual Valuations: A Cash-Flow Approach', *EG* 247:973.

D. Cadman and L. Austin-Crowe, *Property Development*, Spon, 1978.

C. Darlow, *Valuation and Appraisal*, Estates Gazette, 1983.

S. Morley, 'Cash Flow Approach to Financing', *EG* 251:445.

J. Ratcliffe, 'Uncertainty and Risk in Development Appraisal', *EG* 227:603.

K.E. Way, 'Viability in Property Development', *EG* 239:705.

Chapter 9 Analysis

D.P.P. Abayagunawardana, 'Individual Worth Approach', *EG* 256:51.

P.J. Byrne and D.H. Mackmin, 'The Investment Method: an Objective Approach', *EG* 234:29.

M. Harry, 'Portfolio Selections and Capital Budgets', *EG* 230:1681.

L.R. Mason, 'Performance Measurement', *EG* 256:1091.

R. Schiller and M. Lister, 'Portfolio Expansion and Rental Income', *EG* 249:1153.

N.S. Sloam, 'Individual Worth Approach', *EG* 255:45.

General

T.M. Aldridge, *Letting Business Premises*, 3rd edn, Oyez, 1978.

J.F. Andrews, *Business Tenancies*, 3rd edn, Estates Gazette, 1978.

The Appraisal of Real Estate, 6th edn, AIREA (American Institute of Real Estate Appraisers), 1974.

A. Baum and N. Crosby, *Property Investment Appraisal*, Routledge, 1988.

H. Bierman Jr. and S. Smidt, *The Capital Budgeting Decision*, Collier-Macmillan, 1975.

W. Britton, K. Davies and T. Johnson, *Modern Methods of Valuation*, 7th edn, Estates Gazette, 1979.

M. Bromwich, *The Economics of Capital Budgeting*, Penguin, 1976.

R. and H. Cissell, *The Mathematics of Finance*, 4th edn, Houghton & Mifflin, 1973.

C. Darlow (ed.), *Valuation and Investment Appraisal*, Estates Gazette, 1983.

N. Enever, *The Valuation of Property Investments*, Estates Gazette, 1977, 1981, 1984.

M.J. Greaves, 'The Investment Method of Property Valuation and Analysis – an Examination of Some of its Problems', unpublished thesis for the degree of PhD, Reading University, 1972.

C.J. Hawkins and D.W. Pearce, *Capital Investment Appraisal*, Macmillan, 1971.

P.M. Hummel and C.L. Seebeck, *The Mathematics of Finance*, McGraw-Hill, 1971.

S.A. Kahn, F.E. Case and A. Schimmel, *Real Estate Appraisal and Investment*, Ronald, 1963.

W.N. Kinnard Jr., *Income Property Valuation*, Heath Lexington, 1971.

A.J. Merrett and A. Sykes, *Capital Budgeting and Company Finance*, Longmans, 1973.

A.F. Millington, *An Introduction to Property Valuation*, 3rd edn, Estates Gazette, 1988.

P.G. Moore and H. Thomas, *The Anatomy of Decisions*, Penguin, 1976.

J. Ratcliffe, *Urban Land Administration*, Estates Gazette, 1978.

W. Rees (editor), *Valuation: Principles into Practice*, Estates Gazette, 1980, 2nd edn 1984.

D. Richmond, *Introduction to Valuation*, Macmillan, 1975, 2nd edn 1985.

J.E. Roulac and S.J. Maisel, *Real Estate Investment and Finance*, McGraw-Hill, 1976.

L.W.T. Stafford, *Business Mathematics*, M & E Handbooks, 1969.

A. Trott, *Property Valuation Methods: Interim Report*, RICS/Polytechnic of the South Bank, 1980.

D. Turner, *An Approach to Land Values*, Geographical Publications Limited, 1977.

C.A. Westwick, *Property Valuation and Accounts*, ICAEW (Institute of Chartered Accountants in England and Wales), 1980.

E. Wood, 'Property Investment – A Real Value Approach', unpublished thesis for the degree of PhD, Reading University, 1972.

Index